Business Administration

for

Secretarial
Certificates

Business Administration *for* Secretarial Certificates

Jon Sutherland
Diane Canwell

Heinemann

Heinemann Educational Publishers,
Halley Court, Jordan Hill, Oxford OX2 8EJ
a division of Reed Educational & Professional Publishing Ltd

OXFORD   FLORENCE   PRAGUE   MADRID   ATHENS
MELBOURNE   AUCKLAND   KUALA LUMPUR   SINGAPORE   TOKYO
IBADAN   NAIROBI   KAMPALA   JOHANNESBURG   GABORONE
PORTSMOUTH NH (USA)   CHICAGO   MEXICO CITY   SAO PAULO

First published 1997
2000   99   98   11   10   9   8   7   6   5   4   3   2   1

A catalogue record for this book is available from the British Library
on request.

ISBN 0 435 45555 9

Designed by Jackie Hill
Typeset and illustrated by TechType, Abingdon, Oxon
Printed and bound in Great Britain by The Bath Press

Dedication

Dedicated to Richard and Cath

Acknowledgements

The authors and publishers would like to thank the following for permission to reproduce photographs and other copyright materials.

BAA
British Telecom
Community Advice Centre, Southall
First Impressions
Format Photographers/Joanne O'Brien
Format Photographers/Brenda Prince
Format Photographers/Ulrike Preuss
HM Customs and Excise
Ipswich Borough Council
Mobil Oil Company Ltd
Norfolk and Waveney TEC
Oxfam/James Hawkins
Tate Gallery

Contents

Introduction

The aim of this book is to investigate and explain the nature and activities of different business organisations. In addition to this, we also examine the roles of individual working within these organisations and the common administrative services and procedures. It is hoped that we have illustrated the fact that an efficient and effective organisation not only needs to have these systems in place, but also must aim to support and help their employees carry out a variety of roles.

Business Administration has been specially written for students studying for *Business Administration Stage II*, a core module of the RSA Certificate in Administration and Secretarial Procedures, and *Background to Business*, part of LCCIEB's Secretarial Studies Certificate. It will also be essential reading for students studying Business Administration second level.

The book provides a vital source of information for those who are in work or preparing to work in an administrative role which demands some degree of responsibility. It is also hoped that the book will provide you with a useful guide to be able to organise your own work and contribute more effectively to the operations of an organisation.

The format of the book offers:

- an **introduction** to each chapter which gives you a brief overview of what it contains
- **students activities** and **case studies** which provide opportunities for discussion and practical tasks to help with your learning
- **keywords** at the end of each chapter which highlight important topic areas
- **examination practice** at the end of each chapter to help you prepare for the final examination.

Whether you are using this book in your studies towards a secretarial certificate or as a practical guide to aid you in your job role, we hope that you find the information valuable.

We wish you luck in your studies or personal development.

Jon Sutherland & Diane Canwell
March 1997

Business organisations in the private sector

■ Introduction

In the UK economy many decisions are made by private individuals. Some decisions may be small ones, such as how much to charge a customer for a late-night call-out to mend a burst pipe, or the level of an overdraft for a bank or building society customer. Other decisions may affect hundreds or thousands of people, such as a business deciding to locate in a particular part of the country, or the implications of a business deciding to set their production at a particular level. The UK economy is a mixed one, with elements of the private and public sectors. The public sector refers to the part of the economy in which decisions are made by the government or by an organisation which has been given specific responsibilities by the government. We will be considering this aspect of the economy in Chapter 2.

The private sector consists of a variety of organisations which are owned by individuals who are, generally, motivated by monetary rewards. They all have to make business decisions and take risks based on their own judgement of what their customers will buy. They will have to set the price for their products or services so that they can ensure that they sell enough to cover their costs. Ultimately, they hope to make a profit which is the reward for good judgement and successful risk-taking.

■ Types of business organisation

There are a number of different legal types and structures of organisation. However, it is useful to realise that organisations operate in many different areas and, for this reason, they may have different objectives.

An industrial or manufacturing organisation exists to make, construct or assemble products. During this production process the organisation adds value to the raw materials or components it began the process with and will eventually produce some form of finished product. Depending on the size of the organisation, its method of products and, perhaps, its location, it will adopt a certain type of legal structure.

Student activity

Make a list of at least ten local manufacturing organisations and identify the types of raw materials and components they may use.

Service organisations do not actually manufacture products, although the differences between manufacturers and service organisations are becoming less and less obvious. An organisation which produces computer software, for example, could be seen as either a service organisation or a manufacturing organisation. In the past, the major difference between manufacturers and service organisations has been that the former did not usually have any direct contact with the consumer; they relied on service organisations to sell their products for them. In recent years many manufacturers have realised that they have a greater control over their business and a better opportunity to make bigger profits if they become involved in service activities, as well as their more traditional operations. Service organisations, or the **tertiary sector**, is the biggest employer in Europe and includes all of the major retail chains, business-to-business services and the professional advisers that organisations may use.

Student activity

Write a list of ten service industries which can be found in your own local area.

Each organisation will have a particular financial objective. Broadly, these are

- to make a profit
- to improve profits
- to break even or cover costs.

As you will see, dependent upon the type of organisation, and its overall business objectives, these financial objectives may change from time to time. There are a number of aspects which may determine how the organisation sets its financial objectives. These are

- the nature of the market in which the business operates (whether the market is very competitive or constantly changing)
- the period of time during which the business has been operating (as an organisation begins to understand the nature of its business and has a clear picture of the market itself, it may be able to perform cost-cutting exercises in order to become more profitable)
- the needs of the owners or investors in the organisation (shareholders, for example, may not necessarily be interested in the day-to-day running of the organisation and may be interested only in the profits they get from the dividends on their shares, or may judge the success of the organisation on the value of their shares on the stock exchange)
- the availability and awareness of customers (both the number of customers in the marketplace and whether these customers know about the organisation and its products and services)
- the market share held by the business (this is measured in terms of the organisation's percentage share of turnover or level of sales compared to their competitors)
- the size of the organisation (although large organisations can obtain raw materials, components and services at a cheaper rate than smaller ones, small businesses may not have large overheads, such as many employees and expensive premises)

- the range of products and services offered by the organisation (over a period of time the business may decide to concentrate on particular products and services which they know they can sell successfully in the market, or they may decide to broaden the range of products and services they offer)
- the type of organisational structure (organisations need to be flexible and have the ability to respond to change and external threats, so they need to have an effective organisational structure with the necessary employees in place to cope with all sorts of potential opportunities and threats)
- the management style of the organisation (some organisations still have a very strict system of management which does not require their employees to show any kind of judgement or initiative. Other organisations positively encourage their employees to take an active role in decisions and operations).

Each organisation's principal sources of finance can be identified first in terms of the length of time that they are available. In this respect, we will make the distinction between short-, medium- and long-term and permanent availability. We will look at each type of organisation in turn, examining briefly the finance available, length of availability and its probable use.

Table 1.1 gives a summary of each type of business organisation and the criteria under which they operate.

Sole trader

The sole trader is perhaps the most common type of business organisation, although in recent years the numbers of such businesses have been declining, for a number of reasons, which we will look at later. The sole trader is also often known as the sole proprietor.

The sole trader is responsible for all actions that the operation undertakes. This individual will be responsible for borrowing all the money required and actually running the business on a day-to-day basis. Perhaps the most common sorts of sole traders are craftsmen and women – such as, plumbers, decorators, electricians, mobile hairdressers, window cleaners and chiropodists.

Sole trader businesses cover a very wide range of activities, but they all have some features in common, including the way they got started, and the fact that the business can always normally be run by

Organisation	Liability	Use of profit	Source of finance	Control of organisation	Legal obligation
Sole trader	Unlimited	Reinvest Self	Own assets Loans Grants	Direct	All[1]
Partnership	Unlimited[2]	Reinvest Partners	Own assets Loans Grants	Direct	All[1]
Private limited	Limited	Reinvest Shares	Shares Loans Grants	Directors Managers Owners	All[1]
Public limited	Limited	Reinvest Shares	Shares Loans Grants	Directors Managers Owners	All[1]
Franchise	Limited/ Unlimited[3]	Reinvest Franchisor Franchisee	Own assets Franchisor Loans Grants	Managers Franchisor	All[1]
Co-operative	Usually limited	Reinvest Members	Members Loans Grants	Members Managers	All[1]
Central government	n/a	Re-used Treasury	Treasury	Prime Minister Cabinet Ministers Civil servants	Most[4]
Local government	n/a	Re-used	Council tax Rates/rent Central government	Councillors Officials	Most[4]
Quangos	n/a	Re-used Treasury	Central government	Appointees Central government	Nil[5]
Charity	Limited/ Unlimited	Reinvest Cause in question	Donations Covenants Grants	Trustees	Most[6]

[1] Including employment, civil, trade union, health and safety, etc.
[2] Except in limited partnerships
[3] Dependent upon the organisation of the franchise
[4] Except for some laws depending on nature of authorities
[5] Only those imposed by central government
[6] Dependent upon the structure and charitable status

Table 1.1 Types of business organisations

one person, although that person has to be very flexible and needs to be willing to work very long hours.

Like many of the other types of business organisation, the sole trader may have to consider the following points.

- Once a certain level of turnover (sales income) has been reached, the business will be liable to register for value added tax (VAT). This means that the business must charge VAT for its products and services and that it may claim VAT back on the products and services that it uses.
- The sole trader will have to pay income tax and national insurance.
- The sole trader may have to obtain necessary licences from the local authority (particularly if he or she is involved in the sale of alcohol or the provision of public transport).
- The sole trader may have to obtain permission to run a particular type of business from the intended premises (all premises are designated by the local authority as being able to be used for a particular purpose).
- The business will need to comply with a variety of laws including health and safety legislation.

There are a number of advantages and disadvantages to setting up as a sole trader.

Advantages
- There are no real legal formalities to complete before commencing to trade. This means that there are no delays in obtaining legal status or the normal administrative expenses related to the setting up of a partnership or a limited company.
- There are no real legal requirements governing the layout of accounts.
- The annual accounts do not have to be audited.
- Decisions can be made quickly since only one individual is involved.
- The owner has the freedom to run the business in his or her own way.
- All profits can be retained by the sole trader (after the payment of tax, etc.).
- Many sole traders may be entitled to some form of government support in the way of grants.
- The sole trader can determine the hours of work, take holidays when desired and operate the business around other commitments.
- The sole trader can have a close relationship with customers, providing quality (personal) service to them and supplying exactly the kind of products and services that they require.

Disadvantages
- Capital is limited to the owner's savings or profits or any other money he or she can borrow.
- The owner has sole responsibility for debts – if the owner falls into financial difficulties he or she may have to sell personal possessions to meet business debts. This is known as **unlimited liability**.
- Responsibility for a range of activities falls upon the shoulders of one person. The owner is responsible for all aspects of running the business, from

dealing with paperwork and filling in tax returns to day-to-day contact with customers or any employees or subcontractors he or she might use.

- The success of the business is always dependent on how hard the sole trader wishes to work.
- Any unforeseen accident or illness could seriously affect the business since all responsibilities rest on the shoulders of that one person.
- Sole trader businesses are less likely to survive in the long run. This is largely due to the fact that only one individual really understands the nature of the work itself. In cases where the business is passed on to another member of the family, or another individual, there is a very high probability that there will be extreme difficulties in making a smooth transition of ownership.

Main sources of finance

The main sources of finance used by a sole trader include the following.

- Permanent sources of finance – owner's capital, profit reinvestment. Usually used for the purchase of fixed assets and organisational growth.
- Short-term sources of finance (up to three years) – credit, overdrafts, factoring, short-term personal or bank loans, hire purchase. Credit would be used for the purchase of stock. Overdraft and factoring would be used for the purchase of stock, paying wages and provide working capital. Short-term loans and hire purchase would be used for the purchase of relatively cheap assets.
- Medium-term sources of finance (three to ten years) – medium-term bank or personal loans, hire purchase, credit, leasing. Loans would be used for the purchase of fixed assets. Other sources would be used for buying assets in order to maintain sufficient working capital.
- Long-term sources of finance (over ten years) – loans or grants from government agencies, mortgages, long-term bank or personal loans. These sources of finance would be used either for the purchase of fixed assets or as an alternative to using working capital.

Student activity

Using *Yellow Pages*, try to identify ten sole traders who operate in your local area. Is there any type of organisation which is more likely to be a sole trader than another form of organisation?

Partnerships

A partnership may be formed as a way to overcome the problems a sole trader may have in raising capital. A partnership consists of between two and 20 people who set up in business together and share the responsibility for that business. In partnerships, all partners have what is known as unlimited liability. This means that any debts incurred by the partnership have to be met by all the partners. However, traditional partnerships such as solicitors and Lloyds insurers have recently been taking steps to limit their liability. Each partner is required to contribute some capital, and the profits and the losses are shared among all of the partners. The control of the business is the responsibility of all of the partners, and decisions made by one partner are always binding on the others.

The rules governing the formation and running of a partnership are contained within the Partnership Act 1890. This does not mean that there are any really complicated legal formalities to go through in the formation of a partnership, but the partners need to sign a Partnership Deed or agreement which determines the rights of the partners in the case of a dispute.

The agreement usually includes the following.

- The amount of capital to be contributed by each partner.
- The ratio in which the profits and losses are to be shared. Usually, this is worked out in relation to the amount of capital each of the partners has put in. So, in other words, the more capital each partner has put in, the more profits he or she will be entitled to.
- The salaries, if there are any, that are going to be paid to specific partners.
- The rules for admitting and expelling partners.
- The voting rights of partners – they may have an equal or an unequal share of the decision-making.
- The rules for ending the partnership.

On the question of **limited liability**, there is an option which allows a partnership to have limited liability for some members of the partnership – this is known as a **limited partnership**. In such partnerships, certain partners are known as sleeping partners. They take no part whatsoever in the decision-making process of the business, and should the business fail, they stand to lose no more than their original investment in the business. Therefore, they have limited liability. In contrast, the other partners, known as the general partners, still face unlimited liability. In law, there must always be at least one partner with unlimited liability.

The most common form of partnership, however, is the ordinary partnership where all partners play an active role in the running of the business. In the event of losses being incurred, each partner has unlimited liability.

It is very important for people setting up a partnership with unlimited liability that all the partners are trustworthy, honest and hard-working. Otherwise, the mistakes of one may affect all the others financially. Partnerships are commonly found in the accounting and legal professions, where specialists will join together in a partnership to make the business more attractive to prospective clients.

There are a number of advantages and disadvantages in setting up a partnership.

Advantages

- It is easier for partners than sole traders to raise capital because all of the partners can pool their resources and have access to more capital.
- Partners can share their expertise and their efforts.
- Partners can arrange to cover for one another at times of illness or holidays, or even lunch breaks.
- A partnership, like a sole trader, has the advantage of not having to publish its accounts or have them audited.
- Additional capital can be raised by introducing more partners into the partnership.
- Since there are a number of partners, the organisation has the ability to grow at a greater rate than a sole trader. The individual partners, providing that they are all committed to the business, can work to enable the business to expand and incorporate other areas of activity.

Disadvantages

- A partner is personally liable for all of the other partner's debts.
- Disagreements can arise between partners about the amount of effort that each of them puts in.
- Partnerships can raise only limited amounts of capital as compared with businesses like limited companies.
- Decision-making can be slow since all partners have to be consulted.
- The death or retirement of a member can bring a partnership to an end if such a rule is written into the deed of partnership. In any case, the family of the deceased or retiring partner will need to be able to realise the assets. This means that the original partnership will have to be wound up (closed) and a new partnership agreement drafted and agreed at the earliest opportunity.
- All profits must be shared.

Main sources of finance

- Permanent sources of finance – partners' capital, profit reinvestment. These would be used for the purchase of fixed assets and general organisational growth.
- Short-, medium- or long-term sources of finance are the same as for a sole trader.

Student activity

Solicitors', accountants' and doctors' practices tend to be partnerships. Try to identify at least five partnerships in your local area and see how many partners there are in each organisation.

Private limited (Ltd) companies and public limited companies (plc)

The limited company is fast becoming one of the most common forms of business organisation. A limited company is a separate organisation in law from its shareholders and directors. As with a partnership, individuals put capital into the business – these are known as **shareholders** – and they own part of the business and will share any profits that are earned. They elect a number of directors who will actually run the business on their behalf.

The law requires a meeting of shareholders to be held once a year, and minuting of matters that may be discussed is required. Shareholders really have little part in the day-to-day running of the business, although they may also be directors.

A number of Companies Acts have been passed over the years which protect the interests of shareholders, as well as those of creditors who are owed money by limited companies. It is relatively simple and reasonably cheap to set up a company. In order to set up a limited company, two documents must be drawn up. The first is a **Memorandum of Association**. This is really the company's rule book. The types of information that you would find in a Memorandum of Association are:

- the name of the company
- the address of the registered company
- the company's activities
- the type and amount of capital which has been invested to set up the company.

The second document is the **Articles of Association**. These deal with the inside working of the company, and include

- the procedures that have to be followed at an Annual General Meeting, known as an AGM
- the duties of the directors of the company
- the voting rights of the shareholders
- how profits and losses are distributed among shareholders
- details of how company officers will be appointed
- details of how accounts will be kept and recorded
- the rules and procedures of issuing shares and transferring shares to other people.

Once these two documents have been drawn up, the next step is to send them to the Registrar of Companies, Companies House. If everything is in order, the Registrar of Companies will issue a certificate of incorporation, which is rather like the company's birth certificate.

There are essentially two different types of limited company. Both of them have a minimum of two shareholders.

The first is known as a **private limited company**. You can always tell that a company is a private limited company when the word 'Limited' or 'Ltd' is written after the company name. The shares in a private limited company are not freely available to the general public and the transfer of shares is set out in the Articles of Association. Private limited companies are usually family concerns, or were originally family concerns. This is the form of organisation often chosen when a sole trader wants to expand and wishes to retain control of the company.

The second type of limited company is a **public limited company** (plc). These tend to be larger concerns. They are allowed to raise capital through selling their shares on the stock exchange. This gives them greater flexibility in raising capital. Only two people are needed to form a public company and there is no stated maximum number of shareholders.

The process of creating a public company is very similar to that of creating a private company. To set up a public limited company, the following procedures need to take place.

- A Memorandum of Association is drawn up (just as for the private limited company).
- Articles of Association are drawn up (just like the private limited company).
- A Statutory Declaration is prepared. (This states that all of the requirements of the various Companies Acts have been adhered to in the setting up of the organisation.)
- A Certificate of Incorporation is obtained. (This is issued by Companies House, if all of the above have been completed correctly.)

Once a public company has received a Certificate of Incorporation it will prepare a prospectus, which is simply an invitation to the public to buy shares. The people forming the company must decide how those shares are to be sold, and how many shares will be allocated to each prospective buyer. The Registrar of Companies will then issue a trading certificate. This means that the business is now up and running.

One feature common to both types of limited company is that they must file a set of audited accounts with the Registrar of Companies. This set of accounts must include

- a directors' report
- an auditor's report
- a balance sheet
- the source of funds
- an explanation of the accounts.

It is also necessary for public limited companies to file an annual return. This gives the details of the directors, shareholders and any other information that is required by law. All this information is kept on file at Companies House, and is always open to inspection by members of the public for a small fee.

Advantages

There are a number of advantages in setting up a limited company as compared with being a sole trader or partner.

- Shareholders have limited liability.
- It is easier to raise capital through shares.
- It is often easier to raise finance through banks.
- It becomes possible to operate on a larger scale since, when additional capital is required, additional shares are offered to the public.
- It is possible to employ specialists.
- Suppliers tend to feel more comfortable when trading with legally established organisations.
- Directors are not liable, provided they follow the rules.
- It is easy to pass shares down from one generation to another and in this way control may be kept by the same families.
- The company name is protected by law.
- There are tax advantages attached to giving shares to employees.
- A company pension scheme can give better benefits than those that are available for the self-employed.
- The ill-health of shareholders does not affect the running of the business.

Disadvantages

- The formation and running costs of a limited company can be expensive.
- Decisions tend to be slow since there are a number of people involved.
- Employees and the shareholders are actually distanced from one another.
- All the affairs of the company are public, with the audited accounts and annual returns that the company makes being published.
- Legal restrictions, under the various Companies Acts, are fairly tight and there are very heavy penalties for companies which break the rules.
- Large companies are often accused of being impersonal to work for and to deal with.
- Rates of tax on profits are often higher than those that sole traders and partnerships have to pay.

Main sources of finance

- Permanent sources of finance – issue of new shares, building up reserves. Again, these would be used for the purchase of fixed assets and general organisational growth.
- Short- or medium-term sources of finance are the same as for a sole trader.
- Long-term sources of finance (over ten years) are the same as for a sole trader, but, in addition, include debentures and redeemable preference shares. These two new sources of finance would be used for an immediate increase in available working capital.

Case study

Bruce and Julia Thomas set up a home pet-food delivery service in Norwich in 1985. At first their business was a small one, concentrating on the area to the north of the city. They made frequent leaflet drops to the majority of houses in the area, delivering bulk pet foods to domestic users. The business gradually grew and they moved to bigger premises, taking on two delivery drivers and a warehouse person. By 1990 they were in a position to expand into the rest of the city, but unfortunately the recession in the area was still having an impact on their business. Two other local pet-food delivery services had already gone bankrupt and Bruce and Julia noticed that their turnover had fallen and their profits had been cut dramatically.

Bruce decided to return to full-time employment with the local authority, leaving Julia to run the business. They had, by this stage, made one of the van drivers redundant and the warehouse person had left for other employment. After two years profits stabilised and  then began gradually to rise. Julia did not have the finance in order to take advantage of the upturn in sales. She needed someone to join the business and invest a considerable amount of money. A local businesswoman, Heidi Blanchard, made a sizable investment in the company in return for 49 per cent of the shares. This still left Julia and her husband as the major shareholders. Heidi did not wish to have any involvement in the day-to-day running of the business, but was very interested in a good return on her investment.

The private limited company detailed in the case study above is very common. You will notice that there is a difference between the owners and those who directly manage the organisation. How do you think these differences can be balanced? On the one hand, Julia actively manages the organisation and is a major shareholder with her husband, whilst, on the other hand, Heidi is a minority shareholder and does not have any managerial role. Do you think that the demands of these two shareholders are different? Present your findings in the form of an informal memorandum to your tutor.

Franchises

The franchise is a form of organisation which has been imported into the UK and the rest of the world from the USA, where over a third of all retail businesses are operating as franchises. This is becoming a very popular form of business organisation in the UK. The main features of franchising are as follows.

■ Franchising really amounts to hiring out or licensing the use of product lines to other companies. A franchise agreement allows another company to trade under a particular name in a particular area. The firm which sells the franchise is known as the **franchisor**.

■ The person who takes out the franchise needs a sum of money for capital and is issued with a certificate from the franchising company. This person is known as the **franchisee**. The franchisee usually has the sole right of operating in a particular area. Some examples of franchises can be seen in many of our high streets – Pizza Hit, Prontaprint!, Body Shop and Spud U Like.

■ Another important feature of the franchise agreement is that the franchisee agrees to buy all of its supplies from the franchisor and the latter makes a profit on these supplies.

■ The franchisor also takes a share of the profits made by the franchisee's business, without having to risk any capital or be involved in the day-to-day management of the business.

■ The franchisee, on the other hand, benefits from trading under a well-known name and enjoys a local **monopoly**. In other words, each franchisee is the only business to operate under that name in a particular area.

■ The franchise agreement allows people to become their own boss without the normal kinds of risks of setting up a business from scratch.

Student activity

If you were interested in becoming a franchisee, investigate where and when Franchisee Exhibitions are held throughout the company. Discuss this first as a group and then investigate one definite opportunity.

Main sources of finance

■ The availability of finance may be dependent upon the type of organisation that is being set up. For sole trader franchisees, the problems of obtaining long-term finance may be the same as for an individual proprietor. Where the franchisee wishes to become a partnership or a limited company, the availability of finance may be easier, simply due to the decision to set up that kind of organisation.

■ The name and the perception of the franchise may be a considerable factor when the franchisee tries to obtain finance. For franchises that have a good reputation and have been well established, the financing may be much easier. For newer franchises, where the track record is not so clear, the financing may be much more difficult.

- The franchisor may be able to help with the financing in some cases. Obviously, the franchisor (if it is a reputable company) will want to see that the franchisee has sufficient finance available to them to start up the business and pay the costs in the beginning. The franchisor may be able to recommend a finance source that has worked with other franchisees in the past. It may, at the very least, be able to provide franchisees with trade references to help them obtain finance for further development and investment purposes.

Co-operatives

Co-operatives are an increasingly popular type of business organisation. In the past co-operatives were found only in agriculture or retailing. More recently, there has been a growth in the number of co-operatives in services and in small-scale manufacturing. In a co-operative all the people who form part of that organisation join together to make decisions, share the work and also share the profits.

The first successful co-operative was a retail co-operative. It was set up at the end of the nineteenth century in Rochdale in Lancashire when weavers joined together to open their own shop selling basic grocery items. Their profits were shared, as was the amount of money they spent, and everyone had an equal say in how the shop was run.

The basic idea behind the Rochdale Co-op remains and Co-ops may be seen in high streets throughout the UK. Nowadays, Co-ops are registered as limited liability companies.

Another major area in which co-operatives are found is in production, both in manufacturing and food production. In this type of organisation all the members share the responsibility for the success or failure of the business and work together, making decisions together and taking a share of the profits.

These co-operatives suffer from a number of problems.

- They often find it difficult to raise capital from banks and other bodies because the co-operatives are not in business simply to make a profit.
- The larger co-operatives have discovered that they must set up a solid management structure in order that decisions can be made.
- In food production, several farmers will set up what is known as a marketing co-operative, in which each farmer takes responsibility for a particular part of the production of a food, whether it is packaging, distribution or advertising.

Here the more conventional form of co-operative is mainly being considered. Increasingly, an ideal way for smaller retailers (in particular) to compete with larger organisations is to join a co-operative alliance. These alliances, also known as 'buying groups', offer many of the advantages that larger organisations enjoy, particularly when purchasing stock. Independent small businesses through their membership of a co-operative alliance or buying group, can obtain many of the following:

- higher levels of discount
- lower initial basic prices
- cheaper or enhanced delivery services
- greater access to a wider variety of products
- enhanced credit terms
- benefits from co-operative marketing and advertising.

Good examples of these types of co-operative alliance or buying groups are Toymaster, – an independent buying group for toy and hobby shops, and Spar, an alliance of independent grocers and off-licences.

An additional benefit is passed on to the customer (in most cases) by lower prices or at least prices competitive with those of the major chains.

Student activity

Your local Co-op supermarket may be trading under a different name. What is the real name of the co-operative behind this retail operation and what other activities is it involved in within your area?

Charities

Charities view business activity in a different way from many other organisations. Charities have been described as

- **Non-profit making** – they are not necessarily in operation to provide a profit, although a modest profit that could be ploughed back into the operation could be useful. After all, the profit motive is not there as technically charities are not owned by anyone, nor do they have shareholders who require dividend payments.
- **Non-loss making** – the organisation should not have to dip into its reserves to support its activities. Some organisations, throughout the recession, found their income diminishing and had no other choice. Even the Church of England has had to dispose of assets.
- **Profit-making** – this can be said to be true of many charities these days. They do produce a profit from their merchandising and other fundraising activities, but the money is not distributed to shareholders or owners. In most cases, the funds are either used to support new activities, purchase equipment, expand into new countries, or are simply transferred into a reserve fund for contingencies.

An organisation with 'charitable status' is exempt from many of the legal obligations of a normal organisation. However, it still has to comply with such things as health and safety requirements, or contracts of employment, but any

profits it makes are not taxable. In recent times, in addition to the well-known and long-established charities like Barnardo's, Oxfam, Help the Aged, etc., many schools have adopted this particular form of organisation.

The major objectives of charities are

- to raise awareness of a particular issue
- to stimulate action, either from the public or the government
- to provide advice and support to particular groups, the general public or government
- to distribute financial resources or physical resources, such as recreational equipment.

■ Use and distribution of profit

Profit itself is what is left from revenue after the costs have been deducted. Therefore

$$revenue - costs = profit.$$

There are several types of profit, and it is advisable to understand these in basic terms first. A **profit and loss account** is the best place to begin (see figure 1.1). This is simply a statement which records all of the organisation's revenue and costs over a period of time. The statement begins with the **total revenue** (sales total), from which is deducted the **cost of sales** (cost of purchasing the goods and services subsequently sold and any other directly attributable costs). This gives the **gross profit** (not the final profit as more costs must still be deducted).

From the gross profit we must now deduct the organisation's **overheads** (**indirect and fixed costs** such as salaries, rent, lighting and heating). This leaves the **trading or operating profit**. From this the cost of or revenue from 'one-off items' is either added or deducted. This may be revenue from the sale

TRADING AND PROFIT AND LOSS ACCOUNT FOR THE YEAR ENDED 31 OCTOBER 199—

				199—
SALES		451185		367202
COST OF SALES				
Opening stock	20671		23211	
Materials	305001		248966	
Closing stock	(23615)		(20671)	
		302057		251506
GROSS PROFIT		149128		115696
Bank interest received		135		-
		149263		115696
LESS OVERHEADS:				
Wages	9854		6662	
Motor running expenses	5788		5818	
Repairs and renewals	136		1284	
Telephone charges	2312		2557	
Printing, stationery and advertising	2693		3115	
Sundry expenses	892		796	
Heating and lighting	1168		921	
Insurances	1320		1666	
Rent and rates	8388		8280	
Equipment leasing	233		525	
Vehicle leasing	903		4072	
Loan interest	2006		1791	
Bank interest and charges	2080		1972	
Bad debts	1835		-	
Debt collection fees	65		612	
Accountancy charges	1870		1475	
Depreciation	1012		689	
Loss on sale of assets	100		-	
		42655		42235
NET PROFIT FOR THE YEAR		£ 106608		£ 73461
DIVIDED AS FOLLOWS:				
		53304		36731
		53304		36730
		£ 106608		£ 73461

Figure 1.1 Simple profit and loss account

of property, or deductions from the payment of redundancy packages or payments into a pension scheme. After this calculation, we are left with the **pre-tax profit**.

Not surprisingly, we must now take the tax away from this total (corporation tax in most cases, but in smaller businesses, this may be Schedule D – self-employment tax).

The next total, after the tax deduction, is **profit after tax**. In the case of limited companies, they must now pay a dividend to their shareholders. A **dividend** is a share of the profits. The total left is known as the **retained profit**.

So what happens to this retained profit? In most cases, the main use of this cash is reinvestment. This may take a variety of forms, including

- purchase of new materials
- payment of long-term liabilities (such as loans)
- purchase of premises
- acquisition of another organisation
- acquisition of another organisation's product or service (for the purpose of owning and producing it in the future).

Smaller organisations may use profit to expand their operations. A sole trader, for example, may choose to create a partnership with others and relocate to larger premises. Perhaps the sole trader needs to upgrade or replace machinery or vehicles.

Larger organisations may choose to use their profits to acquire smaller or related organisations. This is known as a **merger** (when two organisations mutually agree to join together) or **takeover** (when one organisation buys another one).

As we have seen from the explanation of the distribution and gradual reduction of profits, the cash needs to go to a number of different individuals, groups and organisations. Tax is the unavoidable consequence of profit. The government insists on clear and honest accounting of the transactions carried out by all organisations, regardless of size or structure.

Any owner or shareholder of an organisation also insists on a slice of the profits. After all, the original investments were made to reap the financial benefits of the organisation's activities. As you will see later, larger organisations which have shareholders have a complex job in deciding the level of dividend or profit share.

More simple, in one respect, is the distribution of retained profit to partners. This distribution is usually made on the basis of seniority or the level of the original investment in the partnership.

For a sole trader, the distribution could not be easier. If the organisation is wholly owned and run by a single individual, then he or she will retain all of the profit. Many sole traders will have 'sleeping partners' who do not take an active role in the business. However, they will expect a share in the profits at the appropriate time.

Multinationals or international organisations have complex arrangements in dealing with profits. They are in an excellent position to 'move' profits from one part of the organisation to another to avoid paying tax. In some cases, profit-making parts of the organisation will be deemed to 'owe' another less profitable part of the organisation and thus the profit will have been 'removed' before the stage when tax is payable. This is not illegal, but a much-used benefit of operating in a variety of countries. Profits in this case can often be used to bolster or support struggling parts of the organisation. This can cause animosity between the different parts of the organisation as the successful parts feel that they are subsidising the inefficiencies of another part.

■ Growth from one organisation type to another

Types of change

In a rapidly changing market organisations must be aware of the impact of change upon their operations. Many of the factors which could have been relied upon in the past to be constant are no longer so. Not only can organisations not rely upon a steady level of sales or demand, they can no longer continue producing products and services in traditional ways. One of the major agents of change has been new technology, which has not only affected telecommunications, but has also had a marked impact upon production techniques. Markets have also changed significantly; not only has increased competition affected particular markets, but changes in government policy, such as **deregulation** have opened markets to increased competition. Perhaps one of the biggest changes in terms of markets has been the development of the European Union (EU).

Another major change which also relates to the nature and availability of customers is the fact that the UK and most of the developed world has an ageing population. This is known as the demographic time bomb. Not only has it had an impact upon the workforce, but it also has increasing influence on the purchasing habits of the consumers.

Change can be more generally categorised in one of the four following ways.

1 **Tuning** – to make the organisation operate more efficiently, perhaps by redesigning job roles. This is usually a pro-active approach in anticipation of the need to make changes in the future and is an example of a tactical change in the organisation.
2 **Adaptation** – usually a reactive move to changes in the external environment, often used as a remedy to problems. These changes would focus on selected parts of the organisation. This is also a tactical change in the organisation.
3 **Reorientation** – these are planned strategic changes that anticipate major changes in the external environment. By making these sweeping changes the organisation hopes to maintain or improve its competitive advantage.
4 **Re-creation** – this is the most drastic form of change and would involve significant modification of the organisation. Usually, these changes are made

as a result of potential major changes in the external environment. Without the changes the long-term viability of the organisation would be threatened.

Alternative methods of finance

Traditional sources of finance have often proved to be inadequate if the organisation needs to grow rapidly. Obviously, there is some opportunity for the organisation to plough back profits which have been made as a result of increased demand. However, in many cases, growth needs to exceed profit growth. Consequently, there is often a shortfall in available internal funds to finance this growth. As a result organisations have had to look for alternative methods of finance. **Rights issues** are a more traditional way of achieving this, but other organisations have had to look to **joint ventures**, mergers and takeovers as a way to supplement shortfalls in available funding. Another common way of coping with the immediate need for funds is **sale and lease-back**. At some point, however, organisations will run out of ways in which to raise funds quickly. There may have to be a period of slower growth or considerable readjustment of assets before faster growth can be achieved.

We have looked at the more common sources of capital earlier in this chapter. However, one major area of investment in businesses comes from **institutional investors**. Essentially, these are the individuals who manage the portfolios of pension funds, unit trust groups and insurance companies. They are the major shareholders in the UK. As such, they have enormous influence on the price and availability of shares in the market. Obviously, their principal interest is the performance of the shares which they have purchased. In other words, their concern is for the short-term profit. This, it is said, puts too great a pressure on the organisations that they have invested in to make short-term profits and pay out good dividends. Having said this, many organisations tend to rely on institutional investors to buy the majority of their shares upon **floatation**. Many of the shares offered to the public through the **privatisation** process have found their way to institutional investors in fact a large percentage of the shares are reserved for this purpose.

Changes in the management structure

Major changes in the management structure of an organisation should be as much expected as any other type of change. This is usually driven by the directors of the organisation, the owners or as a result of poor or very good results. Inevitably, there will always be winners and losers in such a change. The main point of the exercise will always be to improve the overall management structure of the organisation. There are three main goals that can be identified here.

1 The management changes should enable the organisation to better fulfill its vision of the future. Within this, the new management positions should involve difficult performance targets and encourage enthusiasm.
2 The management changes should revitalise the managers. The winners of the changes should be held as role models for all.

3   The management changes should also build an effective top layer of management that is able to continue the development of the management practices and support the longer-term change processes.

Growth

With hundreds of thousands of businesses accounting for many billions of pounds of **turnover**, it is inevitable that the relative sizes of various businesses will differ enormously. Most businesses welcome growth. In fact, there are many organisations which specifically aim to do this. At the same time there are many organisations that want to remain small.

If a business has less than £1.5m turnover, then it is considered to be small. Those with a turnover of around £6m are large. Those that fall in between are considered to be medium-sized. Turnover is used as a more accurate assessment of size since organisations with relatively few employees could be extremely profitable, whereas those with many thousands of employees could be relatively unprofitable. There are a great many reasons for growth and consequent changes in size. These include

- the fact that by staying small the organisation may not be able to take advantage of **economies of scale**, fend off possible takeovers or become more profitable
- the fact that the larger the organisation becomes, the greater the economies of scale, leading to lower unit production costs, greater efficiencies and higher profits
- the fact that by growing the organisation should be able to sell more products and services, which would in turn mean a higher level of profitability
- the fact that growth means a greater market share and may be able to have an influence on the pricing structure of products and services in particular markets
- the fact that by growing larger and diversifying into new areas, the organisation can avoid or at best reduce, the level of risks associated with the failure of a particular product or service.

Most growth is internal growth. This is also known as **organic growth**. The organisation will gradually grow in size as it sells more products and services to more markets. Organic growth is a slow process, but it does not have many of the associated dangers of faster growth. Alternatively, the business may choose external growth which would involve a process of acquisition, including the takeover or merging with other businesses. By acquiring a controlling interest or complete control of another business the organisation is able to guarantee faster growth in size, although this does not necessarily mean a growth in profitability. It will, however, mean that greater economies of scale may be achieved.

Takeovers and mergers

The principal reasons for changes in ownership tend to be related to takeovers and mergers. Some changes in ownership may signal significant changes throughout the whole of the organisation and its operations. On the other hand, the change in ownership may not seem to have a serious effect on the business in the short term. Inevitably, changes will be imposed or agreed, and this will affect all levels of the management and the workforce.

Takeovers and mergers tend to occur when organisations choose to (or find themselves obliged to) join together and operate as a single business. The different types of takeover and merger are discussed later, but for now we need to define exactly what these terms mean. A takeover is acquiring full management control of another business by purchasing over 50 per cent of its share capital. An alternative description of the word 'takeover' is **acquisition**. Usually, the buying business is larger than the target business. For this reason, the larger organisation is often described as being a predator.

A merger is an agreement between two organisations to bring their businesses under the control of a single board of directors. Naturally, this has to be agreed by the management and the shareholders to ensure that the merger is a smooth one. There are a number of reasons why these activities take place.

- If an organisation is set upon rapid expansion, then it may be quicker to purchase another business and gradually convert it into its own business (in terms of approach, procedures and name).
- If an organisation has calculated that it would be cheaper if it purchased another business than if it concentrated on growing internally, then it would be a great temptation to consider a takeover rather than gradual growth.
- If an organisation is 'cash rich', it may wish to invest some of its profits in the acquisition of another organisation. This may be the ideal move, particularly as it will mean that the cash can be spent before tax liabilities are calculated.
- If an organisation believes that another business may be a long-term threat to its position in the marketplace, then it may consider acquisition as a purely defensive move. This will mean that at a stroke it will have eliminated the potential threat as well as having acquired the skill and expertise of the growing business.
- If an organisation recognises that the true value of another business is greater than its selling price, then it may purchase the organisation purely to sell off its assets. This is known as **asset stripping**. The purchasing organisation will sell off any valuable part of the acquired business. If the purchasing organisation is not merely interested in asset stripping, then sales may be necessary in order to dispose of duplicated operations and unprofitable areas of the organisation.

Over the past few years, particularly since the 1980s, there has been a marked increase in the number of mergers in the UK. As a direct result of the establishment of the Unlisted Securities Market which allowed potential investors to purchase shares, smaller businesses found it easier to raise finance. They needed this access to finance in order to pay for their merger activities. At the same time, the government appeared to be more willing to allow takeovers and mergers. Many individuals who had not considered becoming shareholders in the past purchased a number of shares during share issues of the utilities and consequently other organisations.

There are a variety of different merger or takeover operations. They can be best described overall as an 'integration process'. These include the following

- **Horizontal integration** – where two organisations in the same area of business activity (particularly at the same stage of production) join together. This allows for greater economies of scale that are evident in larger-scale activity. A typical example of this could be two newspapers joining forces.
- **Forward vertical integration** – this occurs when an organisation merges with another business which is at the next stage of production. A typical

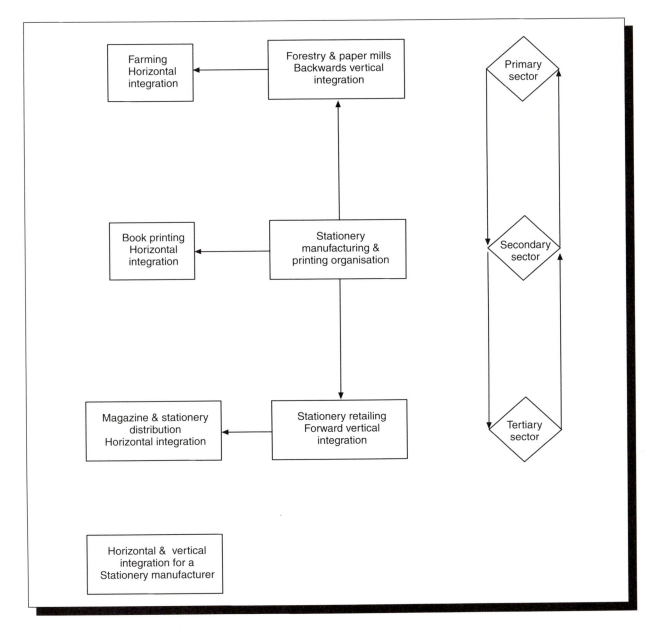

Figure 1.2 Integration process of an operation

example of this would be a food-processing business acquiring a chain of restaurants and grocery outlets.

- **Backwards vertical integration** – this happens when an organisation chooses to acquire a business that is at an earlier stage of production. An example of this would be a newspaper acquiring a printing plant, wood mill or forestry operation. This is done to make sure that the original organisation can make the best use of the advantages of not being reliant upon another supplier, so increasing the overall profits.
- **Lateral integration** – this involves the merging of two organisations that do not have a great deal in common. Perhaps they do have some superficial similarities (such as operating in the same marketplace), but beyond that the acquisition is purely designed to achieve a degree of diversification. Diversification means that the organisation can now operate in different marketplaces that can be designed to be complementary in terms of location, distribution and economies of scale.

Particularly in the latter case, we can see that the organisation's merger activities aim to diversify and form a **conglomerate**. The organisation, as a conglomerate, is no longer reliant on a single market and can divert its efforts and resources to other areas of its activities at the appropriate time.

A predator organisation does not, necessarily, have to acquire 51 per cent of the shares of its victim. Particularly in cases when the share ownership is widespread amongst hundreds of thousands of small investors, the predator may be able to gain control with as little as 15–20 per cent.

If it is believed that the takeover or merger is not in the public interest, the Department of Trade and Industry may require the **Monopolies and Mergers Commission** to investigate the situation.

As you will have realised, some takeovers are unwanted by the present owners or board of directors. These are known as 'hostile takeovers'. The target of the takeover will attempt to gain support in order to fight off the takeover. The board will try to convince the shareholders that it is not in their interest to allow the takeover to succeed. It will then be up to the shareholders to consider the advantages and disadvantages of the takeover and decide whether to support the existing board or throw their shares in with the predator.

In other situations the takeover may be welcomed by the business. These are called 'friendly takeovers'. Businesses which are encountering difficulties may find themselves in a situation where the only alternative is to look for an external investor. The potential investor would bring much-needed capital to the struggling business in return for a share in the ownership.

Management buy-outs and buy-ins

Management buy-outs occur when the managers of an organisation purchase the shares from the current owners of the business. By controlling the organisation the managers hope to be able to maximise the profitability of the business as they have a very definite incentive in ensuring its success. Many examples of management buy-outs have involved the change of ownership of subsidiaries or divisions of larger organisations. The change in ownership has given the new business a considerable advantage as many tiers of management have been dispensed with as it has become independent. The managers need to be very sure that they can make a positive impact on the business. A successful buy-out can mean that the managers stand to make a great deal of money. On the other hand, the managers must also take responsibility for the workforce and their future too. Much of the money that is needed to finance a management buy-out will come from loans secured against the personal property of the managers. This will make the **gearing** of the organisation quite high at the beginning. Whilst the acquisition of a business in which the managers have a significant stake is attractive, they must be prepared to take on a much greater degree of responsibility. They can no longer be wholly concerned with their area of the organisation's operations. They must take an active role in strategic management and the moulding of the business's objectives. In some cases, management buy-outs have signalled either one or the other of the following consequences for the workforce:

■ that manning levels have been significantly reduced and that the workforce lives in a much greater fear of redundancy through reorganisation and rationalisation
■ that the business has become significantly more democratised with the managers actively seeking the cooperation and involvement of the workforce.

Management buy-ins operate in a similar way to management buy-outs, but the managers are not involved in the existing set-up. Individuals, who will take the roles of managers in the organisation buy the shares of the business in the belief that they can manage the business more efficiently and profitably than the existing managers.

■ Importance of each type of organisation to the UK economy

The *Annual Abstract of Statistics,* published by the government, provides some valuable information on the size structure of the UK economy. Actually assessing the size of an organisation in any kind of way presents us with an initial set of problems.

■ Do we simply categorise each organisation in terms of its legal structure?
■ Do we assess the size of a business in terms of its turnover?
■ Do we assess the size of the business in terms of the number of employees?

The most common form of categorisation is that of the level of employment. In this respect, we can break down the manufacturing industries, for example, as shown in Table 1.2. These are broad figures, adjusted to reflect the number of units (number of businesses in existence) and the rough percentage of the total numbers of organisations which exist.

No. of employees	No. of organisations	% of total
1–9	105 125	67.2
10–19	15 952	10.2
20–49	18 003	11.5
50–99	7 883	5.0
100–199	4 855	3.1
200–499	3 318	2.1
500–999	905	0.6
1 000+	408	0.3

Source: Annual Abstract of Statistics 1992

Table 1.2 Size structure of UK manufacturing industry

This offers only one way of assessing the spread and importance of the various types of organisation. In fact, all we can say about this information is that it appears that over 94 per cent of the businesses in this sector of the economy employ fewer than 100 employees. This does not really help us in assessing the legal structure of the organisations involved, but we can make some assumptions. It is highly likely that the smaller organisations (say fewer than ten employees) may be sole traders. The private limited companies probably account for the majority of the other organisations that employ fewer than 200 or so. The remainder, we could safely suggest, are more likely to be public limited companies.

Without doubt, all of the larger organisations in the UK are public limited companies. For example

British Petroleum   BAT Industries
ICI   British Telecom (BT)
Grand Metropolitan   British Aerospace
British Gas   BTR
Hanson   J. Sainsbury
Unilever

A great many of these organisations are also multinationals, ie they have considerable interests outside of the UK.

The single type of organisation that seems to have been charted throughout the twentieth century is the small business. The government uses the unhelpful definition of 'under 200 employees', so again this makes the categorisation difficult. At an all-time high of around 45 per cent of the total number of businesses in the 1930s, the small business was in continual decline until the middle of the 1970s (then at about 28 per cent). From then, they have gradually increased (with a small fall at the end of the 1980s) to a new figure of around 40 per cent.

Keywords

The keywords that should know for this chapter are listed below. Check to make sure you understand the meaning of each word. Discuss those you are unsure of with your tutor.

acquisition
Articles of Association
asset stripping
conglomerate
cost of sales
deregulation
dividend
economies of scale
flotation
franchisee
franchisor
gearing
gross profit
institutional investors
joint ventures
limited liability
limited partnership
management buy-in
management buy-out
Memorandum of Association
merger

Monopolies and Mergers Commission
monopoly
organic growth
overheads (indirect and fixed costs)
pre-tax profit
private limited company
privatisation
profit after tax
profit and loss account
public limited company
retained profit
rights issues
sale and lease-back
shareholders
takeover
tertiary sector
total revenue
trading or operating profit
turnover
unlimited liability

Examination practice

Short-answer questions

1   What is meant by the 'private sector' of the economy?
2   Define 'limited liability' and give two examples of types of organisation that have 'limited liability' and two that do not.
3   What is a franchise?
4   Give two advantages and two disadvantages of co-operatives.
5   Give three objectives of a public limited company (plc).
6   How many individuals can be involved in a partnership?
7   Give two advantages of a private limited company (Ltd) compared to a partnership.
8   What is a merger?
9   Give one example of vertical integration and one of lateral integration.
10 What is the difference between a management buy-out and a management buy-in?

Essay questions

You have recently been employed as an administrative assistant for a sole trader. Helen Kirby has just returned to work after a break of five years in order to look after her two small children. Now that the eldest child is about to start school, she is more able to devote the time and attention she needs to restart her business consultancy company. Helen is extremely good with the clients, but lacks the ability and willingness to devote her time to the administrative work involved. The business is run from her own home, although you work in a converted out-building where all of the records and office equipment are housed.

1 Helen has asked you to prepare a database of all the local businesses in the area.

   (a) She would like you to begin by defining the following categories of businesses: sole traders, partnerships, private limited companies and public limited companies.

   (b) She would also like you to identify the other ways in which you could categorise the different local businesses.

2 Helen's business is not very capital intensive, so she does not really need to attract a large investment of cash in order to grow. However, the business is doing well and Helen cannot possibly look after all of the different clients that are contacting her for advice. Knowing that you have some knowledge about how businesses could expand, she has asked your advice.

   (a) What alternatives does Helen have for transforming her sole tradership into another form of business organisation?

   (b) Should Helen consider taking on a partner, or should she attempt to find someone willing to invest so that she could employ another business consultant?

3 Helen's husband runs his own estate agency business in a town nearby. Sometimes, the services which he offers, such as mortgage advice, insurance and helping clients to find the right premises for their businesses, have proved to be a useful connection for Helen's clients. Her husband, Keith, employs two people at his estate agency and has suggested to Helen that they join forces and move her business into the empty office suite above the shop. This would, of course, mean a major change for everyone.

   (a) What kind of merger would this be?

   (b) What type of business structure would best suit the new company?

(c) How could Helen ensure that the name of 'Kirby Management Consultants' remains known to the clients?

4 After a short period of time, the new combined company is doing very well. Both Helen and Keith are very happy with the structure of the organisation, but realise that if they want to keep growing they will need to change their legal structure again.

(a) What type of legal structure would be most appropriate for them at this stage?

(b) How could they ensure that they still have ultimate control over the decision-making?

(c) If they decided to sell shares in the company to an outsider, what is the minimum percentage of shares that they should retain in order to ensure control?

Business organisations in the public sector

■ Introduction

The public sector consists of organisations which are either wholly, partly or indirectly owned or controlled by the government. As you will see in this chapter, there are a number of different types of organisation which exist to provide a range of services or administrative assistance on behalf of the government, but for the general public or businesses these include the following.

- The central government departments, which include the Department of Trade & Industry (which provides assistance to businesses), the Department of Transport (which attempts to coordinate the UK's transportation needs) and the Inland Revenue (which collects tax from both individuals and business on behalf of the government). Collectively, these departments are known as the civil service.
- The local authorities or local government, which includes county, metropolitan, district and borough councils, who provide a range of services, assist businesses and generally promote their region or area.
- Public corporations or enterprises, such as the Bank of England and the remaining parts of BR, whose task it is to provide specific services within their area of interest. They are also often referred to as 'nationalised industries'.
- Quangos which are semi-independent organisations, funded by government in order to provide a service, but with a level of detachment from normal government business. They include the various utility regulators, such as OFTEL (telephone), OFWAT (water) and OFGAS (gas). Other quangos include the Arts Council and the various bodies which have been created to distribute lottery grants.

Student activity

As a group, try to list at least ten public-sector organisations that operate in your local area.

■ Public corporations and enterprises

When we think about government in the UK we automatically tend to think of Downing Street, the Houses of Parliament and Whitehall. Although these are important and they are places where the government can be seen in action, the government has many other parts, including organisations which are controlled by the government in some way. These are known as public enterprises, or public corporations. Here are some examples of these.

- BR (some of this public enterprise has been sold to the private sector, such as certain routes, former British Rail property, land and track).
- British Coal (many of the coal mines have either been closed down, or have been sold off to private companies).
- The Bank of England.
- The Post Office (much of this has been broken up by the government, or at least de-regulated, allowing other providers of similar services to enter into competition with the Royal Mail).

Since 1979, however, many public corporations have been returned to private hands. Examples of these are: British Telecom (BT), British Gas and electricity generation.

Student activity

As a group, try to think of another five examples of organisations or services that have been privatised.

But why did the government become involved in running these organisations in the first place? Here are some of the reasons.

- One of the main reasons is to avoid waste and duplication. In the past, many services were offered by different companies. Essentially, they were offering the same thing. For example, private railways ran similar services from the same towns, often having lines running parallel to one another.
- Many of these organisations offer services which could not be run profitably. The big debate here is on whether a private company would invest in supplying gas or electricity or water to a remote village when even in the long term it would not be able to make a profit.
- The larger the organisation the more benefits there are in terms of production. Organisations which produce lots of output are able to buy their raw materials more cheaply, their labour can be more concentrated and consequently their prices can be lower.
- The government is always interested in the level of employment. A good example of this thinking is the relocation of tax offices and social security offices, whose vast headquarters have been set up in relatively remote areas of the country where there is high unemployment. In setting up a public

corporation the government might be taking this into consideration.

■ One of the biggest arguments in favour of public corporations is that the government itself needs to control vital basic goods and services which everybody needs. These are known as the infrastructure and include the transport network, water and energy. Some commentators argue that the government has a responsibility to make sure that the infrastructure is supervised and maintained well. The process of privatisation, which turns public corporations into companies owned by shareholders, is proceeding rapidly and is likely to step up in the late 1990s if there is another conservative government.

Student activity

Are these good reasons for nationalising organisations? Can you think of any reasons why the government should not, directly or indirectly, run organisations or services? Discuss this as a group.

One of the ways of safeguarding the running of a public corporation is to set up an independent body which keeps an eye on it. This organisation copes with complaints that are made against the enterprise and tackles the enterprise should it wish to put up prices or cut services.

Although these public corporations operate independently, they are controlled to some extent by government at all times. It is the government's responsibility to make decisions about closing down parts of the business or investing large sums of money to improve it. On a day-to-day basis the chairperson of the enterprise and the other managers will make decisions about wages, prices or industrial relations, but the government does still interfere when these decisions affect the public.

We have seen that a limited company needs to make an annual report to its shareholders. So, too, does a public corporation, but it presents its annual report to the government minister who is responsible for taking care of it. This government minister makes a report in Parliament to the Members, who will then make criticisms or support the corporation and how it is being run. At the same time a committee made up of Members of Parliament meets regularly to keep an eye on the day-to-day running of the corporation and reports back to Parliament on how it is being operated. This is known as a Select Committee.

In addition to public corporations, there are two other areas where the government gets involved in the business world. The first is when an activity is actually run by a government department. A typical example of this is Customs and Excise. It deals with the supervision and collection of taxes due on products entering and leaving the country. The second is when the government has a share-holding in a public company.

■ Local authorities

Perhaps the most common form of government organisation is one which touches our lives the most, and this is local government. In the UK certain

services are run by locally elected councillors. The councils usually run business organisations such as swimming pools, sports centres, bus services, car parks, shopping centres and public conveniences. Just like public corporations, local council activities have been affected by privatisation. The particular process used by councils is that of **tendering**.

The local council details the service it wishes to offer for tender. Companies which are interested in running the service put sealed bids in to the council explaining what it would cost to run the service and what they would be providing. The company that offers the lowest tender is given the job. It is then the council's responsibility to monitor how effective the company is in providing the service. If a company fails to reach certain standards, then the contract is taken away from it. Local government pays for these services by receiving a grant direct from central government and by collecting local taxes. These have been known as rates and community charge and are now called council tax. Local councils also subsidise loss-making activities such as parks which obviously provide benefits to the community.

Student activity

As a group, try to think of any service or organisation that has been put out to 'competitive tender' in your local area. What is your opinion of the organisation? Has it been improved, or has the service that it provides suffered since being contracted out?

■ Quangos

Perhaps the strangest form of business organisation is the quango (quasi autonomous non-governmental organisation). Quangos are organisations that have been set up by the government to carry out a specific task. In other words, they have been set up to take responsibility for a certain area of the government's business. A good example is the Equal Opportunities Commission.

The various publicly owned industries were sold to private individuals during the 1980s and early 1990s. These important utilities such as gas, electricity, telecommunications and water are all necessary services which are used by the majority of the public. Given the fact that they are no longer government-run, there was a very real danger that the new shareholders would be more interested in making a profit than providing a reasonable service. As a result, the government appointed a number of utility regulators or ombudsmen in order to control and watch the activities of these organisations. The key regulatory bodies are

- OFFER (Office of Electricity), which was set up in 1990 and regulates the prices charged by the regional electricity companies
- OFGAS (Office of Gas Supply), which was set up in 1986 to regulate gas supplies to domestic users

Case study

There is one quango for every 10 000 people in the UK. With over 75 000 people involved with quangos at the local level, this means that they outnumber local councillors by two to one. Around 99 per cent of quangos are not subject to any form of investigation or monitoring by an independent body. Only a third of them are audited and over 90 per cent do not invite the public to any of their meetings.

Can you think of any quangos that operate in your area? Perhaps someone you know works for one. You may find your local telephone book to be a useful source of information.

- OFTEL (Office of Telecommunications), which was set up in 1984 and regulates BT and other telecommunications companies, including line rental charges, calls, licences and equipment
- OFWAT (Office of Water), which was set up in 1989 to regulate the supply of water and sewerage services.

■ Aims, responsibilities and sources of finance

State provision of essential services

In nearly all countries, governments have involved themselves in providing for essential needs. These include health, education, law enforcement, transport and housing. Governments provide these services, funded by taxation, to ensure that the basic infrastructure of the economy is maintained. Without the maintenance of these services, individuals and businesses alike would find it impossible to operate. Although some individuals and businesses may be able to provide for themselves in almost all of these areas, the vast majority of the population find themselves reliant upon government-subsidised services. There has been a gradual move towards the privatisation of many of these services, but privatisation does not necessarily mean the elimination of the provision of these services by the government itself. In many cases, the privatisation process merely means that the provider of the service is no longer a government department or agent, but effectively is a subcontractor which provides the service on the government's behalf. The privatisation of prisons, for example, simply refers to private organisations subcontracting from the government the responsibility of running the service. There are two further important points to bear in mind when considering provisions provided for the country as a whole, known as 'public goods or services'.

- **Non-rival in consumption** – this refers to the point that if a particular individual benefits from a public good or service, this does not prevent other individuals from consuming or benefiting at the same time. The level of service should be sufficient for a number of simultaneous demands on the service to be met fairly easily. The state, in providing the service, will try to ensure that the cost of providing that service does not exceed the overall benefit that society gains.

- **Non-exclusive** – if individuals refuse to pay their share towards the service provided, it is very difficult to exclude them from the benefits that all individuals receive. If someone has not paid his or her council tax, this does not mean that the police force (which receives some of its funding from this source) will not respond to an emergency call. Individuals who do not pay their contribution towards services are effectively enjoying a free ride at the expense of those who are willing to pay. In the final analysis, this means that all willing payers will end up paying more to subsidise the free-riders.

Student activity

In pairs, try to find out how much your local authority spends on the various services that it provides. How does the council tax level compare to that of a neighbouring area?

Products or services which fall into the category of **merit goods** could be provided by the private sector. Examples of merit goods include the National Health Service (NHS), museums and education. There are two main reasons why the government chooses to provide these merit goods.

- **Equity** – in a society which recognises equality of opportunity, it is important to give all individuals a fair chance. In this respect, the provision of free education to all tries to address the fact that the poorer sections of the community could not afford a good education for their offspring. Those with high incomes can always choose to use private education, but the majority of the population have no other choice but to use state education.
- **Externalities** – by providing a particular service from which all members of the population can benefit, this has positive benefits for society as a whole. If the majority of the population is literate and well educated, then the assumption is that the economy will be more successful. These are also known as the social benefits, but they are hard to quantify. In some respects, the government may choose to ignore the social benefits and concentrate on the social costs of providing the service. This is a rather negative view to adopt, but an increasingly popular one. The philosophy behind looking at social costs and ignoring social benefits is linked to the desire of many individuals to allow everyone to choose exactly where and how to spend their income. Following on from this, we must assume that if key services are not provided by the state, then we can expect lower taxation – which in turn releases more income to be used as and where the individual sees fit.

Student activity

Do you think that these two reasons are sufficient enough for the working population to be paying the relatively high rates of direct and indirect taxation? Do you think that the country would run much better and more fairly if individuals had to pay their own way through insurances and other personal protection schemes and plans? Discuss this as a group.

Case study

Government activity costs a lot of money and there has been a great change in the last decade in what governments can spend. Bearing in mind that all spending has to be financed through taxation or borrowing, restrictions have developed in both. If the power of government's spending is curtailed, where can investment for vital UK industry come from?

The UK government decided over ten years ago that public ownership should be a thing of the past. It pioneered **privatisation** throughout the 1980s. Perhaps the most revolutionary was the first major privatisation campaign – the selling off of council houses. Telecommunications, airlines, gas, electricity and water soon followed. Instantly these businesses no longer required the government to find money for investment via taxation or borrowing. With the privatisation of coal and the railways in progress, there are very few industries or services left in public hands.

In 1979 the nationalised industries were costing the tax-payer around £50m a week in losses alone. Today the government receives through taxation £60m a week from their profits. From 1983 to 1985 the average investment required to be found out of taxation and borrowing for gas, electricity and water averaged out at around £3.6bn each. In comparison, in 1991–2, these utilities, now in private hands, achieved a £6bn investment level each.

Regional development policy

Government policy on regional development can take a number of different forms. These include the following.

- The siting of central government departments in regional areas. The government operates a policy of positive discrimination in choosing a depressed area to site its services. The Vehicle Licensing Agency, which is responsible for the monitoring and licensing of all motor vehicles within the UK, has been sited in Swansea. This area has been suffering from high levels of unemployment and the move has resulted in many positive effects on the local economy.
- The government offers a range of incentives to industry to help reduce costs in moving to or setting up in a depressed area. The government has built a number of purpose-made factories and lowered the cost of rent and rates to encourage organisations to resettle in depressed areas.
- Labour costs can also be reduced by offering a subsidy to industries to attract them to select a depressed area when considering a move.

Student activity

Can you think of any central government employer in the area? What is the reason for siting the organisation in your area of the country? Does it serve the local community, or is it an organisation that serves the UK?

Certain regions can be designated as special areas which will, in turn, receive additional help and assistance from the government. Development areas can be split into three distinct types.

- **Special development areas** – those in need of the maximum help.
- **Intermediate areas** – those with particularly high levels of unemployment.
- **Development areas**.

The EU assists these regions through its Regional Development Fund and encourages its money to be spent on building up infrastructure as well as encouraging organisations to establish their businesses there.

Fiscal policy

Governments can directly affect an organisation's trading position by altering the amount of direct tax it has to pay on profits (corporation tax) and by using legislation to increase or decrease competition within a particular market. One of the major influences on an organisation's trading position, however, is the availability of finance for investment. An increase in the amount of corporation tax, for example, means that companies have less profit to plough back into the organisation itself. Alongside this, a rise in the rate of interest will reduce the amount of investment as the cost of borrowing money increases. In other words, the higher the rate of interest, the more the organisation has to pay back.

Fiscal policy refers to the government's policy on

- public spending
- various taxes
- public borrowing.

The government uses the above to influence the level of demand, inflation, employment and economic growth. These criteria are achieved in simplistic terms by changing the amount of money it spends in relation to the amount of money it collects and the different tax methods by which it collects it. The government also uses fiscal policy for a number of other reasons.

- To finance its own expenditure on health, education, the armed forces, etc.
- To help lower-income people in the form of transfer payments, such as pensions, social security, etc.
- To give incentives to industry, eg grants, loans, subsidies, etc.
- To discourage consumers from products which may be considered detrimental, eg very high taxes on tobacco.
- To protect domestic industries by controlling imports (this can also help with the balance of payments).

In recent times, the government has nearly always been operating a **deficit budget**. This is when it spends more than it receives in taxes. In order to make up the shortfall, it must acquire money from other sources. This is known as the **public sector borrowing requirement (PSBR)**. A **balanced budget** occurs when government spending is matched by tax income. Recent governments have attempted to reach this balance by spending as little as possible and relying on private individuals to provide for themselves. Rarely does a government have a **surplus budget**, as this would mean that the government had taken in more taxes than it was spending.

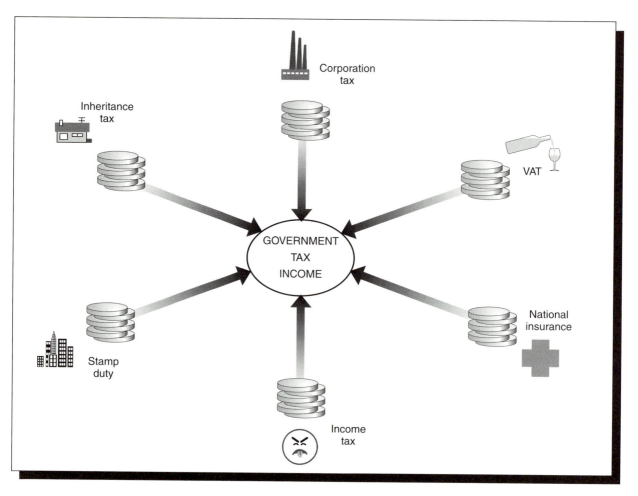

Figure 2.1 Main sources of income tax

There are additional advantages and disadvantages of these various forms of 'balancing the books'. If the government is operating a deficit budget, there is a danger of **inflation** growing, as it becomes increasingly more expensive to borrow money. A surplus budget, on the other hand, can help reduce inflation by cutting down the amount of disposable income each individual has – in other words, reducing demand. The main sources of tax income are

- income tax taken from each individual from money earned
- corporation tax paid by businesses on their profits
- value added tax (VAT) paid on the value of products or services at each stage of their production (this VAT proportion increases as products move from raw materials to finished goods)
- national insurance paid by both employees and employers to provide benefits
- inheritance tax paid on property and money left in wills
- stamp duty paid on financial transactions which involve large sums of money.

The effect of some policies has a much greater and quicker impact on the level of demand than others. The effect of an increase in **direct taxation** such as a rise in income tax has a direct and immediate impact on the level of **consumer disposable income**. This thus reduces the level of demand. Whereas if the government were to increase the level of **indirect taxation** (say VAT), the overall effect is again to decrease the level of demand. However, as indirect taxation is effective only on consumer spending on those items affected by the tax, the decrease in the level of demand obviously takes longer to have an impact.

Monetary policy

The government's monetary policy deals with

- the supply of money circulating in the economy
- interest rates
- exchange rates.

The government uses the above to influence the level of demand, investment, inflation, employment and growth. In simplistic terms, the government can encourage or discourage the amount of money which consumers and organisations spend. This includes not only their personal income, but also the level and ease of obtaining credit.

Monetary policy is concerned with the control of the quantity and price of money in the economy. As long as individuals are spending money at a rate faster than the supply of products or services, then prices will inevitably rise. There is a strong link between the quantity of money available and the level of inflation.

Money cannot simply be described as coins and notes. There are many other forms of money. These include credit cards, cheques and credit payments. In order to control the amount of money available, the government will set the interest rate at a level to deter people from borrowing, or encourage them to do so. As well as attempting to control the quantity of money, the government will also try to set the price of money. Such activity relates also to the interest rate. In addition, the government will keep a close eye on the Retail Price Index (RPI) which serves as an indicator of inflation. By keeping pay settlements below the increase in the RPI, the government will be effectively reducing the amount of money available in the economy. On the other hand, if the government allows pay settlements to exceed the change in the RPI, then it will be allowing the injection of more money into the economy. In the first instance, the RPI will drop, in the latter it will increase. Both of these circumstances may give the government cause for concern.

Direct taxation

Personal income tax and corporation tax are both forms of taxation which are termed 'direct taxation'. These are taxes which are targeted at individual entities and are based upon level of earnings. In other words, income tax is paid upon an individual's income and the more you earn, the more you pay. Corporation tax is paid upon company net profit – the higher the amount of net profit earned, the more tax payable.

Advantages
- This is progressive in the sense that, taken with benefits, it effectively redistributes income in favour of low-income groups.
- The amount raised by direct taxation increases as income rises.
- It is anti-inflationary.
- The exact cost to each individual in society is easily measured and calculated.

Disadvantages
- There is a disincentive effect, in that the more you earn, the more you pay.
- It is said that direct taxation stifles initiative and enterprise by over-taxing.
- It is comparatively easy to evade or avoid payment of taxation – for those who declare their own tax liability, it is comparatively easy to 'hide' income.
- Direct taxation may act as a disincentive to foreign investors as well as those at home.
- It is comparatively expensive to collect.
- By taxing savings, the value of these savings is substantially reduced.

Direct taxation has a higher impact than indirect taxation in terms of a policy instrument as it immediately affects the disposable income of individuals and level of profits returned by companies. Indirect taxation, on the other hand, takes time to filter through. As a means of reducing demand in the economy, an increase in a direct tax such as income tax would have a far more immediate effect than the introduction of an individual tax on a particular product or type of product.

Indirect taxation

VAT was introduced on 1 April 1973 and is an 'indirect tax'. In other words, it is a tax imposed upon people's spending. VAT is collected by the government at each stage of production and distribution. Each organisation pays VAT on the value of goods it purchases, and then charges VAT on to the value of the goods and services it supplies. The business effectively pays no tax as any VAT incurred in purchasing is passed on in sales to the consumer. As indirect taxes are based upon spending, they are often seen as hitting lower-income people harder than the better-off.

Advantages
- Payment is often convenient as indirect taxation may be paid in instalments or at source.
- To some extent indirect taxation can be considered to be voluntary since its payment is linked to consumption.
- Unlike direct taxation, it does not adversely affect incentive or enterprise.
- Since it is often paid at source, it is harder to evade payment.
- Indirect taxation is considered to be a fairly flexible form of taxation.
- The funds received from indirect taxation can be used to fund specific purposes.

Disadvantages

- Although indirect taxation takes a lower percentage of an individual's income, it may not necessarily take a lower amount as income rises.
- Indirect taxation tends to penalise certain types of consumption. If the taxation policy is not sufficiently thought through, then it may adversely affect the ability of a particular industry to operate.
- Unlike direct taxation, indirect taxation is hard to calculate since it is only when specific purchases are made that the indirect taxation comes into operation.

Student activity

As a group, discuss whether you think that direct or indirect taxation is a better or fairer way of collecting funds?

■ Impact of government involvement on the UK economy

It is important to remember when discussing government involvement and the public sector that we are not only concerned with national government (and areas such as nationalised industries and the civil service) and related services (such as police, armed forces, etc.) but also with all those employed by local government as well. Although in recent years there has been a trend towards local government services being offered to private companies on a competitive tendering basis, for example refuse collection, there are still large numbers of people employed by local government, or who are paid by local authorities. An example of this is the payment of salaries to teachers.

Control of government expenditure

One of the easiest instruments that government can use to implement its fiscal policies is the level of expenditure on public-service wage levels and the number of people who are employed in the public sector. Obviously, by raising or lowering the amount of employment and level of income people receive, the government can have a major influence on the level of disposable income its employees possess. This directly influences levels of spending and demand within the economy.

As you have seen, the government finances its public expenditure (on roads, health, education, etc.) by the collection of taxes such as income tax, VAT, corporation tax and many others, for example import tariffs.

The government can control its expenditure in three main ways.

- **Budget deficit** – where expenditure is greater than the revenue collected.
- **Budget supplies** – where expenditure is less than the revenue collected.

- **Balanced budget** – where the government spends the same amount as it collects in tax revenue. This is a very difficult position to achieve as, for example, it is virtually impossible to predict 100 per cent accurately the amount of revenue that will be received from indirect taxes such as VAT.

The reasons for government expenditure can be classified into four main categories.

- The provision of public goods – those goods and services that government supplies because private enterprise may be unwilling or unable to do so, eg national defence.
- The provision of social services, eg health care, education, housing and transfer payments.
- To increase industrial efficiency – firstly, the government believes that certain industries will be more efficient if run by the government, and secondly, the government can use grants and subsidies to improve the performance of the private sector.
- To influence the level of economic activity – an increase in public spending can increase demand and reduce unemployment, for example. Whereas a reduction in public spending can reduce the level of demand in an economy, raise unemployment and lower inflation.

Government competition policy

Increased competition tends to lead to a more efficient use of resources, as those firms which are unable to produce efficiently enough are forced out of the market. An insufficient amount of competition in a market, such as in conditions of **monopoly** or **oligopoly,** can result in some companies having a strangle-hold on the market. The legal definition of a monopoly is a company which possesses 25 per cent or more of the market share and exists due to the existence of barriers of entry of some sort. As a result, such organisations can charge high prices because the consumers have nowhere else to buy the goods and, as mentioned above, this can cause inefficient use of resources as there is no need for the company to produce its products as efficiently as possible due to the lack of threat from any competition.

Since 1948 successive governments have produced a range of legislation in order to stimulate competition within the economy. Generally referred to as competition policy, these Acts try to ensure fair competition in the marketplace. There are five principal Acts of Parliament governing UK **competition policy**.

The 1948 and 1965 Monopolies and Mergers Act

As previously mentioned, we say there is a monopoly when a single organisation substantially controls a particular market. This is not an acceptable state of affairs, as the organisation may be able to control both price and supply within that market. As far as the government is concerned, a monopoly situation is not in the public interest. In recent years, the body responsible for monitoring monopolies has been the Monopolies and Mergers Commission (MMC). With this Act the government provided itself with the means to refer merger proposals automatically to a Mergers Panel. This panel would report back within six months and simply state whether or not the proposed merger was against the public interest. Serious cases are then referred to the Secretary of State who can make an order to counterbalance the state of affairs.

The Restrictive Trade Practices Act 1956

Under this Act, a Restrictive Practices Court was established to investigate and rule upon organisations working together to fix market prices. Such an agreement between organisations is known as a **cartel**. In restrictive practices cases, organisations must prove that it is not against the public interest in order to avoid action being taken against them.

The Competition Act 1980

This Act effectively broadened the scope of activities that could be undertaken by the Director General of Fair Trading and the MMC. They could now investigate public-sector organisations, which were brought into the range of the legislation. Each case is still investigated as regards its particular benefits and costs to the free running of the market, but it is no longer the view that mergers in themselves are undesirable. Indeed, a monopoly may be acceptable under certain circumstances.

The Fair Trading Act 1973

This key Act attempts to tackle the problem of competition. Defining a monopoly as an organisation controlling more than 25 per cent of a market, this Act gave the Director General of Fair Trading considerable powers. Of particular interest to the Director General was any organisation attempting to distort the operation of a market by using anti-competitive pricing practices. Should the Director General rule that the organisation's activities are unacceptable, the organisation is automatically referred to the MMC. Again, the Secretary of State may rule that the organisation must immediately cease this unacceptable behaviour.

The Resale Prices Act 1976

Some suppliers may seek to ensure that retailers do not offer discounts or reduced prices for their products and services. The larger suppliers could, if they wished, try to demand that the retailer follows their pricing policy and rules. Suppliers have, from time to time, threatened to stop supplying retailers who offer price cuts. They have also given better discounts to retailers who follow their pricing policies. The Act attempts to prevent this kind of interference in the way that retailers choose to sell the products supplied to them. If the retailer feels that they are under pressure from the suppier in this way, then they can refer the matter to the Restrictive Practices Court.

Anti-competitive trading practices

The above five parliamentary Acts are the main means by which the government attempts to counteract the anti-competitive practices undertaken by companies. One of the main forms we have looked at is that of mergers and the formation of cartels, ie agreements formed between suppliers to achieve domination of a particular market. These types of agreements can take several forms, including

- agreements to limit the supply of the product to inflate prices
- agreements to fix a standard price
- agreeing to have standard contractual terms (although not as common as the other two types).

However, it is not only agreements between suppliers that take place. Suppliers and retailers may well collude in the formation of a reciprocal trading agreement. In this situation each company involved agrees to purchase only each other's products. This, in essence, effectively eliminates any competition and, additionally, means that suppliers and retailers may enter into long-term contractual agreements. In return for a beneficial price a retailer/distributor agrees to provide only that supplier's products for a long period of time, thus effectively restricting any competitors' products from entering the market.

It should be noted though, that retailers and distributors do not always enter into anti-competitive agreements with suppliers through choice. In some situations dominant suppliers may be able to force distributors and retailers into restrictive trade agreements. For example, as previously discussed in the Resale Prices Act, suppliers may force retailers into minimum resale price or may allow them to stock and sell the supplier's major product only if the retailer agrees to stock the full range of products provided by the supplier. This type of imposed agreement is termed 'full line forcing'. A good example of this may be if a newsagent wished to stock a particular brand and flavour of crisps which he or she knew to be popular and the supplier agreed to provide the newsagent with stock only if he or she agreed to purchase some less popular flavours as well. Another version of this type of agreement is referred to as 'tie in sales' when the purchase of one product is related to the purchase of another. A good example of this is when an organisation purchases a new car – part of the warranty agreement may be that all servicing and parts must be carried out by the manufacturer or dealership.

Student activity

As a group, try to think of an example of a product or service that dominates a particular market. You should try to consider one that is available in many different places and outsells the competition for these reasons.

Other forms of business regulation

Government legislation is often very bureaucratic. As such, it can be very costly and time consuming for businesses. There is also the added problem that enacting new legislation and statutes takes time and often Parliament has more pressing business to undertake. In this respect, the government encourages trade associations to regulate themselves (to some degree) through voluntary codes of practice. These are statements made by trade associations with the aim of achieving a common acceptable standard of trading and behaviour which it expects from its members. These are used instead of legislation and as such, if broken, are not legally enforceable, although they do act as the basis for dealing with customer complaints rather than going through lengthy legal proceedings in court. In recent years governments, through the Office of Fair Trading, have tried to encourage more and more trade associations and other organisations to use such a method as this means

- less legislation and government intervention allows businesses to operate more freely and thus allows the natural laws of supply and demand to do so as well
- if the government enacts legislation, it then has to appoint someone to see that such legislation is carried out and to deal with any breaches of it. The less legislation, therefore, the cheaper it is liable to be for the government.

Another way in which the government may seek to regulate businesses is by using a strategy known as **price capping**. This prevents businesses (usually monopolies) from charging exorbitant prices for goods and services. The way in which price capping works is quite straightforward.

- The government or regulating body (such as OFWAT) sets an upper limit on the price that the industry can charge.
- The limit is then regularly reviewed to take into account inflation, changes in costs of production, etc.

Governments and, in particular, local authorities, use **licences** as a means of regulating businesses in particular industries. The main examples of such industries are the casino and related gambling activities, public houses and off-licences and restaurants. Restaurants come under the Health and Safety and Hygiene Certificate regulations. In this way any business that is seen to be conducting its trading activities improperly simply has its licence revoked and is not granted a new one.

Student activity

Who would actually monitor and control businesses that are required to have licences? What part of the local authority would have trained staff to handle the complexities of the licensing systems? Discuss your suggestions as a group.

Deregulation

In order to promote competition and fair trade it is not always necessary to have more legislation and regulation in an industry. In some cases, deregulation is used. This involves the opening up of a market to more businesses and competition. Deregulation has taken place amongst many of the previously state-owned monopolies such as National Express Coaches (1980), local bus services (1985) and BT (1984). This has been a popular policy with Conservative governments since 1979. The reasoning behind these policies is that by opening up the markets to increased competition, consumers should be able to enjoy lower prices, higher quality of goods and services and, hopefully, increased innovation as companies try to get an edge on each other.

Office of Fair Trading and consumer protection

Despite the government legislation which attempts to counteract anti-competitive agreements and prohibit the formation of mergers and cartels, this by no means ensures that companies are going to conduct their business transactions in a fair and honest manner.

The job of keeping an eye on organisations and their trading activities is primarily carried out by the government's Department of Trade and Industry (DTI) and specifically by the Director General of Fair Trading. This post was created under the 1973 Fair Trading Act which led to the formation of the Office of Fair Trading (OFT). It is the role of the Office of Fair Trading and the Director General to refer any activities which may be seen to be prejudicial to the economic interests of the consumer to the Consumer Protection Advisory Committee, which, in turn, reports to the Secretary of State. The Secretary of State, based upon its recommendations, may then enact appropriate legislation making such practices illegal. These practices may include

- misleading consumers as to the terms and conditions on which goods and services are supplied
- methods of sales representation employed with consumers, ie subjecting consumers to undue pressure
- methods of securing payment causing the terms of the agreement to be deemed so adverse as to be oppressive
- any practice which is considered to be illegal, eg false trade descriptions, dealing in stolen property, etc.

Student activity

If you were in a position where you needed to complain about a local business for some reason, where would you go or who would you contact to do so? Discuss this as a group.

Once a matter has been referred to the Secretary of State and has been found to comprise unfair conduct, then the party concerned must not undertake that activity again or he or she may be liable to imprisonment. Alongside the Office of Fair Trading there is a variety of consumer protection legislation which helps to ensure that fair and honest trading takes place.

- The main legislation is the **Trade Descriptions Acts 1968 and 1972**. These Acts make it a criminal offence to supply false or misleading information about goods, services, accommodation or facilities. However, the legislation applies only to those sales conducted as part of a trade or business and not to private sales. It also makes it an offence to make misleading claims over sale prices.

- The **Consumer Credit Act 1974** allows only firms which have a licence from the OFT to offer credit (including banks, etc.), and includes numerous offences such as failure to supply copies of consumer credit agreements and trading without an OFT licence. It makes firms which supply the credit jointly responsible for the goods and services rendered together with the company which sold them.
- The **Weights and Measures Act 1985** makes it a criminal offence to give a short measure or short weight or even to possess weighing and measuring equipment which does not give accurate quantities. This Act allows for Trading Standards Officers to visit garages, public houses, shops, supermarkets, etc. to check such equipment.
- The **Foods and Drink Acts 1955, 1976, 1982** and the **Food Safety Act 1990** make it an offence to sell goods which are unfit for human consumption. Food intended for human consumption must meet the 'food safety requirements'. This requires that all reasonable precautions in preparation, storage, transport and sale of goods are carried out. An example of this is to make sure that cooked and uncooked meats are not stored in the same container.

Student activity

As a group, divide up the legislation listed above amongst you and try to find out a little more about each Act. You should focus on the way in which the legislation is enforced and by whom. Feedback your findings to the rest of the group.

The **Consumer Protection Act 1987** is primarily concerned with price and the pricing policy of organisations. No doubt many of us have been caught out when purchasing a product, to find that the price quoted is not the price in reality. This may be because the sale period has ended, the price quoted did not include VAT, or the claimed price reduction is untrue. This Act states that the organisation must clearly state the 'real' price of a product, not make unfair or untrue comparisons between products and price, and not make false statements about price reductions. The Consumer Protection Act further covers the consumer who is offered unsafe goods whatever the circumstances.

It must be noted, however, that despite all the legislation that may make you think otherwise, the vast majority of businesses do conduct their trading activities in a fair and honest manner, and will do their utmost to ensure that consumers are satisfied with their products.

Watchdog organisations

Some watchdog bodies have been set up by the government in order to monitor organisations' activities, particularly in their dealings with the public. Others have been set up by a particular industry to keep a check on their member organisations. This has been done to ensure that standards are maintained and

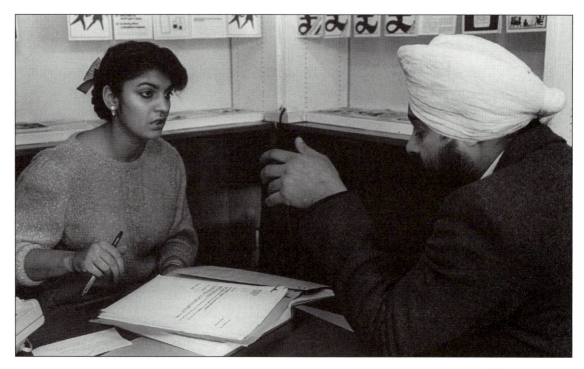

that any bad publicity resulting from a disreputable trader does not damage the industry as a whole. Here are some examples of watchdog organisations.

- **Citizens' Advice Bureau (CAB)** – the principal duty of the CAB is to act as a mediator in disputes between organisations and consumers. It is also responsible for a variety of other advisory matters, not necessarily relating to consumer rights. It operates through a network of local branches.
- **National Consumer Council** – the council is responsible for representing the consumer in disputes and problems with government departments, nationalised industries, local authorities and other businesses.
- **Environmental Health Department** – this organisation operates through local offices which investigate matters relating to food and hygiene. Each has the power to enforce legislation relating to food hygiene and may even close businesses which break the regulations.
- **British Standards Institution (BSI)** – this organisation, which operates on funds received from the government and voluntary donations, is concerned with setting minimum standards in all aspects of business and industry. It is best known for the BSI Kitemark which denotes that a product has reached the standards laid down by the British Standards Institute.
- **Consumer and Consultative Councils** – these organisations monitor the operations of nationalised industries, and attempt to ensure that they do not abuse their monopoly in terms of charging too high a price or providing a poor level of service.
- **Trade associations** – there are a large number of these associations which represent specific industries or services. They offer assistance, information and advice to their members. In addition, they also may devise a voluntary code of practice. A good example of a trade association is ABTA (Association of British Travel Agents).

- **Advertising Standards Authority** – this independent organisation is involved in ensuring that all advertisements are 'legal, decent, honest and truthful'.
- **The Chartered Institute of Marketing** – this is another independent organisation that attempts to ensure that its members have high professional standards, particularly in terms of honesty and integrity. Its British Code of Advertising Practice gives the advertising industry a clear set of rules to follow.
- **Independent Broadcasting Authority** – this organisation monitors the activities of television and radio stations and ensures that particular standards are maintained. Recently, it has been concerned about a new marketing technique known as 'placement' which involves popular programmes featuring and recommending particular brand names or products. Although placement is well established in America, the IBA has ruled that it is unacceptable in Great Britain.

■ Impact of European institutions

The European Parliament

The European Parliament comprises 626 members – 99 from Germany, 87 each from France, Italy and the United Kingdom, 64 from Spain, 31 from the Netherlands, 25 each from Belgium, Greece and Portugal, 22 from Sweden, 21 from Austria, 16 each from Denmark and Finland, 15 from Ireland and 6 from Luxembourg. The Parliament normally sits in Strasbourg. The European Parliament is made up of political groups organised at Union level. Representing 370 million people, Parliament's main role is as a political driving force, generating various initiatives for the development of Community policies.

Student activity

Who is your Euro MP? What party does he or she represent and does your Euro MP offer the constituents the opportunity to talk to him or her?

It is also a supervisory body with the power to approve the appointment of the European Commission and to dismiss it on a censure motion carried by a two-thirds majority. Parliament votes on the Commission's programme and monitors day-to-day management of European policies, especially by putting oral and written questions to the Commission and the Council.

Together, Parliament and the Council form the budgetary authority, with Parliament voting on the adoption of the annual budget (about ECU 80 billion in 1995) and overseeing its implementation. Union legislation is formulated by a three-way process: the Commission proposes legislative instruments, while Parliament and the Council share the power to enact them.

Student activity

Discuss the following as a group. 'Now that we are member of the European Union, we should stop thinking about ourselves as British. We are Europeans and we should follow the lead of our European neighbours.'

The European Council

Established in 1974, the European Council is made up of heads of state or government and the President of the Commission assisted by the foreign ministers of the member countries and a member of the Commission. It meets twice a year, providing the impetus and setting the broad guidelines for future action. Meetings are attended by different ministers according to the agenda: for instance, agriculture ministers discuss farm prices; employment matters are dealt with by labour and social affairs ministers; and general policy questions, foreign affairs and major Union issues are matters for the foreign ministers. The Council's headquarters are in Brussels, though certain meetings take place in Luxembourg. Each member state acts as President of the Council for six months in rotation.

The European Commission

The European Commission has 20 members – two each from France, Germany, Italy, Spain and the United Kingdom and one from each of the other Community countries. The Commission's term of office is now five years, the same as the life of the European Parliament.

In carrying out their duties, members of the European Commission are obliged to be completely independent of their national government and act only in the interests of the Union; only Parliament has the right to censure the European Commission. Each member of the European Commission has special responsibility for one or more policy areas, but decisions are taken on the basis of collective responsibility.

The European Commission is first and foremost the guardian of the Treaties. It is an impartial body which sees to it that Treaty provisions and decisions based on the Treaties are correctly applied.

The European Commission has the sole right to initiate new legislation and can use its influence at every stage of the process leading up to the adoption of a new European law.

Finally, the European Commission is the Union's executive body. This involves issuing rules for the implementation of certain Treaty Articles and administering budget allowances for Union operations. The bulk of these fall within one or other of the major Funds: the European Agricultural Guidance and Guarantee Fund, the European Social Fund, the European Regional Development Fund and the Cohesion Fund.

In 1994, the European Commission sent 558 proposals and drafts and 272 communications, memoranda and reports to the Council. The European Commission has an administrative staff based mainly in Brussels (where it is headquartered) and, to a lesser extent, Luxembourg. It comprises approximately 15 000 officials divided between some 30 Directorates-General and similar departments.

The European Investment Bank

The European Investment Bank (EIB), the financial institution of the European Union, was set up by the Treaty of Rome in 1958 to finance investments in support of the Union's objectives. The EIB is a separate organisation from the rest of the European Union to ensure that it is financially independent of all the member states. Its members are the member states of the Union, and it has its headquarters in Luxembourg. In 1994, it granted loans totalling ECU 19.9 billion, thereby confirming its position as a leading international financial institution.

The priority objective of the EIB is to contribute to the balanced development of the Union. It also facilitates the financing of projects to develop trans-European transport and telecommunications networks, to protect the environment, to secure the availability of energy supplies and to enhance the international competitiveness of industry and small businesses.

The European Monetary Institute and the European Central Bank

In 1997 if possible, and otherwise no later than 1999, a European System of Central Banks and a European Central Bank responsible for issuing and administering a single currency will be set up as part of the process of economic and monetary union (EMU) under the Union Treaty. A European Monetary Institute, based in Frankfurt, has been preparing the ground since 1994.

The single market

The focal point of economic integration is the single market set up by the member states to create a unified economic territory undivided by either customs or trade barriers. This single market rests on the pillars of four fundamental freedoms – the free movement of goods, persons, services and capital. First and foremost it allows capital and labour, two of the basic factors of production, to develop their potential unhindered. Workers can move freely to seek jobs where demand is higher and where wages and working conditions are therefore better. They can settle with their families and work anywhere in the Community. Firms can produce, sell and compete freely wherever it suits them best. No member state may treat its own nationals more favourably than nationals from its Community partners. A single market for the goods produced by industry and agriculture cannot operate smoothly unless uniform conditions of competition apply. This is the only way to safeguard equal opportunities for everyone in a common market and to prevent competition from being distorted through action by the private or public sector or by government. One of the Community's tasks is therefore to create a system to protect free competition within the single market, based on the rules laid down in the Treaties. There is a ban on agreements between undertakings to restrict competition.

Keywords

The keywords that should know for this chapter are listed below. Check to make sure you understand the meaning of each word. Discuss those you are unsure of with your tutor

balanced budget	monopoly
cartel	oligopoly
competition policy	price capping
competitive tendering	privatisation
consumer disposable income	public sector borrowing
deficit budget	requirement (PSBR)
direct taxation	surplus budget
indirect taxation	tendering
inflation	trade associations
licences	voluntary codes of practice
merit goods	

Examination practice

Short-answer questions

1 Give three reasons why the government chooses to provide certain services themselves through a range of publicly owned or directed organisations.

2 What is a quango? Give two examples.

3 What is privatisation?

4 What are the main purposes of the Department of Trade & Industry, the Department of Transport and the Inland Revenue?

5 Give three examples of public corporations or enterprises.

6 Give four examples of services provided directly or indirectly by local authorities.

7 What is a 'public good or service'? Give two examples.

8 What is a 'merit good'? Give one example.

9 Briefly explain what you understand by the term 'fiscal policy'.

10 What is the *Consumer Protection Act* and how does it protect the consumer?

Essay questions

You have recently taken the post of Personal Assistant to the Sales Director of a medium-sized stationery business. Your responsibilities include providing the usual secretarial support for your manager, but he wants you to actively help in the identification of potential new customers. The company has recognised that with the many changes in the public sector, there is an opportunity to offer stationery to the newly re-organised health services, local authorities and other parts of the public sector.

1   The Sales Director wants you to begin your investigations by clearly defining the following types of public-sector organisation and stating their main activities:

    (a) Local authorities

    (b) Central government

    (c) Health services

2   The Sales Director has heard a little about fiscal and monetary policy, but he does not really understand how these policies could affect the demand for the company's products and services. He needs you to explain the policies and how they might affect demand for stationery.

    (a) Define and explain fiscal policy.

    (b) Define and explain monetary policy.

3   Following a recent series of complaints from customers, the Sales Director admits that he is rather rusty in his knowledge and understanding of the various laws which relate to consumer protection. Briefly outline the main implications of the following acts.

    (a) Trade Descriptions Act.

    (b) The Consumer Credit Act.

    (c) The Weights & Measures Act.

    (d) The Consumer Protection Act.

    He would also like you to identify at least three watchdog organisations concerned with consumer protection.

4   Given the fact that the company operates in an area that attracts considerable European funding, it is surprising that no one knows very much about the European Union. The Sales Director, aware that you have some knowledge of the topic, has volunteered your

services in the preparation of a memorandum to be circulated to all senior staff. The memorandum needs to cover the following:

(a) What are the major institutions of the EU and what is their function?

(b) What impact could the EU have on the local area and the business itself?

■ Introduction

Each individual, no matter how senior, carries out a broad range of responsibilities. In order to ensure that the roles and responsibilities are carried out successfully, the employer needs to be aware of the following points:

- that the employer needs to clearly define what is expected of the employee in a particular job role
- that the employee needs to know exactly what is expected in terms of the role and the responsibilities of the post
- that both the employer and the employee are content that the employee is capable of doing the job. If not, then steps need to be taken to ensure that the employee can perform to the best of his/her abilities.

The key terms to consider in our investigation into the common job roles include the following:

- **authority** – can the individual command others to carry out tasks? In other words, does the individual have any real power?
- **accountability** – who is the individual responsible to? How many superiors have authority for the individual?
- **responsibility** – what exactly are the tasks or duties related to the job and what level of independence does the individual have?
- **rights** – what should the individual reasonably expect from the employer? What should the employer reasonably expect from the individual?

■ Job roles

Directors

Directors are essentially members of the board which controls an organisation. The most senior member of the board is known as a managing director. Before looking at directors in general, we shall consider this key role first.

It is the responsibility of the managing director to preside over board meetings. A managing director's main responsibilities are

- to exercise all powers and duties of a director
- to exercise power and responsibility in the name of the board on a day-to-day basis.

The managing director is chosen by other members of the board. In making their choice they will be looking for an individual with a number of important qualities, amongst which are

- wide business experience
- a proven track record of success
- the ability to make decisions under pressure

- to be prepared to answer for any decision made and to stand by those decisions
- to be accountable to the board and ultimately the shareholders
- to be a driving force behind the policies and objectives of the organisation and the fulfilment of these
- to have excellent communication skills
- to act as a representative and ambassador for the organisation in a variety of situations.

It is the managing director who is actually responsible for the implementation of policy formulated by the board, and who represents the board itself at all times. To some extent, the managing director has to interpret the wishes of the board, and develop a clear programme of organisational objectives. Further, he or she must know which key members of staff can be relied upon to follow through his or her policy decisions to successful completion. At all times, the managing director must keep the board informed of any problems, decisions or crises that may occur and of which they should be made aware.

The minimum number of directors depends on the type of organisation. In private companies, there need be only one. In a public company two is the minimum. A directorship has a dual function.

- The direction of activities.
- The management of staff and their activities.

The main difference between these two functions is that direction tends to be longer term whilst management involves day-to-day decision-making.

Direction is essentially the implementation of the board's policies. If a director is an executive director, this means that he or she works full time for the organisation and has responsibility for a particular part of the organisation. A non-executive director may be part time and may concentrate on a particular aspect of policy with which he or she has experience.

Management as carried out by executive directors can be complex as many find it difficult to separate the direction and management roles. They may have a good idea of the nature of the organisation's policies and have a reasonably clear impression as to how this policy may be implemented. Unfortunately, day-to-day decision-making may mean that the executive director has to make decisions which are sometimes at odds with the organisation's policy. One way around this problem is to organise the board of directors into two separate units. Board members will serve on one or other of the units (with the exception of the managing director who will serve on both). One unit of directors will deal with overall policy, and the other unit will concentrate on day-to-day implementation of policy. In this way, any conflict between policy and management of decision-making is avoided.

The main responsibilities of the directors, therefore, are

- to exercise their power and authority in good faith and for the benefit of the organisation

- to put aside their personal interests and always put the organisation first
- to endeavour to be professional when managing the affairs of the organisation.

A director should, therefore, display care and skill at all times. Obviously, non-executive directors, who have been included on the board for their experience and expertise in a particular area, are expected to be even more professional in their conduct on behalf of the organisation. At the same time, these non-executive directors may not have the skill or expertise of a normal board member. Such directors are often helped by an employee who will assist them in procedural matters. Both public and private limited companies are required by law to have a company secretary. Essentially, this is an administrative post and may be at director level. Certainly the company secretary will be expected either to sit on the board or regularly attend meetings. A company secretary has a variety of tasks and duties, the most common of which are

- to keep all records as required by law which include a register of members of the organisation
- to keep minutes of the board and other director's meetings
- to keep the organisation's legal documents secure
- to keep the organisation's seal secure – the seal is the organisation's name and registration number
- to arrange the directors' meetings
- to ensure that any information required by the Registrar of Companies is completed
- to act as the representative of the organisation when the organisation enters into a binding contract.

Managers

Below the level of director, there are a number of layers of managers. It is the duty of a manager to undertake tasks and duties as delegated to him or her by a director. In effect, it is the manager who takes responsibility for the day-to-day decision-making and implementation of organisational policy. A manager will be accountable to the director and ultimately the board and shareholders via any other managers senior to him or her.

A manager would usually have a far better working knowledge of the organisation than even an executive director. Directors, therefore, tend not to interfere with basic decision-making and, providing they consider the managers competent and reliable, are happy to delegate their authority to the various levels of management.

The exact duties of managers very much depend on the following.

- The level of responsibility.
- The department or function of the organisation for which they are responsible.
- The nature of the organisation to which they belong.

Supervisors

Supervisors tend to be the next tier down in the organisational structure below managers. Essentially, they are team leaders or organisers of specific projects or functions of the organisation. It is relatively difficult, in some cases, to recognise the exact difference between a manager and a supervisor. Perhaps it is easier to think in terms of the actual managerial responsibilities involved. Supervisors tend to deal only with day-to-day tasks and to direct individuals under their control in the pursuit of efficiency. Supervisors do not necessarily have wider-scale managerial responsibilities. They will usually answer to a manager who takes on these functions.

There is an interesting point to be made regarding the status of supervisors, particularly in regard to employers' use of the word 'supervisor'. One way around having to offer a higher level of salary is simply to call an individual's job role 'supervisory', rather than 'managerial'. There is a perception that managers should receive higher rates of pay. In order to avoid this, an organisation may choose to call its managers supervisors.

In industrial organisations, there are quite large numbers of supervisors. They have responsibility for specific functions of the production process and have relative independence in their choice of the deployment of employees to achieve success.

In an office environment, a supervisor will tend to have responsibility for ensuring that all individuals have been allocated sufficient work, that the work produced is of an acceptable standard and that the secretarial duties fully support the other operations of the organisation.

Clerical

The term 'clerical' refers to all employees who are not directly involved in the production process. Previously, clerical workers were referred to as 'white-collar workers'. This means that they are involved with administrative and support functions that are usually 'behind the scenes'. They are responsible for all of the functions of the organisation that are necessary to ensure that the business runs smoothly and correctly. Typically, clerical workers would include all of those who work in administration, secretarial support functions and other areas.

Operatives

The term 'operative' is a relatively new one which is applied to a wide range of different job roles. Perhaps the main feature of the term operative is that it infers some form of manual labour. Strictly speaking, 'operative' refers to the operation of machinery or equipment. More recently, it has been adopted to encompass many non-manual activities. Indeed, in a fast-food restaurant, such as McDonald's, the counter staff are referred to as operatives.

Team working

One aspect of the working environment we should not ignore is that employees working in an organisation rarely work on their own. More often teams are created, either formally or informally, to carry out specific tasks. A team is a group of individuals or operatives working together towards a single common objective. When working as a member of a team, people need to know which members of the team have the power and authority, in other words, who is actually directing the efforts of the team. It is common to find a supervisor fulfilling this role. To be a successful team member, a number of skills are required. These include

- the ability to communicate
- an understanding of the objective of the task
- the ability (gained through training) to carry out a variety of roles within the team.

Employers have recognised the advantages of team building and many have been prepared to pay for residential training programmes aimed at enhancing this. We have considered the importance of team working in much more detail in Chapter 4.

Assistants

This job title refers to a subsidiary role in the organisation. Derived from the term 'to assist', an assistant, by definition, helps a more senior member of staff. Typically, we would find the word attached to job titles such as 'shop assistant', 'catering assistant', 'administrative assistant', 'clerical assistant', 'editorial assistant' and 'personal assistant'.

Despite the fact that these job roles may not appear to be particularly key in an organisation, the mere fact that the more senior member of staff needs an assistant means that the individual fulfilling this role is also a vital member of staff. Many managers who have personal assistants working for them would find it impossible to do their jobs without the able support of a well-motivated colleague. Again, the exact nature of the assistant's role within the organisation is very much dependent upon the nature of the job and the organisation itself.

In some cases the term assistant is again used to downgrade the perception of the job. Again, this may be used as a means of offering a lower salary. A shop assistant, for example, may have enormous responsibility in not only the day-to-day shop work activities but also cashier responsibilities, stock-taking and ordering, customer service and security of premises. It should not be assumed that if the job title includes the word 'assistant' this is a junior post.

Support staff

This is another broad area of work that covers a multitude of job roles. Typically, these would include job roles that are designed to assist and back up the activities of 'front-line' staff who have constant contact with customers or clients. The support staff would be responsible for ensuring that the 'front-line' staff have all of the necessary information, equipment and materials to carry out their functions. In some organisations, the support staff would be responsible for the maintenance of machinery and equipment and would probably be qualified to carry out basic maintenance functions that do not require the equipment or machinery to be dealt with by an external contractor.

■ Types of organisation structures

There are many factors which may determine the nature of the organisational structure. These are usually internal – caused by factors within the organisation itself – and external – caused by factors which may not be in the control of the organisation.

Many organisations have been traditionally organised in a form of pyramid structure. Individuals at each level of the pyramid (or hierarchy) are fully aware of their rank and their position in the organisation (see below). Each individual should also know his or her particular role within the organisation. As we will see, this formalised 'chain of command' is better suited to allow orders and instructions to be passed down the pyramid and for information to be readily transmitted up the pyramid. The structure depends on many factors, including the following.

- The number of employees – in effect the actual size of the organisation.
- Type of premises used – a multi- or split-site organisation with a number of

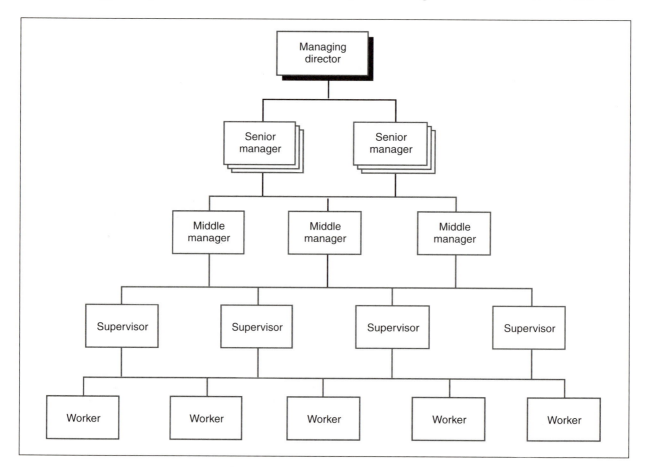

Figure 3.1 A pyramid structure

different branches would need to be organised in a radically different manner from an organisation which is based in a single building.

- Type of business – if the organisation is in the **primary sector**, it is likely to be organised in such a way as to allow as efficient processing of the raw materials as possible, and may be based around a single mine, forest or quarry. A manufacturing organisation may either carry out all of its processing procedures on a single site, or need to transport partly finished goods to other specialist sites. Organisation in this case may be based on the single factory unit, or a cluster of factories which contribute towards the finished product. Distribution organisations tend to be organised on a regional, national or international framework. Depending on the bulk of goods being distributed, the organisational structure will be complex in certain geographical areas and simpler in others. In other words, if the organisation is busy in one area, the size and complexity will reflect this. As with many organisations, good communication between the regions is vital and a separate part of the organisational structure may concentrate on dealing with communication. In the retailing sector the obvious organisational structure is that of the branch. However, many functions of the business are carried out centrally. These services tend to be of a managerial, financial or buying nature, and this allows the individual branches to concentrate on the selling process. Professional services tend to operate on the basis of a number of specialist individuals who are assisted by a variety of support staff. Often these support staff are drawn from a 'pool' of clerical and secretarial employees.
- The number, type and size of the clients may have a bearing on the organisational structure. If the organisation deals with only a handful of clients, then the structure need not be overly complex. On the other hand, if it is dealing with literally millions of retail customers, then the demands on the structure may be much greater.
- The past structure of the organisation and its history may be a good or bad influence on how it is structured. An old-fashioned organisation which has successfully managed to survive for many years may not see the need to change its structure. It may not appreciate the benefits of reorganisation and may be structured in such a way as to prevent the possibility of growth or adaptation to new demands.
- The current structure of an organisation can again be a positive or negative influence on the day-to-day running of the business. If the organisation has recently undergone changes, it will be unlikely to adapt to further changes without encountering considerable problems.
- The future needs of an organisation should directly influence its structure. The need to react constantly to changing demands, diversify into new areas and respond to changes in legislation are all strong reasons to consider how the organisation is structured.

At this point we shall look at all of the different varieties of organisational structure and later try to assess their appropriateness in different situations.

Simple organisational structures

The simplest organisational structure is that of the person who works on his or her own. This person would obviously be responsible for everything that the organisation does. Someone, for example, who set up a mail-order business would be responsible for buying in products, designing the catalogue, getting it printed, carrying out market research to find the kind of person who would buy the products, researching a mailing list, sending out catalogues, taking orders, dispatching goods, dealing with any correspondence, paying bills, banking cheques, doing the accounts and a hundred other things. In this situation the individual who is running the business is at the centre of everything.

Student activity

As a group, try to identify some local organisations that may have a simple structure.

Specialisation

The larger the organisation, the more need there is for people who specialise in a particular area. Good examples of these are bank managers, solicitors,

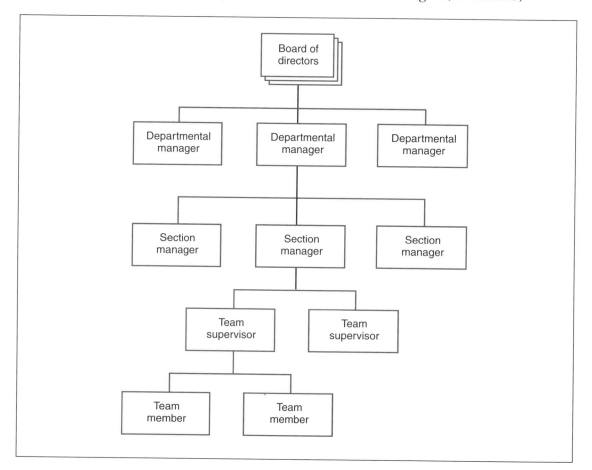

Figure 3.2 A simple organisation chart

accountants. All of these people have specialist skills and can take some of the responsibility off an individual business person's shoulders.

As a business expands it needs to employ people, some part time, some full time. The person who set up the company also needs to think about what has to be done. The business needs to be organised in the best possible way to meet the objectives that have been set for it. The owner of the business needs to define exactly what individuals do. Precisely what departments are responsible for. Who will supervise the employees? Who should tell them what to do? Where does everyone fit into the organisation? And who is ultimately responsible? This is known as the **division of labour** and **specialisation**.

The division of labour involves breaking down the process of producing things or providing services into clearly defined specialist tasks. The fact is that if the process is broken down into these separate tasks, production can actually be increased. Instead of one person trying to do everything, everybody who works as part of the production process of goods or services specialises. Specialisation means being more efficient.

Advantages
- Resources can be concentrated where they are needed most.
- If workers become more efficient at doing a particular job they become more skilled.
- Specialisation allows greater output. This means that each item produced is made more cheaply because the labour involved in producing it is less for each unit.
- If people specialise, then they can pass on their skills and experience to others and help them become more efficient.
- If people specialise, then hopefully they can achieve a better standard of living. By specialising people can develop their own talents and are able to trade what they can do with others.
- By specialising in one job a person can do that job well rather than doing lots of jobs less well.

Disadvantages
- Specialisation can often lead to jobs becoming very boring. Simple repetition of the same task day in day out demoralises people and they can become less efficient.
- Specialisation is always dependent on how good or efficient the specialists in the previous task were. If they are not as efficient or as fast at every stage of production, this can cause bottlenecks.
- There is a tendency in specialisation for workers to become little more than machines. This, in turn, could lead to loss of skill.
- Specialising actually reduces a worker's ability to adapt to change.
- Those who specialise have only a narrow view of the product or service which they are actually producing. Someone who makes an article from start to finish has a better overview and can help to make things more efficient in the long run.

Divisional organisational structures

Larger organisations often need to take a radically different approach to their structure. This is particularly the case in organisations where the operations are complex and span several different countries. They find it impossible to adopt more traditional forms of organisational structure. As we shall see, there are three major methods (which are all essentially divisional in nature) that can be used to facilitate control, efficiency and communication. The third version of divisional structure – the division of multinationals is considered separately later. For now, the remaining two are

- **division by function** – in this form of structure the organisation has identified its key functions and has either an individual (or in the case of larger organisations, a department) which oversees this function throughout all subdivisions of the organisation
- **division by product** – each subdivision is semi-autonomous (partly independent) but has clearly stated goals, objectives and profits to achieve.

Departmentalisation is the process by which an organisation has certain functions which it carries out grouped logically under a particular manager. There are usually five ways of grouping employees or the tasks an organisation does. These are

- by what they produce – the product
- by their function, ie what they do for the organisation
- by process, ie how they do it
- by geographical area, which may be various regional offices or separate companies
- by type of customer, eg they may deal with other business organisations, or they may deal with retail.

Functional organisational structures

A functionally based organisational structure is usually designed around the specific parts of the organisation that produce, market and sell the product or service. The actual substructure of the organisation may take a variety of forms, either hierarchical or flat, for example. Typically, a structure adopting the functional system will be controlled by a managing director who is supported by a range of senior managers. Each of the managers has responsibility for the direction of a specific function of the organisation. These functions could include

- advertising
- finance and accounting
- personnel
- production
- purchasing
- sales.

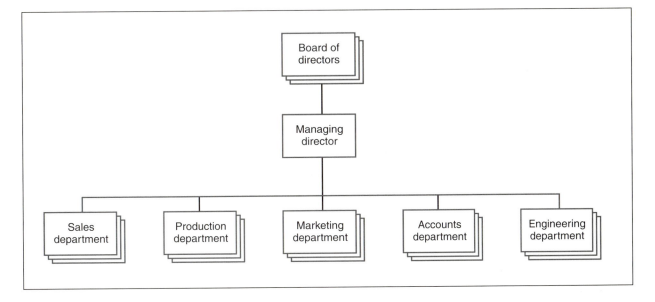

Figure 3.3 A functional organisation chart

Product divisions

An alternative to basing the organisational structure on function is to base it around product(s) or ranges of products. As we shall see when we consider the divisions of multinationals, it is easy to identify how an organisation has grown (organically by acquiring other organisations and incorporating them into the larger organisation, but maintaining their individual identity). An organisation might also value the importance of individual brand names or product names (particularly in cases where the same product is known under various different names across the world). An example of this is the Snickers bar which was known by this name in all countries except the UK. In order to establish its name worldwide, Nestlé decided to give up the name Marathon for ease of marketing, distribution and promotion.

Another reason for dividing an organisation by product is to establish a series of cost or profit centres. Essentially, this means that specific spending related to a particular product can be identified, as can any profits generated by that product. If a multinational organisation acquires another organisation in a different country, it is probably not a good idea instantly to change the 'household name' which may have been trading very well for a number of years. Again, for this reason, we will find divisions by product, in some cases, where the situation was beneficial to the purchaser, and in others, the name will be changed to that of a more internationally known trade or brand name.

Student activity

Do you think that this form of structure is useful only for a large organisation? What would be the advantages and disadvantages of a smaller business adopting this form of structure?

Divisions of multinationals

Large multinationals may have literally dozens of separate companies or divisions being directed, to some extent, by a head office or 'holding company'. Typically, in real terms, the head office is comparatively small. This is always dependent upon the degree to which it involves itself in the day-to-day running of the subsidiaries. Each of the individual companies or divisions is relatively autonomous (or free) to make its own decisions on general matters. It is only at corporate level that the head office exerts its influence upon them. General guidelines would, of course, have been created by the head office to ensure that there is guidance on most decisions that have to be made.

Unilever, the multinational chemicals giant, is divided up into some 500 separate companies, 50 of which operate in the UK alone! All of the 500 operate under guidelines issued by the parent company. In each country there is a national manager who has responsibility for all facets of the organisation's activities. The role of coordinating the efforts of the different national managers is undertaken by a director in the parent company. It is this individual who assists in setting the policies for each country grouping. In this way, the organisation as a whole and in one particular country especially, can respond to developments whether related to the competition, consumers or government.

Matrix organisational structures

In this form of organisational structure, there exists the opportunity to dispose of the more usual departmental boundaries. Typically used in Japan, this system allows for teams to be created that consist of a number of individuals from various different parts of the organisation but brought together to undertake a particular task. This can mean that individuals may have their regular manager to answer to, as well as the project leader.

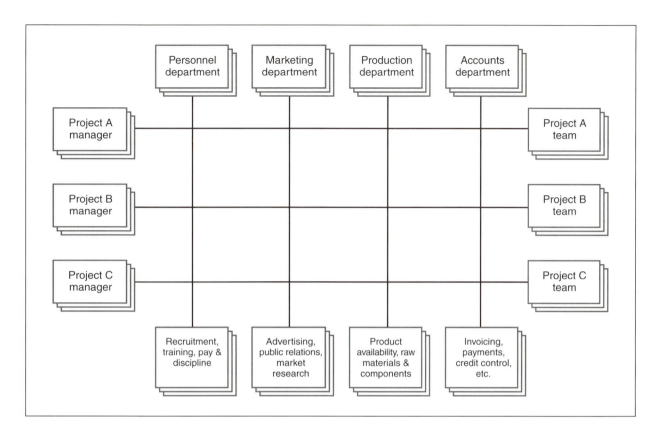

Figure 3.4 A matrix structure

The system appears to work quite well, having the advantage of the team members being able to meet without direct reference to their departments. Also, it allows more individuals to be brought in to use their expertise when needed. Unfortunately, as is often the case, both managers (the departmental and the project) make too great a demand on the time and effort of the individuals. There is also a blurring of the lines of accountability, particularly if the project fails.

Hierarchical organisational structures

The best way to understand what a hierarchical structure looks like is to imagine a pyramid (see Figure 3.1). At the top of the pyramid are the owners or major decision-makers of the organisation. As we look further down the pyramid the shape of the organisation broadens as more employees are involved at that level. At the base of the pyramid are the majority of the employees and below them are the customers.

Responsibility, power and authority are all much greater at the top of the pyramid than at the bottom. Decisions flow down the pyramid, affecting a succession of layers of employees. This form of structure can also be referred to as a 'pecking order' as the higher up the pyramid you are as an employee, the more power and authority you have. Equally, we can see that the lower down the pyramid you are, the less influence you have on the organisation as a whole.

The reason for the hierarchical structure is that important decisions need to be made by those who have expertise and experience along with enough authority to make sure that the decision is implemented. Those at the top of the pyramid may take all the credit for success, but may also bear the consequences of failure.

Typically, we would see a structure that would begin with directors at the top of the pyramid making decisions for heads of department below to pass on to middle managers who would then tell the junior members of staff to implement them. The higher an individual is in the pyramid, the less likely he or she is to understand precisely how decisions are implemented at the lower levels. These individuals may just have an idea of overall strategy and base their decisions on information received via the various layers below them. Each time information passes from layer to layer, the relative importance of what has been said may change. It may therefore be likely that those at the top of the pyramid will have a distorted view of the organisation and how it really works.

For those at the bottom of the pyramid, the directors may seem remote, unable to understand the organisation's needs and unwilling to change decisions which may adversely affect the day-to-day running of the business.

The main advantage of this structure is that each layer sees the organisation in its own peculiar way. Each layer will have different opinions, priorities and interpretation of overall organisational policy.

The main version of the hierarchical structure is the steep pyramid, where there are many layers of management. The reason for the number of layers may be that the organisation operates in several different locations and needs to duplicate the administration in order to function efficiently. Alternatively, the nature of the business may be very complex, requiring the processing of many orders, messages, pieces of information or complaints.

Because the structure is multi-layered and complicated, those further down the pyramid may find it difficult to understand how and why decisions are made, and the organisation may find it impossible to make sure that the employees follow through 'corporate decisions' (general statements of policy and procedures). The organisation may also suffer from being 'bureaucratic'. This means that decisions must pass through so many layers that they take a very long time to put into operation, and the systems designed to help implement them become more complicated than they need to be.

Flat organisational structures

This is essentially a version of the hierarchical structure, but it has a number of different features. It should be remembered, however, that this is still a pyramid-style structure, but one with few layers.

The theory behind having fewer layers in the pyramid is that decisions can be made quickly and efficiently. Each layer is able to communicate easily with other layers and the organisation avoids the danger of becoming 'bureaucratic'.

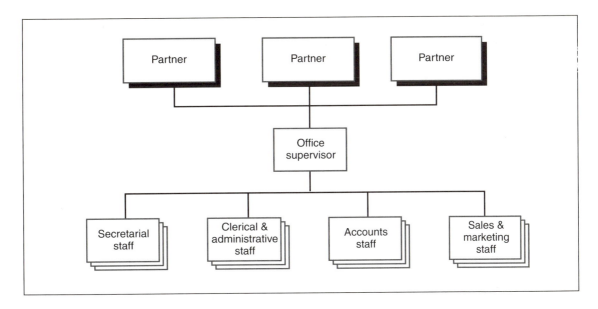

Figure 3.5 Flat structure chart

This simpler structure is generally found in organisations operating from a single site where directors and other decision-makers are readily available for consultation and guidance. Employees find it easier to understand the reasoning behind the directors' decisions and therefore feel more a part of the organisation and less isolated. Equally, junior managers and other employees are more motivated as they are often given more responsibility through delegation.

Student activity

Having looked at some of the types of organisational structure, try to draw out the organisational chart for an organisation that you are familiar with. Bear in mind that this first attempt may be more difficult than you expect.

Centralised organisational structures

There are two different ways of looking at centralised structures, both of which contain features of many of the other types of organisational structures. Indeed, they may be actually organised in another form, but will have centralised features.

- **Centralised services** – this version of a centralised structure involves the reorganisation of key services to provide for the organisation as a whole. In this respect, it would be common to find the reprographics (printing functions) centralised and controlled in such a manner as to provide cross-organisational services. Central control means that the service should be more efficient in terms of work through-put and output, as well as attempting to keep costs down (by the non-duplication of staff roles, etc.).

- **Centralised decision-making** – in larger organisations that do not favour a decentralised approach to decision-making, it may be a preference to concentrate command and decision functions to a few individuals. They will be supported by a variety of employees and will be responsible for cross-organisational decision-making. It is often the case that these organisations are more traditional ones, or rely on the expert knowledge of a handful of individual specialists.

Advantages
- Decisions can be made quickly.
- Specialist staff can be used.
- Larger discounts can be obtained by centralising purchasing.

Disadvantages
- There is little opportunity for total decision-making.
- Individuals lack the opportunity to learn about the decision-making process.
- Centralised power can be misused.

Student activity

Having seen the advantages and disadvantages of centralised structures, do you think that they are more or less efficient ways of structuring an organisation? Discuss this as a group.

Decentralised organisational structures

In recent years, some major organisations have recognised that relying on a pyramid structure has prevented quick and necessary decisions and change from taking place. This new form of structure is known commonly as **decentralisation**. This is the exact opposite to having centralised services which assist individual branches or sites. Each part of the organisation that carries out a distinctly different function in the organisation is given a level of autonomy. This means that it is allowed, up to a point, to make decisions for itself without the permission or consent of the directors or the central office. This allows each suborganisation to be more flexible and responsive to its own needs and customers without having to wait for a central office to consider any points of concern that have been passed on to it. Most typically, the structure consists of a central 'holding' company (these are the owners of several companies who, while they are interested in the profits and decisions made by their companies, do not meddle in the day-to-day business) which has devolved (passed down power and authority) responsibility to each company forming part of the group.

Advantages
- Local decisions can be made by local managers.
- Individuals can learn about the management process.

- Head office managers can concentrate on the strategic decisions.
- There is a greater overall freedom of decision-making.

Disadvantages
- The organisation can be difficult to supervise and control.
- Conflict often occurs between different parts of the organisation.
- Unless the policies are clear, the decisions made can be in conflict with corporate strategy.

Other organisational structures

There are a number of other forms of organisational structure that are really combinations of the main types.

- **Geographically based structures** – retail businesses generally use this form of structure as it best fits with the demands that will be made of regional and local managers. Using a traditional hierarchical structure, in the main, the organisation will take the form of a relatively small head office, which supports a number of regional offices. These regional offices have various support functions to assist the outlets within that area. In other cases, manufacturing organisations may have a similar structure, particularly when they have widely dispersed factories throughout the country.
- **Market-based structures** – some organisations are structured to cater for each of their major markets. If an organisation produces a wide range of different products, it may well be advised to have separate companies or subsidiaries to exploit each market
- **Product-based structures** – in many respects this is a similar structure to the market-based organisation. Each company/division or unit will be responsible for all of the activities related to a particular product. The product divisions will also have their own manufacturing, accounting, sales and purchasing departments.
- **Mechanistic** – these are functionally divided with clearly identifiable chains of command. Each task carried out by the individuals making up the organisation is clearly defined. In this way orders filtering through from the top of the organisation are carried out to the letter. Because of this accountability and rigid structure, organisations like this seem to take on the qualities of a machine, hence the name.
- **Organic** – in these organisations, many of the job roles have been somewhat blurred, as the definition of tasks and duties changes according to the needs of the organisation. Individuals work as part of a network, where communication is easy and the authority to make decisions is readily available. Although there are roles within the organisation that relate to the direction of the work, the actual carrying out of the tasks can differ according to the nature of the work in hand.
- **Bureaucratic** – largely hierarchical in structure, but with a high reliance on adhering to the rules of the organisation and following accepted procedures.
- **Autocratic** – again, usually a hierarchical structure, in which the decisions are made by a single individual who requires unquestioning support and reaction to his or her directives.

Student activity

Now that you have covered all of the different forms of organisational structure, you may wish to amend the organisational chart that you attempted earlier. Once you have done this, try to identify your chosen organisation as one of the types that we have mentioned. Compare your organisation to the others that have been prepared by the rest of your group.

■ Hierarchies and spans of control

Spans of control refer to the number of subordinates who work directly for a manager. The wider the span of control, the more employees a particular manager is responsible for. If the span of control is narrow, then the manager has a responsibility to direct the efforts of only a few employees. There is a definite link between hierarchies and spans of control. If there are managers with wide spans of control, then there is a less complex hierarchy as a handful of managers direct the efforts of a large number of subordinates.

Whilst wide spans of control mean that there is less of a hierarchical nature to the organisation, this does mean that managers need to be very good at delegation as they have little time to devote to each of their individual subordinates. In organisations with wide spans of control there are few 'intermediaries' which does improve vertical communication (ie top to bottom, bottom to top).

With fewer managers to supervise, direct and check work, there can be less opportunity for perfection. In other words, mistakes are not often noticed until

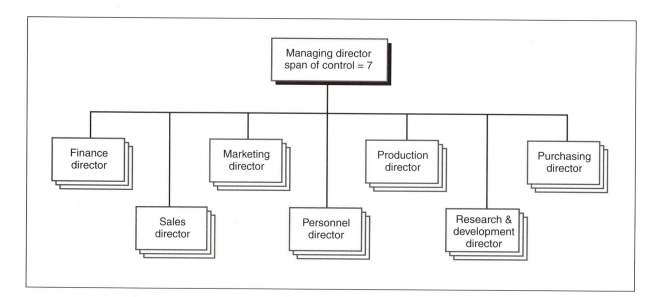

Figure 3.6 Span of control organisation chart

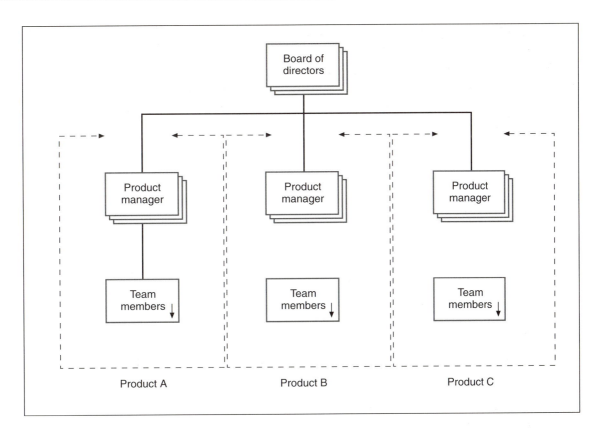

Figure 3.7 A delayered pyramid structure

it is too late. The other major criticism of wide spans of control is that employees notice a distinct reduction in promotion prospects as there are fewer individuals to replace in the next tier of management.

Delayering aims to reduce the number of layers in the hierarchy. In other words, it aims to reduce the complexity of the management structure itself. By doing this the organisation can have a wider span of control, giving greater responsibility to its employees. It does mean that each employee will have a greater workload, but the number of 'intermediaries' between the top of the organisation and the bottom has been greatly reduced. Many organisations have adopted this approach as it leads to enormous reductions in overheads – they do not have to pay for large numbers of middle managers as their jobs have been absorbed by other employees. One of the problems associated with delayering is that employees report greater stress levels as they have increased workloads. Cynics state that delayering is just another term for redundancies.

Accountability and responsibility go hand-in-hand as someone has to be held responsible for a failure or praised for a success. Providing the organisational structure is clearly understood by all employees, everyone will know who has authority to direct activities. It is essential that if mistakes are made, the individual or individuals concerned need to know how to take action to avoid faulty decision-making or poor communication in the future. In many organisations accountability is not seen as an asset but as a threat. Many managers believe that accountability will serve only to show how bad they are at doing their job. This is particularly true of organisations that impose targets on their managers.

Student activity

What is the span of control of your immediate superior? Ideally, this manager or supervisor should be from the same organisation that you have already chosen for the previous activities in this chapter. You will be able to work out the span of control very easily if your organisational chart is correct.

■ Changes in organisational structures

It is important to remember that organisations are never static and are always evolving and changing. Changes in the size and scope of an organisation's objectives can often mean a radical rethink in the structure of the business. Some organisations may opt for a new and more flexible structure as they diversify and expand. Simply 'tacking on' new parts to an existing structure does not always work. The chain of command and the exercise of authority can become difficult if the organisation experiences organic growth. This growth and consequent structure 'add ons' do not really address the need to restructure. Perhaps the organisation is growing too fast to contemplate a radical change and needs to wait until the 'growth spurt' has slowed down. The danger with this philosophy is that the organisation may have outgrown the structure and be experiencing severe difficulties as a result.

Student activity

As a group, try to think of an organisation that has 'outgrown' itself. You may be able to think of an organisation that worked perfectly well in the past, but as it has grown or has changed the emphasis of its operations, it has encountered a number of problems.

Size of the organisation

In terms of size itself, the organisation does need to adopt a structure which not only best suits the nature of its operations, but takes into account the fact that not all operations will be carried out at a single site. Equally, the organisation needs to consider whether it is advisable to maintain a **hierarchical structure** or a more formal structure if the organisation has diversified into a number of different product areas or markets. It is often the case that the senior management, whilst striving to control the organisation as it has always done, does not even understand what some parts of the organisation are doing. If they lack understanding, how can they truly improve any kind of structure or method of decision-making? This can very much depend upon the management style preferred or adopted by the management of the organisation.

This is perhaps the most obvious reason for changes in the organisational structure. Simpler forms of organisational structure are more relevant in smaller businesses, but as the organisation grows it needs to adapt to even more complex requirements.

Growth

Most organisational structures are based on the assumption that the business will expand. This is not the only form of growth. Diversification and changes in the structure are often advisable instead of simply growing bigger and maintaining the general nature of the structure.

As businesses grow, they may need to consider relocation in order to achieve sustained and permanent growth. Moving closer to the source of raw materials, skilled labour, or better distribution points, may be key considerations in this move. More obvious, is the move brought on by growth itself. Perhaps the organisation simply needs larger premises in order to continue its operations successfully. An organisation which has a variety of sites needs to adopt a slightly different structure to accommodate the problems of communication and overall control. Within a single-site operation, the organisation must also consider the most appropriate structure for its business. Again, this may depend upon the nature of the business. In service industries, for example, the organisation would be structured towards providing customer service as a priority. For manufacturing organisations, the bulk of the structure considerations would be related to the production process itself, with other departments supporting and servicing the production unit. Organisational structure may, of course, be related to the premises in which the organisation is located. An inappropriate building may prevent the restructuring of the business since the physical location of each part of the organisation remains fixed. This state of affairs is particularly true of organisations which add extensions and buildings to the site without really considering the implications of their placement or location. In these cases, the organisation may not have had the time to spend considering the future when immediate demands for expansion and new accommodation were pressing.

Type of business

The changes in structure may be brought about by the nature of the business itself. If the organisation has a variety of diversified products or services, it may be logical to organise in such a way as to separate the management and production in order to establish specific **profit centres**. Equally, this organisation (often product-based) revolves around the need to attract expertise in a particular area in such a way as the individuals can identify with a particular product or service rather than a whole organisation.

Function of the organisation

As with the type of product the organisation produces, the specific function of the organisation may bring about changes in structure. As we have already said, businesses have a wide variety of different goals. These differing goals and objectives will determine the historical structure of the organisation, as well as the structure best suited to taking that organisation into future successful years.

Formal organisations can be defined as those that have established the express purpose of achieving a particular goal or aims or objectives. These sorts of organisations have clearly defined rules and instructions as well as quite highly developed communication between different parts of the organisation. Good examples of these sorts of operation include most businesses, governments and international institutions.

Because there are so many different forms of formal organisation, we need to clarify this large group a little more carefully. One of the easiest ways is to separate them into productive and non-productive categories, ie those that manufacture and those that provide a service.

Informal organisations are also known as social organisations. These do not tend to have clearly defined goals and examples of these include families or communities.

Change in type of organisation

As we have mentioned earlier, organisations tend to change their type as they mature or grow. A sole trader may begin a business career with no intention of changing the type of business at all. Growth, changes in legislation or tax incentives may encourage the sole trader to become a limited company. With this change, the organisation will probably need to take on a different structure in order to cope with the new demands placed upon it. Individuals who were employed on a casual and 'when needed' basis may become permanent members of the workforce. Specialists, such as accountants, who had been paid and retained when required may have to be permanently incorporated into the structure.

With this structural and type of business change may come a change in ownership itself. If a sole trader enters into a partnership, the ownership will now be split between the original owner and the new partner(s). Equally, a sole trader or partnership that becomes a limited company (particularly a plc) will have to cope with structural and control changes demanded by the shareholders.

Another form of ownership change is the disposal of an organisation to another party. If this is the case, the new owners will inevitably institute changes merely because they wish to stamp their own authority and presence on the organisation. Many of these changes will be seen by the employees in particular as being changes only for the sake of change and they will have little faith or degree of support for them.

Technology

Technology has a part to play in the changing structure relating to working arrangements. Generally, new demands on the organisation can force change in the working arrangement. These may include

- change in hours worked (shifts, etc.)
- level of staffing (due to technology)
- greater supervision (quality control)
- total hours worked
- relocation of new premises
- multi-skilling (undertaking new and varied tasks)
- redesigning of job tasks.

Gradually, computerised management information systems are making it possible to streamline management and structures. On a higher level, the use of computers allows much greater flexibility in structural terms. It is no longer essential to locate all employees in one large building or a connecting set of premises. Outlying units can be directly 'plugged into' the organisation regardless of their location. Technology also changes the nature of the structure relating to production itself. Automation means fewer employees on the shop floor and more in management and supervisory positions.

Student activity

Consider the organisations that you know. Have they been affected by any of the factors mentioned above?

Customer needs and competition

There is, quite rightly, a greater emphasis on the customer and meeting the customers' needs. The traditional concerns with the internal problems and running of the organisation, and, indeed, 'office politics' have slowly given way to other concerns.

Customers require and demand greater levels of service, advice and after-sales service. To this end, the restructuring of the organisation will be needed to provide support for these services, not to mention the training of all staff to cover these considerations.

The competition can have a direct impact on the organisational structure. Any organisation which ignores what the competition is doing may be doomed to failure. Structural changes are often copied within a business sector, particularly if the first organisation to restructure is obviously more competitive and successful.

Apart from the obvious effects on the internal functions and activities of the organisation, competition may force the organisation to consider restructuring in order to stay competitive. A competitive edge, or the ability to 'stay ahead' of the competition can mean the difference between success and failure. All aspects and parts of an organisation can have a role to play in maintaining this advantage over the opposition. Here are some examples of how the structure and the consistent parts of the organisation can contribute.

- Administration – by streamlining procedures and cutting down on wastage.
- Sales – by following up sales leads, providing customer service and ensuring that key customers are especially well provided for in all aspects.
- Marketing – by ensuring that products and services are fully researched and supported with appropriate advertising and promotion.
- Distribution – by swift, efficient and reliable delivery at all times to all customers.
- Accounts – by ensuring that all invoicing, statements and other financial documents are correct at all times.

Student activity

Again considering the organisations that you may have contact with, have any of them restructured themselves to cope with any of the above?

Requirements of the market

The organisation must always be aware that the currently stable (if this is so) situation will not always remain. The organisational structure may need to change radically if there is a sudden or unexpected market change. Principally, the organisation may need to ensure that the following are addressed.

- employee levels are sufficient to take up extra work, or are capable of redeployment
- employees are multi-skilled and require minimum retraining to undertake new duties
- production facilities are flexible enough to respond to changes in production at short notice
- the management is aware of the necessity to 'keep an eye' on the market, including regular checks on the competition and market trends
- the product or service is not wholly reliant on a single market.

The availability of suitable employees and the proximity to a large market (in population terms) can have an influence on the structure of the organisation. In the first instance, the structure may have to be adaptable and include more part-time or casual employees than the organisation would prefer.

Closeness to markets may be a problem for certain organisations. If the organisation produces goods which are either inappropriate for the immediate market, or the population density is low it must consider having more employees located in various places around the country where they can be closer to the market. In this sense, conventional organisational structures may not be appropriate since the level of autonomy at these remote sites will need to be developed and accepted. In this respect, the organisation must be willing to allow local decision-making (within set guidelines).

Keywords

The keywords that should know for this chapter are listed below. Check to make sure you understand the meaning of each word. Discuss those you are unsure of with your tutor.

decentralisation	informal organisations
delayering	primary sector
departmentalisation	profit centres
division of labour	spans of control
formal organisations	specialisation
hierarchical structure	

Examination practice

Short-answer questions

1 Give three duties of a director.

2 How does a manager differ from a director?

3 Explain the role of 'operatives' in an organisation.

4 Outline four factors which may determine the structure of an organisation.

5 Give three reasons why specialisation can often mean greater efficiency.

6 What is departmentalisation?

7 What is 'hierarchical structure'?

8 Give two advantages and two disadvantages of decentralisation.

9 What is a 'span of control'?

10 What are the major differences between a formal organisation and an informal organisation?

Essay qestions

As part of your induction package, you have been given a useful organisation chart (Figure 3.8). There is no explanation of what the chart is actually showing apart from the basic structure of the organisation or the department. In order for you to understand exactly how the organisation works, you will need to analyse this chart and draw some conclusions from it.

1 The chart overleaf shows the overall structure of the organisation; by carefully considering how the structure has been put together, answer the following questions:

a What is the average span of control of the directors?

b Approximately how many employees work for the organisation?

c In your position, as a personal assistant to a brand manager, how many levels of management are above you?

d In an ideal world, the organisation would like to re-structure itself. Suggest three simple ways in which the structure could be improved.

2 You are still unsure of the exact roles of some of the job titles, identify the key responsibilities of the following:

a directors

b managers

c supervisors

d clerical

e operatives.

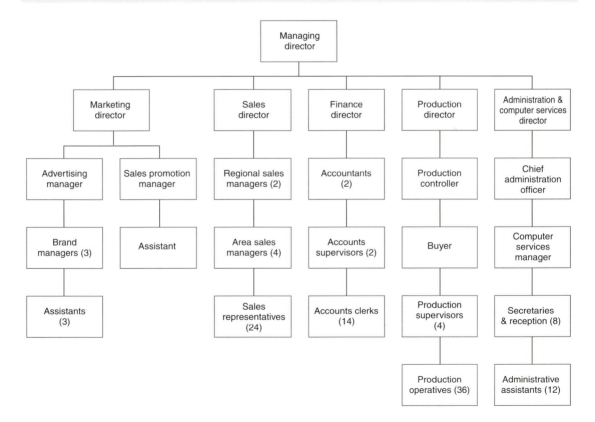

Figure 3.8 Organisation chart

3 The organisational structure is clearly departmentalised. Briefly explain the following:

    a The advantages and disadvantages of departmentalisation.

    b The alternatives that could have been adopted by the organisation as opposed to the departmental structure.

    c How easy would it be for the directors to keep a close and informed understanding of the activities of the organisation? What could they do in order to stay in touch with developments lower down the hierarchy?

4 The organisation is seriously considering the structure of the company; there have been numerous jargon words used to describe the ways in which this might be achieved. Briefly define the following:

    a centralised and decentralised

    b matrix

    c functional.

Work patterns

4

In an increasingly competitive market, organisations realise that they will have to become far more flexible in the ways in which they operate. Obviously, measures such as adopting the latest technology and making sure that they are aware of trends in the marketplace go only some way in achieving this aim. Over the past few years, a number of radical developments have occurred not only in the structure of the workforce (such as the increasing percentage of women in full- and part-time employment), but also in the 'modes' or patterns of work.

As a result of these developments, all aimed to not only increase the flexibility of the organisation, but also to facilitate the employees in being able to balance their other commitments with work, new working patterns have become widespread. In this chapter we will examine the work patterns and trends in the UK. We will identify the new developments, relating to working practices and new technology, that are having a considerable effect on the working lives of employees.

■ Work patterns and trends in the UK

It is widely recognised that there has been a recovery in the labour market. Unemployment itself has been steadily declining since early 1993, although from the summer of 1993 to the summer of 1994 employment actually increased by 230,000. It is expected that the longer-term unemployment growth will continue, but at a slower rate. Projections carried out by the Institute of Employment Research suggest the following.

1995–7 – employment growth of 0.6 per cent per year.
1997–2001 – employment growth of 0.9 per cent per year.

If these figures are correct, then by 2001, 1.6 million new jobs will have been created.

The census of employment which measured the workforce in employment in June 1994 identified the following figures.

- Male full-time employment – 96 million
- Male self-employment – 2.5 million
- Male part-time employment – 1.1 million
- Female full-time employment – 5.7 million
- Female self-employment – 800 000
- Female part-time employment – 490 000

The Institute of Employment Research looked at the overall employment changes between 1993 and 2001 and discovered the following.

- Primary and utility sector will lose 12 per cent of the workforce.
- Manufacturing will lose 8 per cent of the workforce.
- Construction will gain 7 per cent of the workforce.

- Distribution and transport will gain 6 per cent of the workforce.
- Business services and other related services will gain 23 per cent of the workforce.
- Public services will gain 8 per cent of the workforce.

This means that the whole economy will gain around a 6 per cent increase in the workforce.

Male and female employment

Since the 1960s female employment has risen whilst at the same time male employment has fallen. The predictions of changes throughout the 1993–2001 period suggest that whilst female employment will increase by 1.2 million, male employment will fall by 200 000. The consequence of this means that whilst in 1981 women accounted for only 42 per cent of employees, they had gained a 49 per cent share by 1993 and will be expected to outstrip for the first time their male counterparts in 2001 with a figure of 52 per cent.

Since women will outnumber men in all other areas except self-employment, this will not mean necessarily that they will make up the lion's share of the employment workforce. Predictions vary, but the current 54 per cent majority of males in employment will fall to at most 52 per cent by the year 2001.

Female employment is still concentrated in certain sectors of the economy; specifically women outnumber men in the areas of

- health
- education
- other services
- textiles
- clothing.

In the construction and mining sectors of the economy, women still represent a mere 10 per cent of the workforce.

Men in the 35–44 age group still have the highest level of participation in work. By 2000, this figure is likely to be 94 per cent. At the same time men over the age of 55 show a considerable decrease.

Women will play a much greater role in employment than they have ever done in the past. In fact, their participation rates are rising whilst men's are falling. The growth rates of women aged 25–34 will reach 77 per cent by the year 2000. This is in comparison to 61 per cent in 1984 and 72 per cent in 1994. In the next age group of women aged 35–44, some 81 per cent will be in work by 2000 compared to just 71 per cent in 1984 and 78 per cent in 1994. During the period 1983–90 almost two-thirds of all new jobs went to women. From the 1960s there has been a continual rise in female employment.

Full-time and part-time work

There has been a trend away from full-time employment. It now accounts for around 62 per cent of employment. This is projected to decrease by a further

300 000 by 2001, giving a percentage of just 57 per cent. This is in the light of the fact that many other forms of employment offer considerably more flexibility to both businesses and individuals.

Part-time workers are those individuals who are working for less than 30 hours per week. There has been considerable growth in this type of employment. Indeed, some 1.4 million extra jobs have been created between 1981 and 1993. During the same period the number of full-time employees fell by 2 million. As a direct result of this, the overall percentage of employees engaged in part-time work rose from 21 per cent to 28 per cent.

The Institute of Employment Research further expects part-time employee positions to rise by a further 1.3 million. Coupled with this is a comparative fall in full-time employment of 300 000. This will mean that as the number of part-time employees increases, it will outstrip the total increase in employees. In other words, by 2001 part-time employment will account for some 32 per cent of all work.

Core and peripheral workers

In order to be leaner and more competitive, some organisations have taken the radical step of reducing significantly their levels of employment. Using this model, the organisation identifies core workers who will have the responsibility of providing a regular and essential level of service at times when demand and business activity is low. However, they will take on a more important role when demand increases. Working around and for these **core workers** will be a number of peripheral employees. Typically, these will be either on short fixed-term contracts or, perhaps, on temporary contracts via employment agencies. Alternatively, some of the **peripheral workers** could be freelance individuals who can carry out a series of activities for the business at another location.

The key advantages to having identified core and peripheral workers revolve around the organisation's ability to adapt to change in demand and activity at fairly short notice. The core workers become an extremely important asset for the organisation and the peripheral workers can be dispensed with once busy periods have passed.

Temporary work

In the temporary category of employment, nearly half of all jobs are in the secretarial field. Very much behind secretarial are publishing, industrial and technical areas of employment. Just ahead of computing and accounting comes catering. Normally, the definition of a temporary full-time post will mean that the individual is working on a short fixed-term contract, as discussed above. As you will see a little later when we evaluate types of employment with business needs, the use of the temporary worker has become a steadily more attractive prospect for employers.

Self-employment

Self-employment has shown very strong growth throughout the 1980s. However, this growth trend was severely interrupted by the recession. It is now widely believed that the growth has recommenced. By 2000 it is projected that a further 500 000 people will be self-employed.

Small businesses themselves also account for a growing proportion of employment. During the 1980s there was a growth from 1.9 million to 3.1 million. They were, however, the main casualties of the recession and in 1992 only 2.8 million had survived. Again, this short-term 'blip' has come to an end and there appear to be underlying trends which suggest that small firms and self-employment have recovered and are growing.

Job sharing

Job sharing offers the two individuals involved the opportunity to divide the working week according to the share that they have agreed. Normally, this means a simple halving of the working hours so that one employee covers the mornings and the other is available in the afternoons. In other cases, the working week may be split at Wednesday lunch time. The job share concept becomes a little more complex when the share is not equal, commonly one employee will have a 0.6 (or 60% of the working week) contract and the other will have 0.4 (40% of the working week). In either case, the positive advantages of job sharing are:

- that this organisation of the working week allows two individuals to cope with their other commitments outside the working environment (such as child care or caring for an invalid) without having a drastic affect on their working life
- that the organisation has the advantage of 'two for the price of one' in that they have the energies and attention of two individuals for the wage bill of one employee
- that the organisation can be assured that in the event of illness, for example, at least half of the job is still being done.

The disadvantages are:

- that there may be a tendency for the work output to be different and somewhat disjointed
- that it is unlikely that the work load over the day or the week is the same, so there may be a tendency for one of the job sharers to be doing more than the other
- that the employer has the legal responsibility for two employees instead of one, with the requirements to pay sick pay, maternity pay, provide holiday entitlements and other statutory obligations.

Freelancing

Freelancing can be another alternative to the more conventional forms of employment. In this respect, the employer has no long-term commitment to the employee who will simply work when, and if, there is work available. Under normal circumstances, freelancers are used to cover particularly important posts in an emergency and to take on specific projects as required by the employer. Most freelancers will be very experienced and will be able to adapt to most situations with the minimum of disruption. As they are reliant upon the employer to offer them work, they will also tend to be far more reliable and hard-working than someone on a permanent contract. For this reason, despite the disadvantages of not having a permanent member of staff to cover the work, the employer will be willing to enlist the aid of the freelancer.

Homeworking, teleworking and flexible working

Homeworking is becoming a growing trend as a form of working conditions. The traditional forms of home-working were often restricted to the clothing, textile and simple assembly occupations. Increasingly, however, very complex and technologically based tasks are undertaken on a routine basis within the home environment. Not only does this new form of occupation offer greater flexibility to the employee but also it offers significant cost savings for the employer. As there are about 640 000 people currently engaged in some form of homeworking, this does represent a major minority which cannot be ignored. There is every indication that the trend towards homeworking, which involves **teleworking** too, will continue to increase at a growing pace.

Contract and non-contract

There are still numerous employees who work without the benefit of a contract. These individuals, although they may not be strictly breaking the law, involve casual workers and hourly paid employees. Some employers prefer to pay a slightly higher gross pay and rely on the employee (who may be technically classed as self-employed in this respect) to worry about their own tax, national insurance and pension schemes. If you refer to Chapter 6, you will discover that employers are legally obliged to provide contracts to their employees. Work without such a contract is rather like jumping out of an aeroplane without a parachute – there is no protection.

Skilled and unskilled work

At this point we shall have a look at the unskilled workforce in general terms. There are a number of current skill supply issues. There are three ways of assessing skills.

- **Core skills** are very general skills applicable to almost every kind of job. They, of course, include basic literacy and numeracy, the ability to work with others and some understanding of information technology.
- **Vocational skills** are skills which are needed for a particular occupation but are often less useful outside of this occupation. These skills are still in part transferable. An individual who can operate a specific computer package would be more likely to be able to use a new one.
- **Specific job skills** are often limited to a fairly narrow range of occupations. It would be perhaps more accurate to call these specific job skills knowledge.

The availability of jobs in a particular region of the country is often related to the present skills mix within that region. Certain areas will have a predominance of occupational types and consequently will require significantly more individuals skilled in those areas. If we return to the nature of skilled and unskilled work, we will discover that the boundaries between them are becoming increasingly blurred. To this degree it is obvious that even some of the more routine unskilled occupations do require a little more than basic core skills. Increasingly, the need to communicate at a number of different levels coupled with the flexibility of **multi-skilling** is equally as relevant to those involved in more straightforward occupations as to those who are involved in complex operations.

Multi-skilling can prove to be extremely useful, particularly in production situations. The ability of an individual employee to stand in for unavailable colleagues may ensure that the production process is not interrupted by their absence. Equally, multi-skilling allows the organisation to employ its workforce more flexibly in a variety of different ways which would be determined by current demands. Multi-skilling implys that the production process should be **batch production** rather than **mass production**.

De-skilling, on the other hand, implies that the organisation is more interested in mass production, conveyor-belt-driven processes. Consequently, rather than the job being reliant on particular skills, the employee is now required to carry out a series of mundane and repetitive tasks which are predetermined by the speed of the machinery or conveyor belt.

Both approaches have their own advantages either in the speed of production or the quality of individual products. Whilst it could be argued that mass production requiring de-skilled labour is more likely to mean faster production, in many cases this is not so. Several major organisations, such as Nissan and Volvo, have moved across to multi-skilled workforces who are equally capable of producing products quickly and, above all, of a consistently high-quality standard.

On balance, the multi-skilled approach offers greater flexibility when change is required. Organisations which have a multi-skilled workforce will be able to deploy their employees into a variety of different related work activities, dependent upon the level of demand and the availability of work space and machinery.

■ The impact of changing work patterns

Pay

Changes in types of employment will obviously have an impact on the basic requirements and expectations that employees may have of their job.

If we begin with pay, there has been a tendency for certain employers to move over to part-time types of employment. Employers will keep only a core of staff on full-time contracts to provide some degree of stability and continuity within the work place. With a change in the form of employment individuals may not necessarily suffer any difference in their job security but they will experience a considerable drop in their weekly or monthly income. Similarly, if individuals move across to a temporary contract, they may experience lulls or periods of inactivity between contracts. This will obviously have a detrimental effect upon their ability to make long-term plans and commitments. Pay, in most cases, is essential to ensure that the individual remains committed and motivated to the organisation.

In many organisations, employees enjoy a variety of different benefits, such as pensions, sick pay, maternity pay and profit sharing. For those employees who are not considered full-time or permanent, many of these benefits may not be available. In many cases, the availability of additional benefits is a positive attraction to potential employees, but poses a difficult problem if the benefits are not offered to them.

Career progression

A great many employees would not cite career progression opportunities as being a readily available possibility for them. This is perhaps an additional concern for individuals who are not working on a full-time basis. Not only are the job roles and duties limited and somewhat curtailed compared to their full-time counterparts but also there are severely limited options available to them in terms of career progression. Despite the fact that these individuals may be very experienced and have more than adequate educational qualifications, they are often overlooked by the organisation as merely part-time workers who can address the short-term demands made by the organisation and its customers.

For individuals who are not on a permanent contract, job security is the paramount concern. At the end of their contract they will not know whether they will have a job or not. This uncertainty not only undermines their motivation, but also puts into question their loyalty to the organisation. If the organisation has not given them sufficient job security and a commitment to long-term employment, then the former cannot realistically expect these employees to give loyal and dedicated service. This is not to say that those on temporary contracts do not provide a valuable and essential service to the organisation. On the contrary, they are often the most motivated members of staff, albeit for a short period of time. If they are engaged on a short-term basis, then many of the long-term complications and falls in levels of motivation will not occur.

Working conditions

The physical surroundings and atmosphere of a work place are an important factor in the motivation of employees. Poor working conditions lead to demotivation, whereas there is a tendency for good working conditions to be accepted as the norm and employees receive no positive satisfaction from them. For an individual working on a part-time basis, the availability and use of the physical benefits that may be gained from a good working environment may have a tendency to be only incidental. They may not be in the working environment long enough to appreciate or take advantage of the working conditions, or any additional features which make the working conditions more agreeable may not be available during their working hours. This is particularly true of individuals who are working in an alternative employment mode to the standard 9am – 5pm (see Table 6.1).

Shift/work pattern	Total no. of employees	As percentage of all employed
Saturday working	6 289 000	24.6
Shift working	4 138 000	16.2
Sunday working	3 110 000	12.2
Night working	1 577 000	6.2

Source: Department of Employment 1994

Table 6.1 Employees usually engaged in weekend working, shift work and night work

The drive towards greater **flexibility** in working conditions has made businesses look towards alternatives to full-time employment. These include the following.

- Varying the number of employed to match demands. It has been shown that amongst the largest organisations over 80 per cent use temps. Temps account for around 5 per cent of the total number of employees in all sectors.
- Subcontracting. In 1990 the Workplace Industrial Relations Survey found

that 72 per cent of organisations subcontracted services to another business. Equally, a slightly later study showed that 70 per cent of 'non core operations' are contracted out. This flexibility offers considerable benefits to the business

- There is a strong growth in part-time work and indeed new working conditions such as annual hours contracts and flexitime have increased to 9 per cent and 12 per cent respectively in all occupations since the beginning of the 1990s (1993 figures). Table 6.2 shows the percentage of full-time employees with flexible working patterns. Table 6.3 considers the percentage of part-time employees with flexible working patterns.

Type of flexible working	Male (%)	Female (%)	All employees (%)
Flexible working hours	9.7	15.4	11.7
Annualised working hours	5.6	6.4	5.8
Term-time working	1.1	4.7	2.4
Job sharing	–	0.2	0.1
Nine-day fortnight	0.7	0.4	0.6
Four-and-a-half-day week	3.2	3.1	3.1
Total number of employees	10 573 000	5 681 000	16 245 000

Source: Department of Employment 1994

Table 6.2 Full-time employees with flexible working patterns

Type of flexible working	Male (%)	Female (%)	All employees (%)
Flexible working hours	7.3	9.1	8.8
Annualised working hours	3.1	5.3	5.0
Term-time working	4.9	10.3	9.6
Job sharing	1.8	2.5	2.4
Nine-day fortnight	–	–	–
Four-and-a-half-day week	–	0.3	0.3
Total number of employees	745 000	4 760 000	5 506 000

Source: Department of Employment 1994

Table 6.3 Part-time employees with flexible working patterns

- Teleworking/homeworking. In 1992 it was estimated that some 10 per cent of employers use home-based workers and 5 per cent use teleworkers. Some large firms may use as much as 20 per cent teleworking or homeworking employment systems. In 1994 the Labour Force Survey calculated that there were around 640 000 homeworkers.

- Functional flexibility involves the organisation being able to switch staff from one task to another, or in other words multi-skilling. In 1990 some 68 per cent of businesses said that they were actively using this form of flexible working practice. In the same survey 72 per cent of businesses reported that their productivity had increased. This is a good comparison with organisations that did not use this system who claimed only a 56 per cent productivity increase.
- Restructuring. In surveys carried out during 1993–4 around half of all major organisations reported considerable structural changes. Unfortunately 80 per cent of these organisations also reported job losses at all levels and 70 per cent significantly reported a loss of at least one layer of management.
- Flexible pay bargaining. During 1990 surveys showed that **collective bargaining** at organisation level had increased significantly. Local pay bargaining now accounts for 48 per cent of manual workers and 43 per cent of non-manual workers.

The ability and willingness of employees to adopt different methods of working can be an essential part in being able to cope with change. Many organisations strive to obtain a multi-skilled workforce that is not resistant to changes in its working practices. This means that not only do the employees need to be multi-skilled, but also they need to be willing to dispense with rigid demarcation which separates one job function from another.

As an alternative to this, the employment patterns may have to be changed in order to cope with differences in the need for particular job tasks to be undertaken. This may mean that some jobs will remain permanent and full time, but others may have to be either temporary or part time.

Some organisations have used shift working for a considerable number of years. This is often seen as a way in which the organisation can ensure that production and staffing levels remain constant throughout the whole day. The level of manning and consequent production at different times during the day may be related to particular production patterns and determined by deliveries of components and raw materials or the need to dispatch orders at particular times of the day.

Other organisations, mindful of the need to ensure that maximum staffing levels are achieved at busy times of the day, have introduced flexihours which go some way towards catering for the individual needs of the employee. Under flexitime, the core periods of the day have optimum staffing, whilst the less vital periods either side of the busy times have a skeleton staff available.

■ Team working

Working in any job role will require an employee to be both a competent individual worker and a willing and able team contributor. Any team is simply a collection of individuals with very different skills and motivations; no one should expect to have all of the abilities necessary to complement the attributes of the other team members. Some individuals prefer to concentrate on the job in hand and let others do the organising. Others are good organisers and poor doers. Whenever a team is established, for whatever reason, there will instantly be 'insiders' and 'outsiders'; this is particularly true once the team has established its own way of doing things. Team members will tend to support one another to the exclusion of all 'outsiders'.

Teams are encouraged within the majority of organisations for the following reasons:

- that it is often very difficult for individual employees to feel a part of a large organisation
- that teams offer the opportunity for individuals to have a sense of belonging, where their own contributions are recognised and valued
- that by having shared goals and objectives, individuals can help one another in achieving them
- that individuals who routinely work with one another on a daily basis may automatically form teams in order to complement one another's activities
- that teams often bring together a group of individuals who share common interests and ideas
- that individuals will naturally seek out others who are in similar circumstances and positions in the organisation
- that individuals may seek to become part of a team that is visibly achieving and getting results (and being noticed by the management too).

Effective team members are those who have the following characteristics:

- a willingness to co-operate
- a desire to share in the decision-making
- an ability to be adaptable and open to different views and approaches
- an ability to work to deadlines set by the team
- a willingness to allow praise to be given to the team as a whole even when they have carried out the majority of the work
- a willingness to offer suggestions regarding the approach to the work, despite the fact that their suggestions may not be adopted
- a strong desire to support all of the other members of the team at all times
- a willingness to accept both the praise and the criticisms as an equal member of the team
- an ability to trust the other members of the team.

Problems and benefits

Employee awareness and commitment to the organisation's policies are the key aspects of team working. Through team briefings, the organisation should aim to put over the culture and philosophy of the company.

In order to do this, the organisation needs to be clear about its culture and philosophy. It may be, as is often the case, that the organisation wishes to encourage employees to make decisions at an operational level. This is a more open style of management where good and bad times are shared.

It is essential that employees can feedback to the management through a recognised process. At team leaders' meetings, the management should attempt to provide clear and short answers to any issues that have been raised. They need to admit mistakes and be prepared to change policy.

Team briefings and hence team work, if treated in the right manner, can

- help to motivate employees
- open up channels of communication between employees and management
- build trust between the two groups
- prevent unnecessary misunderstandings
- reduce the detrimental effect of rumours
- explain why changes are necessary
- reduce frustration on the part of employees who are concerned about their fears and worries of the unknown
- improve company loyalty
- provide a valuable source of information
- reduce the 'them and us' syndrome
- lead to a greater cooperation between different teams.

There are three basic approaches to consider here.

The gatekeeper model (closed management style)
- Senior management prepares the policy.
- Managers relay the policy to team leaders.
- Team leaders relay the policy to the staff.
- Staff receive the policy at third hand.

In this model

- there is no opportunity for feedback
- everyone does get the same story
- there is no discussion.

Hierarchical model (semi-participation style)
- The policy is prepared by senior management.
- Senior managers relay it to managers.
- Managers relay it to team leaders.
- Team leaders translate it into their own words to make it relevant to staff.

In this model

- there are different methods of delivery
- questions are encouraged
- employees have a better chance to understand.

Open management model (continuous improvement style)
- The policy is prepared by the senior managers.
- The policy is relayed to managers who add their own information to it (specific to their department).
- The policy is then relayed to team leaders who are encouraged to deliver it

to employees in their own words; while at the same time the latter are encouraged to ask questions.

In this model

- there is effective communication
- there is ownership of the policy by all
- the statements can include questions to be answered by those lower down the chain
- the system encourages ideas and involvement.

Quality circles

A **quality circle** is a discussion group which meets regularly to

- identify quality problems
- investigate solutions
- recommend suitable solutions.

The members of quality circles are ordinary members of the workforce and may include an individual with specific skills such as

- an engineer in the case of complex products
- a quality inspector (if the organisation has a quality control department)
- a sales person to give information on customer perspectives.

Quality circles were first created in the 1950s in the Toyota motor company. In the 1980s this Japanese form of employee participation and consultation was adopted on a large scale in both Europe and the USA. Quality circles aim to use untapped knowledge from the factory floor, as well as giving employees the opportunity to show their knowledge and talents in terms of problem solving.

Autonomous work groups

This is a useful participation scheme that does not, necessarily, require a great deal of financial input. The work carried out by the employees is delegated down to teams of workers. The teams have full independence to decide how to complete the tasks that have been set. They have the right to elect a team leader and decide how the division of the various duties and tasks should be allocated.

■ Employee representation

Many organisations, while recognising that employees are a valuable resource in terms of their work output, have largely ignored their ability to offer specialist knowledge which could aid the operations of the organisation. Some employers, however, have introduced schemes aimed at tapping this hitherto unused resource. Sceptics often claim that many of these schemes are simply paper or public relations exercises aimed at trying to appear to be more enlightened. Many progressive organisations have installed very effective forms of employee representation and consultation. As regards representation, the traditional forms obviously included trade union organisations. As we have seen in recent years, many of these trade unions have decreased in size and power, whilst at the same time staff associations have become more common.

There are various forms of employee representation and consultation. Some organisations have formed a 'joint consultative committee' in which employees are given the opportunity to involve themselves in the organisation's decision-making. These committees hold regular meetings at which decisions made by the management are relayed to the workforce and a forum for discussion is provided. Such committees also meet to discuss and negotiate matters relating to industrial relations, such as working conditions, disciplinary procedures and pay.

These committees will take the form of

- an advisory body
- a consultative body
- a negotiating body.

Another form of employee consultation is known as employee participation. This has come about because organisations have recognised that the workforce has considerable skills and good ideas which could be used for the mutual benefit of employer and employees. There are various versions of employee participation and they include the following.

- Employee briefing sessions – where employees are given useful and relevant information regarding the objectives of the organisation.
- Quality circles – where employees meet voluntarily to discuss their work and how systems and procedures may be improved.
- Transfer of responsibility – when employees take on some of the management-related decision-making.

- **Worker directors** – where employees attend meetings of the board of directors. In Europe this idea has proved to be very successful in improving the quality of decision-making at board level. It also gives the board the opportunity to hear the views of the workforce at first hand rather than relying on the various layers of management to relay employees' wishes and ideas. Further, this system tends to mean that employees are more committed to decisions made by the board. Finally, it helps reduce employer/employee conflict as employees have a greater idea of the overall problems faced by the organisation.

Worker councils

These are also known as **works councils**. Essentially, they are regular meetings which encourage discussion between the workforce and the management. At these forums the workforce is represented by a number of individuals. These forums are not meant to replace the role of the trade unions, as such – works councils do not discuss pay, productivity or working conditions.

The precise role of works councils differ from business to business, but the key focus is to examine and review the plans of the organisation and to suggest possible changes. The second major function is to consider the suggestions of the workforce as to how to improve the general working of the organisation.

Some critics of this system of employee participation have said that whilst works councils may be useful in certain organisations, they are not as effective as quality circles, for example. The main reasons for this lies in the fact that the membership of the works councils are intended to encompass the whole of the workforce. For this reason, the members, collectively, do not have a grasp of one particular aspect of the organisation. As a result, they can talk only about improvements in general terms.

Worker directors

This form of employee participation and consultation is not very widespread in the UK. In the rest of Europe, on the other hand, the practice is common and is seen as a solution to the prospects of industrial problems within the workforce.

Many more traditional managers do not largely embrace this initiative, which effectively democratises the whole of the decision-making process. They have the following reservations.

- It actually slows down decision-making as more individuals are involved in the process.
- Some sensitive information about the business, its finances and plans may leak out and be made available to competitors.
- Above all, it reduces the powers of the directors as the workforce will have a say at board level.

You may think that UK trade unions would be in favour of such an initiative. They are not. They state the following reasons.

- Worker directors at board level become as responsible for the decisions made as traditional directors.
- Because worker directors are sitting on the board, the union's ability to negotiate is weakened.

Many of the causes and implications of change in an organisation are as a result of new office technology. With the new developments in office technology such as the lap-top computer, Internet access and voice recognition, employers need to make decisions on how various activities are carried out. For the employees, there is always a period of uncertainty, coupled with the fact that they may face redundancy or a new set of job responsibilities.

The need for efficient management

In any proposed change in either job role or working conditions, the whole process is very much reliant upon the ability of the management. Assuming that the manager has the following characteristics, we can expect a fairly smooth implementation of change.

- An effective manager manages the relationships with employees rather than managing the employees themselves.
- An effective manager recognises that management skills, particularly in terms of negotiation, communication, learning ability and the setting of goals, are essential management techniques.
- An effective manager learns from the experience of management rather than having a theoretical knowledge.
- An effective manager recognises that no two individuals are the same and people cope with stress or change in many different ways.

The difference between effective managers and poor ones is their ability to recognise goals and identify methods by which these goals may be attained. The first stage in implementing change is to identify the goal itself. The following questions need to be asked at this stage.

- What is it we are trying to do?
- What is the point of the change?
- Who will it affect?
- What is in it for the organisation?
- What are the short-, medium- and long-term prospects?
- What are the constraints involved?
- What is the time scale?
- Do we have the technology, equipment or machinery?
- How will the employees respond?
- Who has overall responsibility for the change?

Student activity

Can you think of any other criteria which may be relevant in establishing goals? Discuss these in pairs.

Planning for change

Individuals set about the process of planning in many different ways. In general, however, we can recognise the following features of the planning process.

- In relation to the objectives, a plan should include what needs to achieved and by whom.
- The plan should also identify the key factors involved.
- Above all, the plan should include a list of actions and timings.

Having determined what is to be achieved, the plan should address the following.

- What will be the changes in working conditions?
  - Will managers have to delegate more?
  - Will there be a change in the location of the work?
- Will there be a change in the way in which teams work?
  - Are new procedures necessary?
  - Does the organisation have to be restructured?
- What are the training requirements?
  - What new skills will need to be learnt?
  - How will they be acquired?
  - What will be the format of the training?
- Will there be changes in the communications procedures?
  - Will it make communication more difficult?

- Does the organisational structure support the new conditions?
  - Does someone need to be appointed to oversee the new changes?
- How will individual employees be affected?
- How will groups in general be affected?
  - Who will be affected?
  - Who will not be affected?
  - Who, therefore, needs to be informed?
- What information has to be relayed?
  - Who needs to be consulted?
  - When should they be consulted?
  - How will the changes be presented?
- What are the likely reactions or resistance to the change?
  - What are the anticipated reactions?
  - Who will present the greatest resistance?
- What is the estimated cost of the change?
- What is the timetable for introducing the change?
  - Should milestones be identified?
  - What steps need to be achieved?
- How will the changes be measured and monitored?
  - By whom?
  - How?
  - When?

Once the effects of the changes have been thought through in detail, the following needs to be addressed.

- The more complicated the change, the more there is a need for schedules to be drawn up.
- Assuming there are limited resources, how realistic is the timetable?
- What will be the net effect on the day-to-day running of the organisation whilst the changes are being undertaken?

Setting identifiable targets

The establishment of milestones, or means by which the process or progress of the change is progressing, is essential. Certain targets or objectives must be readily identifiable in order to assess not only the progress of the change but its current impact on the organisation. When we consider significant structural changes relating to the premises of an organisation, it is fairly easy to recognise and establish these targets. However, when we are considering less tangible changes in working conditions, we must, perhaps, turn our attention to either the reactions of the employees or their gradual acceptance of the changes. To this extent, the measurement or the recognition that the target has been reached may be rather problematic. Regular meetings and the subsequent feedback from employees is essential in ensuring that changes are being made in the smoothest and most beneficial manner.

Programme of training

With any change in working conditions, there may be a need to train, retrain or refresh individuals' understanding and knowledge. Included in the overall implementation plan should be a rolling programme of training. Obviously, dependent upon the nature of the change in working conditions, more or less training will be involved. In the field of health and safety, particularly relating to new legislation, significant amounts of training may be required. If, for example, individuals are required to wear protective clothing or maintain equipment, this may have a significant impact upon the productivity for a short period of time. If new equipment or machinery has been installed to be used in the manufacturing process, again significant retraining may have to be undertaken. It is often the case that the suppliers of new equipment include in their quotation to the purchasing organisation a basic training programme for all operators or users of the machinery.

Monitoring and evaluation

There is probably, in many cases, little or no real attention given to the monitoring of the change or the progress. If the organisation has not clearly thought through how it will ensure that the change has kept to its timetable, delays may be inevitable. In more formal situations, the organisation may require that certain documentation is completed and feedback given at the identified milestones.

Generally, when changes are implemented, a specific individual will be responsible for the monitoring and evaluation process. Indeed, this individual's time and effort may be solely directed at the implementation of the change. Unfortunately, this is not always the case and the monitoring and evaluation process will have to be undertaken by an individual as well as his or her normal day-to-day duties. In this case, the individual may find it difficult to address both job roles.

If, as is often the case, things do not go according to plan, the organisation and the individual responsible for the implementation may find themselves in a difficult situation. If the production process has been drastically affected by the change(s), but the change is not significantly completed as yet, then this may have drastic effects upon the viability and profitability of the organisation.

The relaying of information is essential throughout the whole process of change. Organisations should call regular meetings, particularly with those mostly affected by the change. These feedback opportunities should not be ignored as employees may have good ideas or suggestions to overcome problems and aid development and implementation.

Keywords

The keywords that should know for this chapter are listed below. Check to make sure you understand the meaning of each word. Discuss those you are unsure of with your tutor.

batch production	multi-skilling
core workers	peripheral workers
collective bargaining	quality circles
de-skilling	shift work
freelancing	teleworking
homeworking	worker councils
mass production	worker directors

Examination practice

Short-answer questions

1 What is homeworking?

2 What is job sharing? Give an example of how it might work in practice.

3 What is short fixed-term contract?

4 Give three advantages of team work.

5 What is the fastest growing work pattern in the UK and why?

6 Explain what you understand by the terms 'multi-skilling' and 'de-skilling'.

7 What do you understand by the term 'job security'? Give two examples of how an individual's work pattern may provide more job security.

8 What are 'worker directors'?

9 What is 'teleworking'?

10 Give three examples of alternative work patterns that could be considered to be 'unsociable'.

Essay questions

You work for a very traditional family business which manufactures chocolates and boiled sweets. Although the demand for the products is fairly constant throughout the year, there are periods, such as the run-up to Christmas, Easter and St Valentine's Day that put the business under extreme pressure to deal with the orders. Naturally, the goods have to be ready for dispatch well in advance of these periods. The business has, until now, relied on permanent full-time staff working overtime to meet the demand. Lyndsey Williams, your direct line manager is the Personnel Officer and she wants to investigate other ways in which the business could avoid the chaos and the problems of encouraging all of the staff to take on overtime during these periods.

1 Lyndsey has asked you to begin by defining the nature of the various options open to the business in terms of changing the working patterns of the staff. Specifically, she wants to know about the following.

   a What are the general trends in full-time and part-time employment in the UK?

   b What are the 'core' and 'peripheral' workers?

   c Would the business be more likely to attract male or female employees and why?

2 Lyndsey understands that she could offer some new employees fixed short-term contracts, or she could decide not to employ any more staff beyond the current levels and try to convince the management to subcontract the extra work when the demand is high.

   a Define and explain fixed short-term contracts

   b Define and explain the advantages and disadvantages of sub-contracting

3 Although the business has managed to cope with the present machinery and equipment the Production Manager is actively trying to convince the Board to make a considerable investment in new technology in all areas of the business. He maintains that not only will an automated production line be far more efficient than the current practice of making the sweets and chocolates by hand, but the use of computers all networked and integrated throughout the company will mean great savings in the long run. The vast majority of invoicing, stock control and other administrative activities is still done manually. Lyndsey is concerned about the impact of these potential changes and has asked you to put a short report together which outlines the following.

   a What would be the probable impact on the number and skill level of the current employees if the new technology was introduced?

   b How could the new technology enable the company to be more efficient and competitive?

   c What qualities of the company would be lost or improved upon by the introduction of the new technology?

4 Lyndsey is convinced that sooner or later these changes are inevitable. The company does value the hard-working and committed workforce. To this end, she wants you to suggest ways in which the introduction of the new technology could be implemented in such a way as to allow the employees to take an active role. She would like you to prepare a short set of notes on the following alternatives.

a What are quality circles and how could they be used by the company?

b Would the introduction of work teams be a good idea?

c What other ways could the company involve the employees in the decision-making?

d How would the company allay the fears of the employees in terms of their job security?

Business functions

5

■ Introduction

As you will have already appreciated, all business organisations are different. Not only do they have different priorities, but they also have different structures. In consequence, it is difficult to make any broad generalisations about the functional areas of a typical business organisation. There is no such thing as a 'typical organisation'. In this chapter we investigate the main activities that are undertaken in the majority of medium to large organisations. You should bear in mind that in smaller organisations many of the activities are undertaken by relatively few individuals who will need to juggle their time and resources in order to cover all the needs of the organisation.

For many of the functions that have been identified as specific departments, we could make some logical conclusions about the grouping of certain functions.

- Accounts may also include purchasing.
- Production may also include research and development.
- Sales and marketing may be part of the production department.
- Computer services may be a part of administration.

You will be able to get a clearer picture regarding the grouping of business functions and activities when you see the range of work carried out by each of the specific areas and the nature of each of the specific job roles, it may become apparent that some of the roles are broad enough to encompass other areas of work or are simple duplications of role, but in another departmental area.

■ Accounts

The main function of accounting systems is to provide managers with the means to exercise financial control over their departments so that they may implement budgetary control. A budget relies on a plan, which is made on the basis of estimates of future spending and income. The budget will also try to allocate any expenses in relation to particular objectives set by the organisation. Depending upon the size of the organisation, this may be across the whole of the organisation, or on a departmental basis. Budgetary control is established by careful consideration of the following.

- The organisation will define its objectives and try to allocate the expenditure related to each of them.
- The organisation will establish standard operating procedures which relate to specific strategies in meeting the objectives.
- The organisation will establish systems to monitor the actual spending on each objective, as opposed to the estimated expenditure.
- The above monitoring of the objectives in relation to the standards set will be made at various times and take the form of interim reports.

- The organisation must have in place a series of procedures in order to react to any differences between the estimated and the actual spending. This is particularly important if there is an overspend and may result in the re-examination of the organisation's operating systems. Most organisations expect constantly to have to redefine their operating standards and monitoring systems in order to maintain efficiency.

The accurate monitoring of budgets is essential to all businesses for the following reasons.

- It allows the organisation clearly to define its aims and policies.
- It allows the organisation to develop an overall corporate strategy.
- It allows the key decision-makers of the organisation to keep a careful eye on all budgets.
- It allows the organisation to monitor actual performance against estimated activity.
- It should improve the organisation's efficiency and the deployment of resources towards the meeting of specific objectives.

When considering the creditworthiness of individual customers, most organisations will have set a particular policy at high management level. In large organisations, there may be an individual with specific responsibility for credit control and the setting of customers' credit levels. In small organisations, as we have mentioned, an individual may have to take on this responsibility in addition to other tasks. Regardless of the particular situation in the organisation, an efficient credit system should include the following features.

- **Credit checks** – these include the taking up of bank and trade references and reference to credit agencies.
- Establishment of credit levels and what terms apply to these limits.
- Action to be taken in the case of credit breaches – this will involve a system being created to determine at what particular stage action will be taken. It will include a series of letters requesting payment. The style and tone of these letters is important in order to avoid unnecessary complications, both legally and personally, with the customer.

Credit ratings are often based on sales experience with a particular customer. Credit ratings given to customers should reflect their ability to pay at some point in the future.

Specifically then, the major requirements of the administrative system within a finance or accounts department are:

- to record information
- to store records either manually or using a database or specific accounts software
- to have these records available for inspection by the Inland Revenue (for tax purposes)
- to have these records available for inspection by Customs and Excise (for VAT purposes)

- to have these records available for inspection by the company's auditors
- to report on the financial health of the organisation at the end of the year.

It is vital that these systems work, as the organisation will need them for planning, decision-making and financial control.

Job roles

The main job roles within an accounts department are as follows (see Figure 5.1)

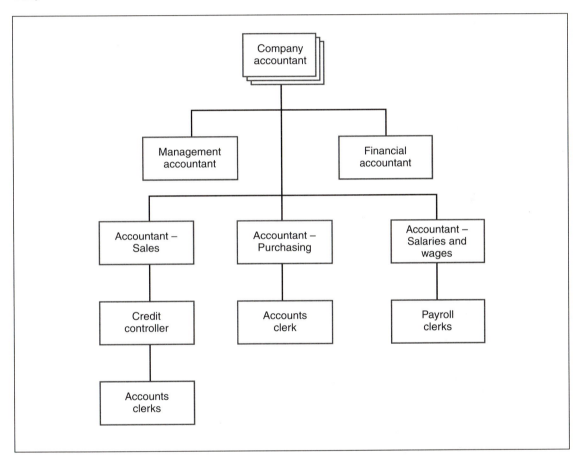

Figure 5.1 The accounts department

Company accountant

It is the company accountant's responsibility to maintain an up-to-date record and analysis of income and expenditure. The company accountant has a number of accounts specialists who monitor, on his or her behalf, various financial aspects of the organisation. At any time, the company accountant may be asked for detailed information about the financial status of the organisation, and must be able to respond immediately. There are a number of legal and statutory requirements that an organisation must fulfil and it is the responsibility of the company accountant to ensure that all of these obligations are met. The company accountant is directly accountable to the board of directors for his or her actions and decisions. It is usual, particularly in larger organisations, for the accountant (or equivalent) to be a member of the Board of directors.

Accountant

Various accounts specialists are employed to carry out specific monitoring and analysis of financial data. These accountants oversee the flow of data received regarding sales, purchases, running costs and other expenses. In addition, they provide essential accounting information such as gross profit, net profit, turnover and relative profitability of different areas of the organisation. In larger organisations they may keep track of the performance of investments in other organisations and regularly monitor the financial strengths and weaknesses of subsidiary companies.

Credit controller

The credit controller monitors the orders placed and the payment history of customers in order to establish their reliability as payers. Each customer has a set credit limit (rather like an agreed overdraft) and the credit controller must endeavour to make sure that customers do not exceed this limit. In cases of late or non-payment of invoices, it is the credit controller who contacts the customer in question in an attempt to secure payment. The credit controller takes into account how long the customer has been purchasing from the organisation and may well look back into the past to see if there have been any previous problems with regard to payment.

Accounts clerk

The accounts clerk carries out routine day-to-day accounting duties, as directed by either the chief accountant or senior accountants. This may involve either manual figure work, or the use of the increasingly popular range of accounting software. It is usually the accounts clerk's role to prepare figures for analysis by the more senior accountants. In some organisations, one duty of an accounts clerk is to maintain and issue petty cash to those who request it by the presentation of a validly signed voucher.

Payroll clerk

Working closely with the personnel department, the payroll clerk is responsible for ensuring that the correct wages or salaries are paid to every member of staff. The payroll clerk must be familiar with income tax and national insurance and pension scheme contributions. Depending on the size of the organisation, the payroll clerk may have to undertake these tasks manually, or in a larger organisation, he or she may be assisted by a software pay roll package. In some organisations where the wages structure is complex, or is related to performance and output, this job may not be straightforward.

■ Sales and marketing

The sales department's main responsibility is to create orders for goods and services. Many organisations employ a large sales force which operates either, in the case of retail stores, on a local level, or, in the case of organisations which supply to other organisations, on a regional basis.

The greater the emphasis on selling to individual customers, the larger the sales force. Those organisations which rely on heavy advertising to stimulate interest in their goods or services may have a relatively small sales team.

In terms of organising the efforts of the sales employees, the sales department draws up a detailed sales plan which includes targets to be met by each area or region of the sales force. Also included in this will be the level of profit which can be expected from each and every product.

Working closely with the marketing department, the sales department regularly supplies information on sales levels, activities of competitors and requests from customers for new or improved products. Individual members of the sales force compile the raw data about their sales figures on a weekly basis for interpretation by the sales manager, who will then pass this information on for analysis by the marketing department. In order to stimulate sales, the sales department may develop a range of point-of-sale material (including posters, leaflets and boxes with the company logo) and other promotional materials.

The main function of the marketing department is to try to identify customer requirements. There is also an element of trying to predict future customer needs. The marketing department works very closely with the sales department, and it is important that the two communicate well.

The starting point for most marketing functions is to carry out extensive research on a particular market to try to discover exactly what customers want, where they want it, how much they want to pay for it and the most effective way of getting the message across. This is known as the **marketing mix**.

The marketing department will need to work closely with the research and design department and the production department in developing attractive and saleable products. This work will also include the constant updating of existing products to cater for changes in taste and demand.

One of the more obvious responsibilities of the marketing department is the design and development of advertising ideas and marketing campaigns. This design and development process will take account of the needs of the sales department and any other interested area of the organisation.

As part of its regular market research procedures, the marketing department will monitor changes in trends and fashions that affect its customers. Some information is readily available as statistical tables published by the government which is known as secondary research, but much information must be researched as required by the organisation itself. This is known as primary research. Both these market research methods are looked at in more detail on pages 227–228.

Customer service

This function includes the parts of the organisation which have direct contact with the customer. We also include marketing here, since it may have a responsibility for customer service in terms of advertising, promotion and quality assurance. The exact relationship between customer service (sales) and marketing will very much depend upon the organisation itself.

The key functions of sales staff are to control and organise the selling and distribution of the organisation's products and services. The sales function may often be found within the marketing department of an organisation, but the sales operation will always be supported by administrative personnel and various sales representatives. As with any other managerial function, the sales manager will be responsible for the establishment and revision of systems which will ensure the smooth running of the sales operation. In addition, he or she may have specific targets to meet and must maintain budgetary control over these. Communication is a key feature of a good sales department, as the staff must be able to handle all communications with customers. They will also be responsible for the maintenance of any relevant records and exercise some control (via a credit controller) over the availability of credit to customers.

Dealing with customers requires the establishment of systems to handle enquiries and problems efficiently. These systems will also require the sales department to keep records of any enquiries made, orders received and other documentation which maintains an up-to-date record of customer transactions.

When sales staff have contact with customers, whether this is by telephone or personal visit, administration systems must be in place to ensure that the details of any conversation, negotiation or problems have been recorded accurately. This information will be held by the sales department and will mainly include

- the name and phone number of customer's chief buyer
- discounts agreed
- creditworthiness
- specific customer requirements
- delivery arrangements
- size of customer order
- frequency of customer order.

The documentation and administration systems used by the customer service section of an organisation will very much depend upon the nature of the organisation itself. However, some generalisations can be made about the types of information that should be recorded.

- Processing of sales information (through invoices/order forms and letters, etc.).

- Marketing research (including data collection and analysis).
- Customer care details (guarantees or warranties, etc.).
- Customer service (dealing with complaints, etc.).
- Sales promotions (all non-advertising marketing such as special offers, etc.).
- Advertising (planning, monitoring, etc.).
- Support services (via personnel for training and development, etc.).
- General sales administration.

Student activity

Although many organisations do not actually sell a physical product, they do still need to have a customer service function in order to ensure that their clients are receiving the best possible service from the organisation at all times. Considering a non-product-based organisation, how will customer service differ from organisations that actually sell a physical product?

Sales department personnel

Sales department personnel include the following (see Figure 5.2).

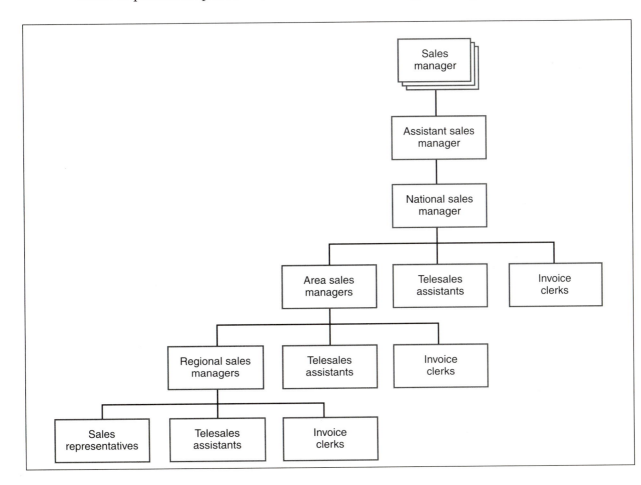

Figure 5.2 The sales department

Sales manager

This job entails the coordination of the organisation's sales efforts. The sales manager is usually located at the head office with an administration staff who monitor the performance of the various national, regional and area sales managers and teams. In positions such as this, a considerable amount of salary is related to sales performance. Periodically, the sales manager visits his or her sales team in the field to assess its effectiveness and to keep in touch with current customer demands.

Assistant sales manager

Deputising for the sales manager, this individual takes on a range of sales-related responsibilities and may often be the first point of contact for the various members of the sales force. It is the assistant sales manager's role to help the sales manager formulate the sales policy of the organisation.

National sales manager

In larger organisations, there is a need to coordinate the sales efforts on a country-by-country basis. National sales managers are usually given considerable freedom to formulate a sales policy which is the most effective for the country in which they operate. Normally, national sales managers will have a wide knowledge of the country in which they work and may even be a national of that country. Other organisations may not have national sales managers, as they may have entered into an agreement with a foreign company to represent the interests of the organisation in that country.

Regional sales manager

Just as different countries have their own peculiarities, regions within a country also have theirs. Different sorts of industry and commerce tend to cluster around particular towns or cities. The regional sales manager will have an intimate knowledge of the needs of these businesses, which may be different from the national needs. The regional sales manager is located within the region for which he or she has responsibility and is required to analyse regularly any changes in the local economy which may affect sales.

Area sales manager

Working under the direction of the regional sales manager, the area sales manager is responsible for a part of the region. In some cases, this may mean a single city or county. Again, a good working knowledge of the needs of the area is essential in coordinating the sales effort. The area sales manager regularly accompanies sales representatives when they visit customers and is able to offer on-the-spot advice and guidance.

Sales representative

Sales representatives form the backbone of the sales team. Constantly on the road, visiting both existing and potential customers, they will be in direct contact with their area sales manager via mobile or car phones. Since the bulk of their salary is directly related to the sales they generate, they are always under pressure to meet their targets in order to achieve their bonuses. The image of the sales representative in a company car is well known. In reality, they may be very well-trained sales people, with an expert knowledge of their field and extremely useful to their customers. They are, after all, the first point of contact and may well become a useful 'partner' in building up a business.

Telesales assistant

Working from central, national, regional or area offices, telesales assistants take direct orders for goods and services from the customer. They also receive regular orders from customers and from the sales representatives. Operating with up-to-date lists of customer contacts from the sales representatives, they attempt to gain new sales or arrange for one of the sales representatives to visit the business. They are particularly well trained in telephone skills and normally have useful information to hand via a desktop computer.

Invoice clerk

The invoice clerk processes all orders generated by either the sales representatives or the telesales team. Essentially, the documents produced form both a list of required products for the warehouse to dispatch and a record for the accounts department of products sold. The invoice clerk is in regular contact with the warehouse to ensure that the sales team is aware of the stock levels of each product.

Marketing department personnel

The staff in this department include the following (see Figure 5.3).

Marketing manager

The marketing manager is responsible for planning, organising, directing and controlling the marketing efforts of the organisation. Increasingly, these are professional individuals who are well versed in formulating a marketing plan which is workable within the limitations of the organisation. In effect, they are responsible for establishing the organisation's marketing objectives (known as

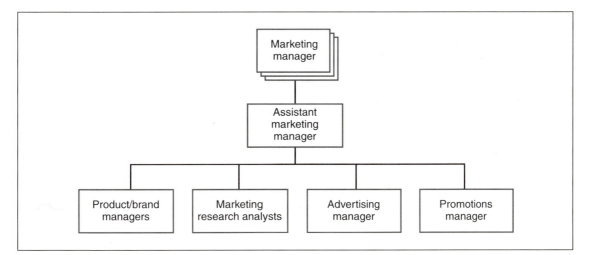

Figure 5.3 The marketing department

the strategy) and deciding how the overall objectives may be achieved (known as the tactics). All organisations have a **corporate image**, which means that everything the organisation produces, from letterheads to finished products, has the same overall look. The marketing manager decides exactly how the corporate image relates to each and every aspect of the company.

Assistant marketing manager

Deputising for the marketing manager, and coordinating the efforts of each of the product/brand managers are the main responsibilities of the assistant marketing manager. It is this individual's role to implement the marketing strategy across all aspects of the organisation and to ensure that the corporate image is consistent.

Product/brand manager

A product manager is responsible for coordinating the marketing plan relating to a single product. A brand manager, on the other hand, may be responsible for a range of products which have the same brand name. In both cases, the individuals organise all activities relating to their product(s), including advertising, sales promotions, launches, relaunches and packaging.

Marketing research analyst

Millions of pounds are spent each year on marketing research. Nearly 10 per cent of the retail price of every item is spent on marketing research alone. Marketing research is the systematic collection and analysis of data which looks specifically at the customer's attitudes, needs, opinions and motivation and anything which influences these. In order to minimise the risks involved in launching a new product, the organisation needs to know as much as possible about the potential customer, competition and any other factors which may affect sales. This specialist uses existing statistical data, as well as commissioning new market research as may be required.

Advertising manager

An advertising manager is responsible for coordinating the advertising budget of the organisation. Working in close cooperation with various other members of the organisation, the advertising manager should be able to identify the best media for the advertising of the product. Additionally, the advertising manager negotiates with magazines, newspapers, radio and television companies to achieve the best possible price. In many organisations, the advertising manager's function is taken over by an outside advertising agency which places and coordinates all advertisements.

Promotions manager

There is a narrow line between the responsibilities of a promotions manager and an advertising manager. Essentially, the promotions manager coordinates all other marketing strategies apart from advertisements. These include special offers, competitions, trial offers, money-off vouchers, point-of-sale material and exhibitions.

Student activity

In the role of marketing manager, where would you look for information on changes in customer trends and fashions? Discuss this as a group.

Procedures for dealing with customers

Increasingly, organisations have begun to recognise the value of not only responding to customer needs by adapting or expanding the products and services offered but also by employing staff who are trained to deal with numerous different customer-service problems.

If customers are happy with the service, then there is a tendency for them to use the service more often. This is known as repeat business. Equally, they may tell their friends, family and colleagues at work about the good service that they have received and this will enhance the reputation of the business. If both of these things happen, then the business will, of course, get increased sales. This is not only good for the business, but it is also good for the customer. The business can provide a better and wider service and ensure that standards are always maintained at a high level.

Case study

Surveys have shown that no matter how successful an organisation may be in providing a good customer service, customers do not return to a business after the first visit for the following reasons.

- 1 per cent of customers die.
- 3 per cent of customers move away.
- 4 per cent of customers float from one business to another.
- 68 per cent of customers stop dealing with the business because sales staff are indifferent or show little interest in them.
- 8 per cent of customers are chronic complainers and would find fault in anything.
- 9 per cent of customers change because they can find the products and services more cheaply elsewhere.

Source: Maggie Hardy McKee, Personnel Manager *at Granada Studios* (1995).

The customer/public relations department

The customer relations department is the main point of contact for customers who have complaints about products or services supplied by an organisation. A smooth, efficient and courteous response to customer complaints is a key feature in making sure that the organisation's reputation is maintained. Many products now have on their labels a short sentence stating that if customers have any problems with the product, they should simply return it to the manufacturer for a refund or replacement. This is an offer in addition to the legal requirement that a product must be fit for the use for which it was intended, and has gone a long way to enhance organisations' reputations for being fair.

A public relations department traditionally was the main way which an organisation passed on news and information about its activities and products to the media and other interested parties. In recent years, organisations have realised the need to project a strong, positive image to the public. This role has expanded to include close contact with the public. Requests for information about an organisation and its operations are dealt with by the public relations department, which may well have developed a range of booklets and other materials for this purpose.

The staff of a public relations department include the following.

Public relations officer

The job holder is responsible for fostering a good relationship with the media, in the hope that they will consider giving the organisation both editorial space and favourable news reporting. He or she maintains a comprehensive database of media contacts, from which extensive mailshots are made. The public relations officer is also responsible for the writing of press releases and also produces a range of booklets and leaflets concerning the operations of the organisation.

Customer relations officer

While the public relations officer is concerned with media and news coverage, the customer relations officer concentrates on existing and potential customers. He or she responds to customer enquiries, providing a range of information packs on request. In addition, the customer relations officer also coordinates activities within the community projects department. In cases where a customer has a serious complaint about the products or services of the organisation, the customer relations officer will be available to assist in the solving of any problem.

The community projects department

This is never a particularly large part of an organisation, but many organisations, having recognised the need to form a closer relationship with the local community, have appointed a community projects officer. In several respects, the duties of this individual are somewhat similar to those of the customer relations officer. However, the community projects officer tends to concentrate on the immediate locality. He or she organises, with the assistance of other local organisations, a range of activities in order to heighten the public's awareness and appreciation of the organisation. This may take the form of sponsoring local events, financing community projects, or offering the organisation's facilities to local groups.

■ Production

The production department is involved in all functions which revolve around producing goods or services for the customer.

This department monitors levels of **wastage** to ensure the most efficient use of resources and checks the cost of raw materials and parts purchased to make sure that **profit margins** are maintained.

As new products are developed, and technology changes, the production department will be responsible for purchasing all the necessary plant and equipment required, as well as organising the production process.

In consultation with the sales department, the production department must make sure that it can manufacture or supply customers with the quantity of goods required at the time they have been requested. The tight monitoring of production levels means that the production department should know how long it would take to produce sufficient products to fill a particular order. Advance planning and close liaison with the sales department are vital to ensure that deadlines can be met.

Regardless of how many units of products are being produced, the production department is also responsible for the maintenance of quality. Each product must meet a number of strict quality standards and must, to all intents and purposes, be exactly the same every time. Periodically products will be randomly selected from the production line and tested by either the R & D department or the quality assurance/control department.

A good production department will monitor methods of production used by all major competitors and allied industries and will take steps to implement any useful methods of production used elsewhere.

Increasingly, as production becomes steadily more automated, the production department will also have to design computer programs which can handle the new processes.

Purchasing

In some organisations, the purchasing or buying function is centralised in order to ensure that budgets are strictly adhered to, that recommended suppliers are used and that only correctly completed and authorised orders are processed.

For many organisations, the **devolved budgets** system (where each department takes responsibility for its own purchases) has meant that purchasing, as a department in its own right, has ceased to exist.

Purchasing departments still exist in name only in many organisations and are often found as a part of either the production department, accounts or administration. In a manufacturing operation the majority of purchases tend to be related directly to the production itself.

Student activity

Think of a few organisations that you know well. Do they have a separate purchasing department? If not, which part of the organisation takes the responsibility for purchasing decisions? What part of the organisation makes sure that deliveries are correct and monitors the stock levels?

Production/Purchasing personnel

The staff of this department are as follows (see Figure 5.4).

Production manager

The production manager's responsibility is to manufacture products to the correct specification, quality, price and safety levels. Production managers tend to be quite technical individuals, who understand the production process intimately. He or she works closely with the R & D manager, as well as the sales manager. It is the production manager's role to turn new product ideas into finished products and supply the regular needs of the sales department.

Assistant production manager

This individual is given the responsibility by the production manager to oversee the smooth running of the various production lines. He or she works in close cooperation with the production line managers to ensure that production levels and product quality are maintained in relation to demand. The assistant production manager is technically competent and may have a good working knowledge of the machinery.

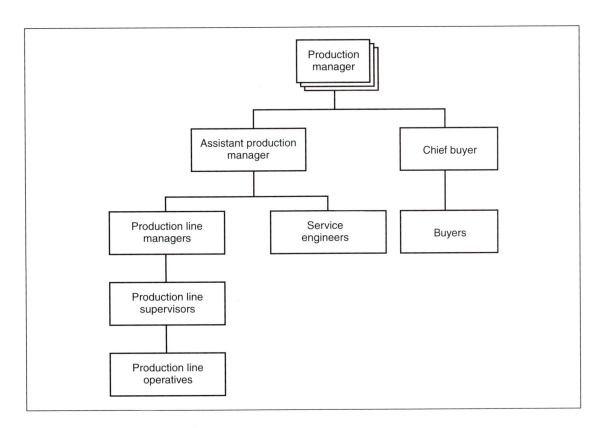

Figure 5.4 The production department

The buyer

The buyer is required to ensure that he or she has purchased sufficient stocks of raw materials and components to enable the production lines to run efficiently. The buyer must be able to predict demands for all raw materials, components and machinery by close examination of sales figures, past, present and projected. An essential duty of the buyer is to obtain all items at the best possible prices. The buyer may be able to negotiate favourable extended credit terms from regular suppliers. He or she is also responsible for making sure that all items ordered are received in good time.

Production line manager and supervisor

The production line manager is responsible for the smooth running of a part of the production department which produces a single product or product range. He or she is given quotas to achieve by the production manager or assistant production manager and has to organise his or her staff to meet the deadlines.

The supervisor monitors the performance of both the work team and the machinery and regularly reports to the production line manager regarding any potential problems. The supervisor is the main point of contact between the employees and the management structure of the organisation. In the event of potential problems with the machinery, he or she will liaise with the service engineers.

Service engineer

It is the service engineer's role to ensure that any defects or breakdowns in machinery within the production department are swiftly and efficiently dealt with. He or she will inform the production manager and the relevant production line manager regarding any need to close down a production line for the purposes of maintenance, service or cleaning. The service engineers need to keep a stock of basic components in order to repair machinery on the spot.

Production line operative

Depending on the type of production employed by the organisation, production line operatives are responsible for either a repetitive task or a series of related tasks. Many production lines have been developed so that only routine duties need to be carried out by humans. In these cases, production line operatives tend merely to feed the machines with raw materials and components and do not actually take part in the production process itself. In situations where the production is less automated, production line operatives are involved in the production of goods to completion. Many organisations run their production lines continuously and therefore require their production line operatives to work shifts.

Student activity

In the role of a production manager, design a time sheet for completion by employees. Your time sheet should be produced using computer software.

The stores/warehouse and distribution departments

The stores/warehouse department is a service department which keeps a careful check on the stock levels of all items for which it has overall responsibility and informs the relevant department should stocks begin to approach their minimum stock level.

Staff in this department are as follows.

- The warehouse manager is responsible for the smooth running of the warehousing facilities of the organisation. He or she coordinates all warehouse staff in an effort to ensure that goods both inwards and outwards are dealt with in a quick and efficient manner. The warehouse manager designs the storage facilities in such a way as to enable easy access to the most used items. He or she must also keep a close eye on the stock levels of all stored equipment, products, components and raw materials.
- The warehouse operatives take their instructions from the warehouse manager. They are responsible for reporting any problems to their immediate manager, and for ensuring that they carry out their tasks in a quick and efficient manner. Upon receiving an order via the sales

department, warehouse operatives 'pick' the order and pack it ready for distribution. Others may be concerned with the goods inwards part of the warehouse operation, and check goods received against orders made by the organisation. Should there be any discrepancies, the warehouse manager should be informed and he or she will contact the relevant person. Some warehouse operatives operate machinery such as fork-lift trucks.

Student activity

There are many rules and regulations which control the working conditions of a driver. Research the legislation and restrictions which relate to this occupation. Choose one law in particular and when you have carried out your research, present your findings to the remainder of your group.

The staff of the distribution/transport department are as follows.

- The distribution manager's duty is to design, run and maintain a cost-effective way of ensuring that products reach their correct destination, in a suitable state, at the right time. The distribution manager works in close cooperation with the sales department which informs him or her of orders placed by customers, as well as expected delivery dates. The distribution manager tends to control the operations of the warehouse and all storage facilities. He or she informs the production department when stock levels reach the re-order level. This information is received from the warehouse manager.
- The transport manager's responsibility is to maintain and run the fleet of delivery vehicles which service the distribution requirements of the organisation. He or she liaises closely with the distribution manager, the warehouse manager and the sales department. The transport manager is also responsible for keeping service records and vehicle registrations, as well as any related insurance for the fleet. He or she also negotiates any leasing or purchasing agreements relating to vehicles and directly coordinates the efforts of the drivers, vehicle service engineers and the administration staff within the department.
- The drivers are directly answerable to the transport manager, who issues them with delivery rounds. In certain cases, particularly in larger organisations, there may well be a need to have regional distribution points which will have small warehousing facilities and attached drivers/delivery personnel.

■ Research and development (R & D) and design

By working closely with the marketing department, which keeps a constant check on competitors' products and services, the research and development department (R&D) may be informed of the need for a new product. Equally, R & D staff may be developing new products or ranges in their own right.

The main function of the R & D department is not only to design new products, but to work out the most efficient and logical method of producing them. The R & D staff will, after a number of exhaustive tests, pass on their designs and proposed methods of production to the production department. This department will then be responsible for putting the product into production.

Routinely, the R & D department will test random samples of products being manufactured to ensure that they comply with the quality standards set by the organisation, as well as by government legislation. In some organisations, this function is separated from the R & D department and is supervised by a quality assurance/control department.

The R & D department will also test competitors' products to see how they have been manufactured and whether the organisation's products compare favourably with them. Additionally, it will monitor the technological advances made within their area to see if the design and production processes can be improved.

Key personnel

Key research and development personnel include the following.

Research and development coordination manager

It is the responsibility of this manager to coordinate the development of products and services to prototype level. All products and services must be rigorously tested before they are put into production and offered to the customer. The job holder is likely to be a technical expert within a specific field. He or she will be aware of the technological requirements and any production problems related to these. Normally, this manager will be given clear instructions as to the organisation's requirements for a new product or service, but will have to work very closely with the production manager in order to develop a product which the organisation is capable of producing.

Researcher

Once the departmental manager has been given a brief to develop and test a new product or service, researchers investigate all aspects of this product or service. They refer to any scientific reports which relate to the area of interest, as well as investigating competitors' products. In effect, they produce a report which offers a series of alternatives from which the developers can work. This report is also circulated to any other interested party in the organisation.

Product/service developer

These individuals are specialists in their own field. They will have been chosen for their knowledge and ability to apply their skills. It is their responsibility to work from the information given to them by the researchers and to develop a working version or versions of the product. This product is then subjected to exhaustive testing to ensure that it meets the requirements of the organisation, safety tests and the needs of the customer. At all stages of the development, the production department advises the developers of any production considerations.

Student activity

What kind of R & D would be carried out by a manufacturer of frozen foods? Discuss this as a group.

■ Personnel/Human resources

The key consideration of the personnel department is the management of the human resources of the organisation. In addition, the department is responsible for the well-being of the workforce so that employees can contribute fully to the organisation itself. Specifically, a personnel department will deal with

- hiring and firing of employees
- education and training of employees
- staff welfare
- industrial relations.

In order to carry out these functions, the staff must deal with a range of administration work, which mainly relates to the maintenance of personnel records. The personnel department will maintain records on all members of the workforce, both full and part time. The organisation will require the personnel department to store the following information about each employee.

- Name, address and date of birth.
- Gender, marital status, number of dependents and next of kin.
- Nationality and place of birth.
- National insurance number and tax details.
- Education and qualifications.
- Past and present employment record.
- Present job role(s) and responsibilities.
- Salary details.
- Appraisal interview(s) and outcome(s).
- Disciplinary action taken, if any.
- An assessment of his or her potential.
- Any staff development undertaken or required.

The system by which this information is collected and stored must be flexible enough to be updated regularly. The information on particular employees should be available to relevant members of staff upon request (but only those with the authority to access such records).

Specifically, the human resourcing department or personnel department is responsible for providing the administrative systems which relate to

- statutory and legal requirements
- confidential personnel records
- organisations and provision of support for employee activities and relations.

The information which must be recorded to comply with statutory and legal requirements falls into the following main categories.

- Records of **Statutory Sick Pay** (SSP) which the employer has to pay to any employee who is absent from work through illness for more than four days. These records must be kept for inspection by the Department of Social Security. SSP is payable for up to 28 weeks.
- Records of Statutory Maternity Pay (SMP) which the employer has to pay employees who are absent from work to have a baby. SMP is payable to women who have been working for the organisation for at least 26 weeks.
- Taxation records – the employer is required to deduct income tax on behalf of the Inland Revenue. This system is known as Pay As You Earn **(PAYE)**.

Student activity

What other departments would the human resources or personnel department have regular contact with? Where would the personnel staff obtain information about a particular job vacancy and draw up the necessary job descriptions and devise the advertisement for the post? Discuss your own experiences and thoughts with the rest of the group.

Job roles

The staff of this department include the following.

Personnel manager

The personnel manager is ultimately responsible for the recruitment, retention and welfare of all staff. In this role the personnel manager is involved in the designing of job descriptions and job specifications, the interview process, any training required by employees, staff problems and handling any necessary documentation relating to termination of employment for whatever reason. The personnel manager is also involved in the coordination of staff facilities such as catering, sport, leisure and social activities. He or she monitors and fulfils any staff development requirements. The personnel manager is the first and main point of contact with the management structure in trade union negotiations.

Assistant personnel manager

This individual deputises for the personnel manager in various situations, and has regular duties delegated to him or her. The assistant personnel manager is usually the first point of contact for employee problems and individuals enquiring about possible vacancies within the organisation. The personnel manager and the assistant personnel manager between them offer a confidential counselling service to all employees. The assistant personnel manager is also responsible for the maintenance of comprehensive staff records.

Clerical assistant

Routine personnel duties, such as the maintenance of staff records and work logs are carried out by clerical assistants in the personnel department. Various duties are delegated to them by either the personnel manager or the assistant personnel manager and it is essential that these are carried out with confidentiality always in mind.

Student activity

In the role of personnel manager, draft an advertisement for the following position:

Job title: Administrative assistant
Hours: 18 hours per week
Payment: £9000 pro rata
Previous experience preferred

Once you have decided on the content of your advertisement, produce two copies using computer software.

■ Computer services

The information technology or computer services department's responsibility includes computing (hardware and software), maintenance of databases, telecommunications and other technological office developments. As most organisations are now incorporating computers into almost everything they do, the number of truly separate information technology or computer services departments is diminishing.

The information technology or computer services manager must not only be aware of new developments in technology but also know how to use them. These managers will also supply all support and guidance to help others accomplish this too.

New technologies have made devastating changes to administration systems and their procedures over recent years. These changes are not restricted to the acquisition of computers, but extend also to fax machines, advanced and sophisticated telecommunication systems and robotics for production departments.

Student activity

Using either your college centre or place of work, try to assess the importance of this area of activity to the organisation. Is there a separate computer services department? If this does not exist, what department of the organisation has responsibility for this area of activity? Compare your thoughts and findings with the rest of your group.

Job roles

The staff of the computer services department are as follows (see Figure 5.5).

Departmental manager

It is the responsibility of the departmental manager to provide a round-the-clock and comprehensive service back-up for the organisation's computing and data-processing requirements. Within his or her area of influence, the manager coordinates the design of computer programs to manipulate data for the various departments.

Assistant departmental manager

Under the direction of the departmental manager, the assistant manager is responsible for acquiring and maintaining all computer software and hardware. In order to carry out this task, he or she delegates various aspects to specialist managers. In conjunction with the departmental manager, they ensure that

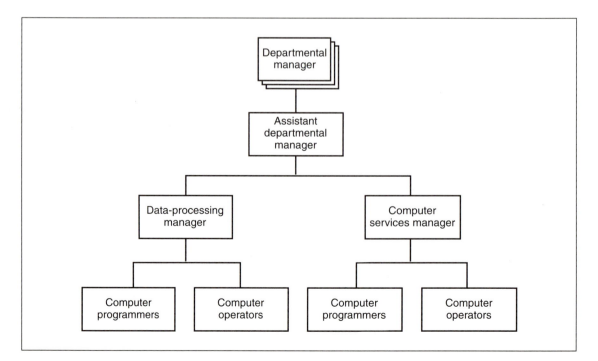

Figure 5.5 Computer services department

sufficient support is given to all computer-based communication systems within the organisation.

Data-processing manager

This individual maintains a detailed record of the organisation's stored information, which is constantly updated and always accessible. The manager also ensures that sensitive information is protected from access by an unauthorised person. The data-processing manager also regularly makes sure that back-up copies of all data stored have been made and are kept in secure and fireproof locations.

Computer services manager

The computer services manager keeps a constant overview of new developments in order to inform the departmental manager of more efficient ways of storing and manipulating data. It is also this individual's responsibility to install and maintain new or updated versions of software as they become available. In addition, his or her team of servicing engineers will regularly check all of the organisation's computer equipment. In some organisations, this service function has been bought-in from computing service specialists.

Computer programmer and operator

Computer programmers create computer software needed by the various departments, so that information may be processed and analysed according to changing needs.

Computer operators are responsible for the inputting of data and the manipulation of existing information at the request of various departments within the organisation. Routinely, they update information from a variety of sources, deleting or modifying as required. Increasingly, organisations have become more reliant on computer-based information and need constant access to reliable and contemporary data.

Student activity

As a group, discuss the following statement: 'Computers have taken the human factor out of too many business decisions.'

■ Administration

The majority of organisations will have a centralised administration service or department. The main function of this department is to ensure that it supports all the other departments within the organisation and generally to control the storage, flow and dissemination of information throughout the organisation.

In some organisations there is no administration department as such since the administration has been devolved to the individual function of the departments which are then responsible for their own administration. You may know the administration department as one of the following: administrative support, office services, secretarial support and administration.

Administrative systems play a vital role. They are the means by which the organisation is able to operate as a whole. Any organisation can have good ideas and well-motivated personnel, but without systems to ensure that functions are carried out, these may be unsuccessful. Organisations need not necessarily rely on their own personnel to provide the design and running of systems. They may employ outside specialists or consultants.

Figure 5.6 explains information handling. As you will see, information received into the organisation has to be processed in some way before it can be either stored (in which case it could later be retrieved) or disseminated around the various departments. Alternatively, the information may need to be sent out from the organisation in a different format.

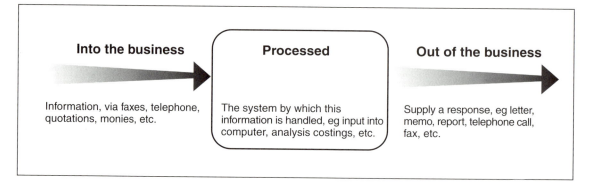

Figure 5.6 Information handling in organisations

In effect, we can split the 'process' part of Figure 5.6 into two parts.

- Storage of information (either manually or by computer).
- Analysis of information.

The running of an organisation requires an organised approach if it is to be efficient and effective. Administrative tasks will be carried out at all levels of the organisation. In a larger organisation, administration will be carried out by the administration department, but in smaller businesses the administration may be carried out by a single individual who will be responsible for all forms of administration. Whoever is responsible for carrying out these administrative tasks, the basic purpose for these procedures remains the same.

- To provide support systems for all resources used by the organisation.
- To keep records relating to the activities of the organisation.
- To monitor the performance of the business's activities.

The activities of an organisation may be classified as routine or non-routine. We need, at this stage, to look at these in a little more detail.

Routine activities mean those carried out regularly. Some individuals will be responsible for administration functions which will not differ regardless of any other activities carried out by the organisation. Examples of such functions may include.

- the processing of invoices
- the filing of business documents and information.

Student activity

Write down another five routine activities which would be carried out regularly by an organisation.

Other individuals will carry out a series of non-routine activities. They will have to be more adaptable as the demands of each day will differ greatly. These individuals will not be able to predict the demands upon them with any great accuracy. On a single day they may have a series of meetings or tasks to perform without prior notice or instruction.

Routine functions of an office can be easily organised through the establishment of systems to handle them. An office organised in this way will base its procedures upon previous experience and will know with considerable accuracy the demands that will be placed upon it. In situations where individuals or departments must carry out a **non-routine function**, they must be able to rely upon a separate series of procedures to support them. It may be the case that a support system has to be created for that specific purpose.

Student activity

In pairs, discuss the amounts of time you think would be spent by the following individuals on routine and non-routine tasks:

a   an accounts clerk
b   a receptionist
c   a shop manager
d   a telesales assistant.

Many organisations have found the need to provide administrative systems or procedures in order to support the resources used by the organisation. These resources can fall into the following three main categories:

- human resources
- financial resources
- physical resources.

In the managing of any of these resources, it is a priority that the organisation establishes a series of systems to assist in the efficient running of the administration function. An administrative system would need to be in place to track the following transactions which relate to the activities of the business:

- purchases made
- sales made
- organisations and individuals with whom transactions have been made
- dates of transactions
- payments received and pending
- personnel records
- stock levels
- staff training and development
- accurate minutes of meetings.

The gathering of information requires certain skills if an individual is to perform efficiently whilst carrying out the duties required of him or her at work. Basically, this means that the person would need to know where to obtain the necessary information. This information could take the form of data from books, periodicals or leaflets. It could also relate to information gathered from other individuals, either from within the organisation itself, or from another organisation.

The storing of information would relate to both documents which may be filed in a manual or paper-based system and to information which is stored using a computer-based system. In other words, the person who is responsible for storing information in whatever form on behalf of the organisation would need to be efficient, well organised and have a good knowledge of the systems in use.

The coordinating of information would usually be the responsibility of one member of staff on a particular project, or alternatively, for one particular aspect of the administrative system. Only one person is normally responsible so that information does not go astray. In addition, for security reasons, an organisation would choose just one person to 'manage' or 'bring together' the information. The person carrying out this task would have to be able to locate easily any information about the specific project or duty. Also, he or she would have a good knowledge of the other individuals working closely beside him or her on the project and would be able to identify immediately who else would be able to assist or provide information.

The word '**retrieval**' means find again or take out of the system. Once the information has been stored, it may be needed again at a later date. The person responsible for retrieving the information may be doing so for different reasons. It could be that the information simply has to be copied or reprinted. On the other hand, the information may have to be amended in some way. Whatever the reason for the need to retrieve the information, the person responsible for this duty would have to be fully aware of the exact location of that information and the quickest and most efficient method of accessing it.

Another word for **dissemination** is 'breaking down' or it could mean distributing information. Part of the information handling system in place within an organisation might mean the distribution of one document (or files) to various different people within the business or that only selected pieces of information have to be distributed. The individuals responsible for this task would need to be aware of the project being documented and be fully aware of the security restrictions on the information they are dealing with.

Administration personnel

The main staff of an administration department are as follows (see Figure 5.7).

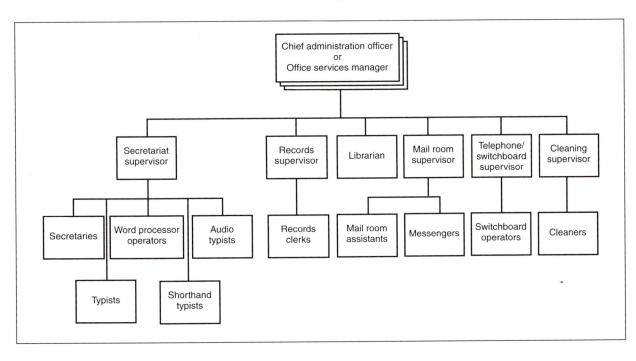

Figure 5.7 The administration department

Chief administration officer or Office services manager

This individual oversees all major functions of the department, allocates work received from other departments (and routine administrative duties) and is responsible for the smooth running of the department.

Secretariat supervisor

The secretariat supervisor allocates and monitors all work carried out by the secretaries, audio typists, shorthand typists, word-processor operators and typists.

Word-processor operator

Under the guidance of the secretariat supervisor, the word-processor operator undertakes work from a variety of different sources and is responsible for the presentation and safe storage (on disk or hard copy) of this work and for ensuring that any deadlines related to the work are met.

Secretary

The secretary usually works directly for one or more managers. It is the secretary's responsibility to ensure that any information in the form of messages, memos, letters, reports, etc., is brought to the attention of the manager. In addition, a secretary is responsible for routine letter and note-taking, on behalf of the manager, as well as keeping track of all his/her diary commitments (sometimes his or her personal diary too). Secretaries may also arrange meetings for which their manager may be responsible. At all times secretaries must ensure that only relevant information and individuals who really need the time of the manager are brought to his or her attention. A secretary's skills may include the ability to work with audio tapes, word processors and to take shorthand.

Audio typist, shorthand typist and typist

The *audio typist* work for several people in the organisation, possibly based in a 'pool'. Duties include typing from audio tapes which have been prepared by various individuals and the audio typist will need to ensure that this work is completed to the given deadline, in a neat and accurate way.

The *shorthand typist* works for several individuals within the organisation. He or she takes dictation from the manager and is responsible for transcribing this and typing up the document in a neat and accurate way. A shorthand typist is usually present to note the decisions taken at any meetings.

The *typist* types routine documents within the organisation. To a great extent this role is gradually being taken over by word processor operators, as organisations are increasingly tending to buy word processors rather than typewriters.

Messenger

The messenger distributes both internal and external documents. The role is particularly useful in organisations which have a number of sites close to one another, or in situations where the organisation's customers are located in the immediate vicinity. Messengers are still used in the City of London. However, many functions traditionally carried out by messengers have been replaced by the use of fax machines, modems and e-mail.

Records supervisor and clerk

The *records supervisor* is responsible for ensuring that all necessary documents are safely, securely and accessibly stored. Despite the fact that technology has substantially reduced the need to store vast amounts of paper documents, there are many reasons why organisations still prefer to have hard copies of documents available for inspection. Upon receiving a request for information, the records supervisor instructs a records clerk to retrieve and deliver the required documentation.

The *records clerk* is responsible for retrieving the required information and ensuring its safe delivery by internal mail, personal delivery or by messenger. The records clerk also takes note of who has requested the information, the date of the request and the date of return. An 'out' card is completed in order to keep track of the documents and ensure their safe return.

Librarian

This individual is responsible for acquiring and maintaining resources relevant to the organisation's activities. These may take the form of books, reports, periodicals and newspaper cuttings. This resource is then available to all members of the organisation who may need to conduct research into a specific area related to their work. It is the librarian's task to ensure that the information is as up to date as possible and that all staff are aware of its availability.

Mail room supervisor and assistant

The *mail room supervisor* is responsible for the handling of all internal and external mail. The office is commonly known as the post room. This location acts as a central collection point of letters, packages and parcels. Some may be bound for literally any part of the world whilst others may be internal mail or bulletins. The various pieces of mail are either collected by a mail room assistant or delivered by various individuals within the organisation. It is the mail room supervisor's responsibility to make sure that all outgoing mail is weighed, franked and made ready for collection by the Post Office. The mail room supervisor also notes (for internal cost allocation) the postage totals for each department within the organisation.

Working under the direction and instruction of the mail room supervisor, the *mail room assistant* may carry out a variety of different tasks, including

- collecting mail from the various departments
- delivering mail received each morning to the relevant person(s). Before this can be done, the mail needs to be sorted and perhaps re-routed to another site
- weighing, franking and putting outgoing mail into the correct Post Office bag ready for collection or delivery to the Post Office
- noting postage costs of each department and ensuring that the mail room supervisor has up-to-date figures for these
- ensuring that the Post Office leaflets kept in the mail room are current.

Telephonist/switchboard supervisor and operator

Since many organisations rely heavily on the internal and external telephone system, the *switchboard supervisor* is vital to the smooth running of most operations. This individual ensures that all telecommunication needs are met and that the switchboard system is capable of fulfilling the demands of the organisation. In addition, the supervisor makes sure that the switchboard is constantly staffed and that, at times when the organisation is closed for business, an answerphone can record incoming calls, or can give useful information to callers.

In many cases, a customer's first contact with an organisation is via the telephone. It is therefore most important that the *switchboard operator* answers the calls swiftly and is helpful and responsive to the caller. A good switchboard operator knows exactly who the caller needs to speak to about a particular matter (despite the fact that the caller may not ask for a named individual) and knows from memory the extension number of most members of staff.

Cleaning supervisor and cleaner

All organisations, whether or not they have a constant flow of visitors, need to ensure that the premises are kept as clean and tidy as possible. Organisations which have sensitive technological equipment may even need to ensure that the work areas are as dust-free as possible. The *cleaning supervisor* allocates his or her cleaning staff according to the demands of each particular work area. Periodically, floors and windows may need to be given special attention and may require specialist equipment/subcontractors to carry out the necessary work.

Each *cleaner* is usually given a particular area of the premises for which he or she is responsible. The main cleaning duties include emptying of bins, clearing away of empty boxes and packing materials, hoovering and dusting and routine general cleaning duties. Specialist cleaners may be employed to sanitise telephones, clean word processors with anti-static sprays and clean carpets or polish floors.

■ The interaction of functional activities

Although it is helpful to an organisation to sub-divide or departmentalise their various operations, it is essential that the senior management ensures that adequate communication and cooperation is maintained between the different departments. It is obvious that the creation of departments allows individuals to specialise in particular areas and develop their expertise without having to concern themselves with activities that could be adequately dealt with by others. The larger the organisation, the more difficult the coordination of the different departments becomes. As an organisation grows there is always the tendency to divide the new activities and the existing ones into more clearly definable and manageable sections.

The following problems can be associated with creating separate departments.

- Even when a department is created, there may still be too many individuals in that department to ensure effective communication and coordination.
- Creating departments or divisions is inevitable if the organisation is operating on several different sites. There needs to be an effective way of ensuring that all of the different departments in these dispersed locations actually talk to one another and coordinate activities.
- Individuals who are deeply involved with a specific function of the organisation may find themselves unable to understand or relate to the needs of others in different departments. As a result of this mistakes can occur simply because one department does not understand what another needs.
- In setting up departments the organisation needs to be aware of the fact that rivalry may develop between the different departments, particularly if one

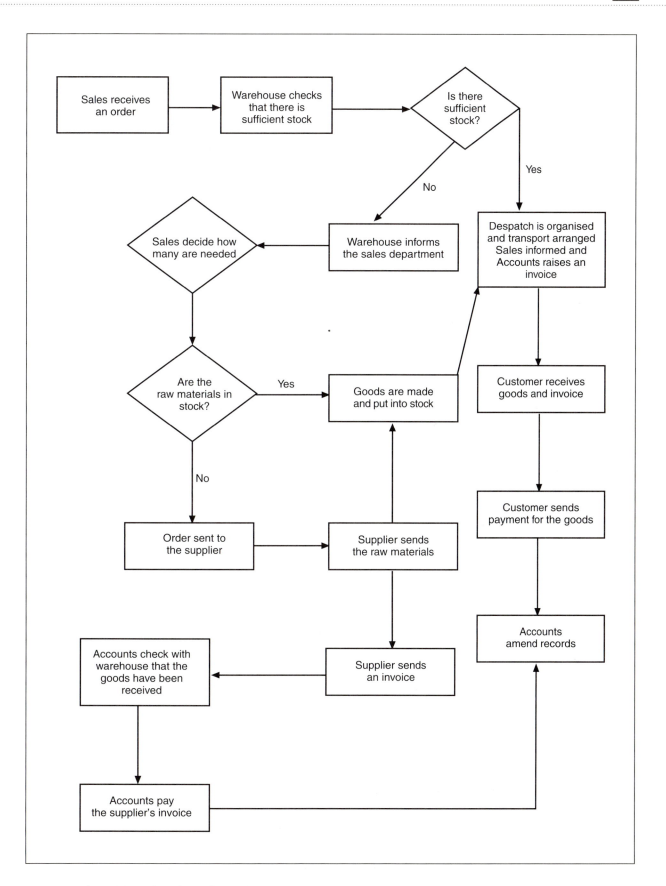

Figure 5.8 Flow chart of an order

department is seen to be favoured by the management, or is seen to be performing extremely well against targets or objectives. If the rivalry is allowed to develop, this could undermine the whole of the organisation's objectives and efficiency.

■ Although specialisation is a good idea in certain cases. It does tend to make the individuals involved rather short-sighted and unable to see how their actions may affect the whole of the organisation. They will be simply interested in meeting their own targets and objectives, possible at the expense of other parts of the organisation.

■ In creating a series of departments the organisation is creating a new set of smaller, pyramid structures within itself. Each of these small pyramids is, in fact, a hierarchy, with senior managers, middle managers and supervisors. All this will add to the problems of communication and coordination.

Organisations need to ensure that their departments cooperate as closely as possible in order to be both efficient and effective. A typical **chain of integration** will incorporate the following.

1 Research and development carry out market research and test new products. The successful ones go into production.
2 Production manufactures the products developed by R & D and ensures that quality is maintained and deadlines are met.
3 Production is dependent upon individuals involved in purchasing to buy cost-effective materials and components to aid their production role.
4 Accounts will record all of the financial transactions carried out throughout the whole of the process.
5 Administration will ensure that all of the departments involved are kept supplied with office equipment and consumable materials, as well as handling legal considerations.
6 Personnel, meanwhile, will be ensuring that all of the departments are adequately staffed with well-trained individuals and will also take care of pay and matters relating to working conditions.
7 At the earliest possible point the marketing department will be informed that the new product or service is being developed and will get busy, creating various marketing communications aimed at the target customers.
8 The sales department, working closely with all of the other departments, will be involved in actually selling the products and services to the customers or distributors. This will generate the necessary income to pay for all of the other departments' activities.

Keywords

The keywords you should know for this chapter are listed below. Check to make sure you understand the meaning of each word. Discuss those you are unsure of with your tutor.

chain of integration	non-routine functions
corporate image	PAYE
credit check	profit margins
devolved budgets	repeat business
dissemination	retrieval
functional area	statutory sick pay
marketing mix	wastage

Examination practice

Short-answer questions

1 State three main functions of an accounts department.

2 State four services which would be provided to other departments by the administration department.

3 Why is it unlikely that the majority of organisations have separate computer services departments?

4 What is the role of the research and development department?

5 Outline one specific administration role that could be found in the following departments: human resources, sales and marketing, accounts.

6 Sketch out a typical organisation chart for the administration department.

7 What is the role of the personnel department?

8 Briefly list one example of a typical purchase that would have to be made by the purchasing department for any four other departments of your choice.

9 Explain why the role of customer service is important to most organisations.

10 Considering the sales and marketing department, list four specific sales-related roles and four specific marketing-related roles.

Essay questions

Your role in the personnel department of a small manufacturing organisation had been fairly simple until now. With only 40 employees, the personnel department really needed only two people. Your boss, Richard Penhaligon, had warned you that things were about to change and that you should make the most of the calm before the storm. No sooner had the organisation signed a manufacturing deal with a Japanese car producer, than the whole organisation had to be radically restructured. Not only was the organisation due to treble in size within the year, but also many of the existing employees would be carrying out radically different jobs. There was also a change of premises on the cards. Although Richard had been promised extra help in the personnel department, you realise that this is your opportunity to make a name for yourself.

1 Richard has asked you to clearly identify the separate functions of each of the typical departments. He needs the following information:

   a what are the most common types of department?

   b what is their role?

   c how would they inter-relate with one another?

2 Richard wants you to begin by defining the functions and roles within production and purchasing, since these will be the areas that are most concerned with the new contract. You will need to cover the following:

   a assuming that you do not have to state exactly how many individuals will be in each department, draw up a proposed organisation chart for each section.

   b having created the organisation charts, you must now briefly outline the roles of the key individuals within each of these proposed departments.

3 The next area that Richard wants you to consider is the accounts and administration functions. Although he is fairly clear about how these two departments would look, he is unsure about what areas of responsibility each should have. Therefore, he needs you to:

   a clearly state the main differences between these two departments.

   b outline how these two departments would cooperate with one another.

   c explain how these two departments would support the activities of the rest of the organisation.

4 Richard feels that there will be no need to have a separate research and development department or a computer services department, although he does realise that he needs to integrate the activities of the currently separate sales and marketing departments. To this end, he wants you to:

a draw up a proposed organisation chart which incorporates both of these departments, bearing in mind that there needs to be an active sales force in all areas of the country.

b briefly outline the key roles in at least the top two levels of management which you have identified in your organisation chart.

6 Employer and employee rights and responsibilities

■ Introduction

The relationship between the employer and the employee is a formal one. As we will see, the vast majority of relationships are governed and set down within the contract of employment. These specifically state the terms and conditions under which the employee will operate on behalf of the employer, as well as a series of undertakings to be made by the employer.

The vast majority of conditions which determine the nature of the contract of employment and the future relationship between the employer and the employee are governed by law. Throughout this century a series of pieces of legislation have come into force in order to protect the rights of employees and employers. For example, some legislation specifically relates to individuals who had been discriminated against for various reasons by employers. These seek to equalise the treatment of all employees, regardless of their age, gender or cultural background.

We also need to consider the fact that an employee who is given the opportunity to develop by being given gradually more complex job roles, as well as training, will serve only to improve the overall prospects of the employer. With considerations such as quality assurance uppermost in employers' minds, the need to ensure that they have a motivated and effectively trained workforce is extremely important.

■ Identification and communication of business objectives to employees

Obviously, it is in everyone's interests to identify the exact business objectives as laid down in either the **mission statement** or other company documentation. The specific business objectives can be wide and somewhat imprecise. In addition, business objectives may differ from time to time. Objectives are the medium- to long-term targets which help the business to achieve its mission statement. The strategies and tactics involved in achieving the objectives are usually those which will have a direct impact upon employees.

There are numerous methods of ensuring that employees understand current business objectives, rather than employers relying on rumour and misinformation (which is usually rife in many organisations). These include

- staff meetings
- newsletters
- company newspapers
- bulletin boards
- noticeboards
- e-mail
- press statements

- corporate videos
- letters sent direct to all employees.

An organisation which fails to ensure that its employees are informed of any key changes in company policy or objectives may find itself working 'against' the employees. Suddenly to impose radically different working practices or procedures without consultation can lead to unrest and a loss of motivation among employees.

It is also advisable to clarify the business objectives in order to prepare employees for possible training and development. An organisation which is able to look ahead and, to some extent, predict its business objectives, is an organisation which will find that employees not only understand, but are also in step with, the new business objectives.

■ Contracts of employment

The employer has a number of duties towards the employee. This can be seen very clearly in a **contract of employment**. This document really formalises the relationship and is seen as legally binding on both the employer and employee. A contract of employment should lay down

- job description, ie the precise nature of the job
- job title
- pay details, ie how it is paid, frequency of payment
- additional payment details, such as which salary/wage scale the individual will be placed on
- when overtime can be undertaken
- how bonuses can be earned
- how commission can be earned
- start times and finishing times of work
- total number of hours to be worked per week
- number of paid days off for holidays, etc. (and any restrictions)
- sick leave details, duration and entitlement
- maternity leave details, duration and entitlement
- pension schemes, including contributions made by employer and employee
- grievance procedure details
- period of notice to be worked or given
- resignation or termination details.

The employer may also wish to inform the employee of

- company rules and regulations
- codes of behaviour (including dress code, etc.)
- availability of social activities.

Just as the employer will be expected to fulfil his or her obligations as set out in the contract of employment, so too will the employee. The employee will be expected to comply with all aspects of the contract of employment, and furthermore, will be required to accept responsibility for his or her actions at work. Confidentiality is important; the employee should also take care not to release any information of a sensitive or secret nature to the media or competitors.

Student activity

You may be working either full time or part time and possibly will have seen a contract of employment. Compare your contracts with those of other members of the group. Can you identify any common parts of the contracts? Are there any significant differences?

The employer must take care when advertising a job, as the advertisement is considered to be the beginning of the formation of the contract of employment. Once a candidate for a particular job accepts employment on the basis of the advertisement details, then, to some extent, much of the contract of employment has already been decided. Before an employer finally accepts a candidate as an employee, he or she will usually take up references. If a prospective employer receives unfavourable references about the candidate, then he or she is quite within his or her rights to withdraw the job offer.

A contract of employment is like any other contract. It gives both parties rights as well as obligations. The contract identifies formally what was agreed during the interview or selection process. Normally, a contract of employment will contain the following commitments.

- The employer will pay wages/salaries.
- The employer will provide work.
- The employer will pay any reasonable losses or expenses incurred by the employee in the course of his or her work.
- The employer will provide a reference if required by the employee.
- The employer will provide safe working conditions and practices.
- The employer will not act in such a way as to breach the trust and confidence given by the employee.
- The employer will provide necessary information relating to the employee's work, pay, conditions and opportunities.
- The employer will always act in good faith towards the employee.

Employees have a responsibility to the employer to work in a loyal, conscientious and honest manner. They are also expected to accept any reasonable and legal directions from their superiors. In essence, this means adhering to the terms of the contract of employment. As you have seen, the contract of employment can be a very detailed document and is considered to be legally binding once both parties have signed. By law, all employees must have received a contract of employment within 13 weeks of commencing employment.

■ Recruitment and selection

The recruitment and selection process can be complex and time consuming. The purpose of recruitment is to attract a sufficient number of well-qualified or appropriate candidates to fill the requirements of a job. The purpose of selection is firstly to define exactly what the requirements are and then adopt an effective 'filtering system' to ensure that the candidates fit those job requirements. Organisations may have radically different approaches to the way in which they recruit or select individuals. Clearly, depending upon a number of criteria, the organisation will choose to recruit employees by one of the following methods.

- **Casual recruitment and selection** – where an individual is usually recommended by a current employee, or an individual has been working on a part-time basis for the organisation and is well known to them. In this instance, the individual may not necessarily go through the standard recruitment and selection process, but may simply be appointed to the job.
- **Formal (objective and scientific)** – where the organisation has developed complex recruitment and selection procedures. It may use expensive selection techniques, such as handwriting analysis or assessment centres. This formal process is usually found in larger organisations, or when unemployment is high and it is relatively easy to attract a large number of potentially appropriate candidates.

Whichever recruitment and selection process is employed, organisations frequently find themselves in the position of failing to select the correct candidate. The main reasons behind this include

- the organisation's inability to have clearly defined the exact nature of the job
- the organisation's inability to brief interviewers correctly – to ensure they are all looking for the same thing
- a failure to realise what the selection process has been designed to achieve
- a failure to use the correct selection procedures relating to the job itself.

There are many reasons why an organisation may find itself in a position to have to recruit or select new employees. Expansion or diversification may involve the employment of new members of staff. Equally, changes in technology or working practices may involve the gradual replacement of employees. If an organisation has a disproportionate number of employees in the older age bracket, it may find itself with a constant need to replace retiring members of staff. Termination or resignation of employment, as a result of an employee's decision, may make recruitment and selection an immediate priority. This is particularly true if the employee leaving the organisation held a key post at a particularly crucial time in the development of the organisation. This form of termination of employment cannot be predicted easily by the organisation, but the organisation should be prepared (at fairly short notice) to advertise, recruit and select a replacement.

In all cases, the organisation is faced with a potentially expensive and time-consuming activity which does not stop when the individual signs his or her contract of employment. The gradual integration or induction of the new employee may not happen over a period of days. It may take the new employee a matter of weeks or months to be a fully functioning and effective member of staff. The organisation needs to take all possible steps to ensure that particularly key members of staff are retained and highly motivated.

The main purpose of offering a new post to prospective candidates is to meet an identified organisational need. As we have mentioned, it will involve the definition of

- a job description
- a job specification
- a person specification.

Internal recruitment

It is often possible for an employee currently working for the organisation to fill a job vacancy. There are advantages and disadvantages for both the individual and the organisation in considering internal recruitment.

Advantages
- The individual knows a great deal about the organisation.
- The organisation can save considerable sums of money on recruitment costs.
- The organisation can save considerable sums of money on induction costs.
- Promotion within the organisation is seen as an incentive to other employees.

Disadvantages
- Since the individual already knows the policies and procedures of the organisation, it may be that he or she can offer no new ideas or innovations.
- An external candidate usually works very hard in the initial period of employment.
- The individual who has filled the vacant job position will have to be replaced.
- By choosing one individual the organisation has had to ignore or overlook other individuals within the organisation.

Student activity

As an applicant for a job within the organisation in which you are presently working or studying, what real advantages do you think you would have in succeeding in your bid to gain a new post? Discuss this in a group.

⬥JOB VACANCIES⬥

Office staff

Able, qualified PA or secretary urgently needed for part time assignment. Work from home when it suits. Must be able to deal with people at a variety of different levels by telephone. Generous £ package for the right person. Call me now if this is for you. Call 233647

Able to temp? We could be the answer to your long- or short-term unemployment problems. Have you office skills, especially secretarial, word processing, VDU, reception or accounts, etc.? If so, call us now at Find-A-Job Recruitment. 258277

Bright, enthusiastic person required for an administration position, office environment, knowledge of estate agency work an advantage. Salary of £10,000 plus. Call 246122 now.

Capable versatile and experienced secretary required for busy Surveyors office. Please ring Richard Stevenson on 895422.

Enthusiastic and qualified administration person required for a lively office. Experienced computer use and ability to type essential. Management of people and a sense of humour a bonus! Able to work under pressure 8 a.m. – 5 p.m. Mon – Fri. Hours/ wages neg. to suitable applicant. Ring 644780. No time wasters please.

PA with good audio and copy typing skills, knowledge of EXCEL an advantage required for a local company. Friendly personality and a sense of humour are essential. Salary c.9,500. Call 388388.

Part-time PA or secretary with excellent typing skills and WP skills. To cover for maternity leave, possibility of full-time permanent post maternity post. Free parking. Salary around £4,000. Ring 453432.

Receptionist/Secretary needed. Are you between 18 and 35 years of age and would you like to become part of a team working in a busy office? If yes, contact Julie Crisp at Ambrose Went Curtiss on 676767.

Return to work courses starting now. Update your skills, brush up your speed, effective CV and letter writing. Future training 323663.

Start right now! Secretarial Courses for all levels. Ring 323663.

Start right now, courses in MS Office, Word For Windows, Power Point, EXCEL, Access, Teeline, Shorthand. Gregsons Training 556556.

Starting soon, courses for all interests and levels. Learn valuable career skills at times which suit your lifestyle. Word processing, spreadsheets, databases, desktop publishing, typing, shorthand and book keeping. For more details and expert advice call 217080.

Secretary/PA
c£10,000

Working with a friendly team, you will provide a full secretarial service including drafting letters and reports, maintaining the appointments diary, taking minutes at meetings and handling special projects.

To be successful, you will need to have RSA II in Word Processing. You should also be a good communicator and a professional with an outgoing personality. Shorthand would be an advantage.
If you are interested, please ring Marion Hobbs at Bookham Technologies on 896410

Admin Officer
c£9,000

Varied work, applicants should be flexible.

Call Brian on 776689

Fleet Service Administrator part-time post

A motivated person with the ability to meet deadlines is needed for an immediate start. The applicant should have very good keyboarding skills. RSA Stage II. Word 6.0. Some service administration experience an asset but not essential as training will be offered.
Please apply in writing with CV, to Andi Brough, at City Tec 124 High Street

---

Figure 6.1 Advertising administrative vacancies

External recruitment

Advertising the vacancy

In order to seek external candidates, the organisation must begin its recruitment campaign by advertising the vacant post. An advertisement should include

- the job title
- a brief job description
- the nature of the organisation's business
- the market sector in which the business is active
- the geographical location of the vacancy
- the salary range
- the organisation's address
- a specific person to whom all applications must be made
- a telephone number for candidates to contact
- qualifications required
- experience required
- any limitations the organisation may wish to place upon the post (age or additional skills required).

Another method is to use a commercial employment agency which will attempt to recruit on the organisation's behalf for a commission or a fee.

Government-run employment agencies fulfil a very similar role to that of a commercial employment agency. The major difference is that such agencies do not, at present, require commission or a fee to fill a post. Local job centres, career services or employment services are the main agencies involved.

Student activity

What facilities and services do government-run agencies offer? Investigate your local office in the course of your research.

Present your findings to the remainder of the group.

Exactly where the employer chooses to place the advertisement, if this is the route preferred, will very much depend on the job itself. There are countless magazines and newspapers that offer the chance of finding the right person for the job. A useful start is a regularly updated guide called *British Rate and Data*. This lists most of the magazines and newspapers published in the UK. It includes the cost of advertising, the circulations and a brief profile of the type of readership. It is also wise to contact the advertising manager for additional information and a 'rate card', which details all of the available discounts, introductory offers and special issues. This may be of enormous help in deciding where to place the advertisement.

Generally speaking, the higher the circulation, the higher the cost of advertising. The employer will have to balance the cost of the advertisement against the level of response likely from a larger-circulation publication.

Recruitment agencies and consultants will take on the task of actually sifting through the candidates and fielding the enquiries from applicants, but the employer still needs to do the basic work in drawing up the job description, job specification and details relating to job title and pay and conditions.

The private recruitment agency will place the advertisement in relevant magazines, newspapers and journals for the employer. They will also have a database of potential employees who have already registered with them. In return for their assistance in obtaining the right person for the job, they may charge the employer anything from 6 per cent to 20 per cent of the employee's first year's earnings.

Depending on the type of job vacancy, employers usually advertise to find recruits for particular jobs through a variety of sources. Job centres, colleges/schools, local advertisements and letters of enquiry may be the usual source of recruitment chosen to advertise for a trainee.

National and professional magazines and journals, recruitment consultants/agencies, letters of enquiry from potential candidates may be the chosen advertising route to recruit for a senior management role. Employment agencies, local advertisements (press) and specialist magazines (such as free papers/journals, etc.) may be the best advertising medium to recruit secretaries.

Student activity

Discuss in pairs the media you would use for the following occupations

a   a personal assistant to a managing director
b   an accounts clerk
c   a credit controller
d   a customer service manager.

Short-listing the candidates

Employers devote considerable amounts of time to recruiting employees. It is perhaps at the **short-listing** stage of the recruitment process that many mistakes may be made. An employer might do one or more of the following:

- be over-critical – when the employer fails to recognise a good potential applicant by too rigidly adhering to preconceived ideas about what he or she is looking for
- be under-critical – when the employer finds it hard to sift out the good candidates from the less relevant and useful ones and may end up needing to interview all of the applicants
- fail to set criteria – when the employer has all of the applications and finds it difficult, due to lack of preparation, to sift through the applicants and make any form of decision about them
- make snap decisions – when the employer looks at the applications and decides that one of the candidates is ideal, and having formed this

impression, he or she cannot really make an objective judgement about the other applicants

- take too much time – when the employer either finds it difficult to make the sifting process work, or is unable to devote enough time to the task.

Once the candidates have been ranked, these are the ones to call for interview. If, and sometimes this is the case, even the short-listed candidates do not 'fit in' after the employer has seen them, then the whole process may have to be repeated. It is for this case, in the main, that the short-list process is so important.

Taking up references

Taking up references should, in most cases, merely confirm the employer's impression of the candidate. The references should also confirm that the candidate has had particular work experience and has achieved certain qualifications.

When taking up references, it is advisable to provide a straightforward form for the **referee** to fill in. It is also a matter of courtesy for the employer requesting the reference to provide a self-addressed, stamped envelope. In most cases, the employer should also include a brief description of the job involved. At this stage it may be a good idea to confirm whether the potential employee has to work a particular length of notice or has to complete studies until a specified date.

Some employers include on their application forms a box to tick concerning the taking up of references. Usually, this refers to the timing. In some cases, employees would prefer that their current employer does not know about their applications until the last possible time. The employer should note this; it is not a question of secrecy but more to comply with the candidate's wishes. In most cases, references will not be taken up until the candidate is short-listed with the probability of being asked for interview. It is perfectly acceptable for both the employee to make this request and for the employer to respect it.

When writing references, particularly in cases when the requesting potential employer does not give guidelines, the following are normally covered:

- duties/responsibilities
- current salary (including bonuses, etc.)
- job role and title
- service record
- absences (sickness, etc.)
- honesty and integrity, etc.

Student activity

In pairs, compose a reference for your partner. He or she has applied for a position as a clerical assistant in a large engineering organisation. Word-process your reference and compile a covering letter to accompany it.

Assessing candidates – the selection interview

If a candidate has reached this stage, then the employer needs to be absolutely certain that the individual on paper (the details on the application form) matches the individual who is attending the interview. This might sound rather strange and it is not meant that the interviewee may be an impostor! In many cases, a good candidate 'on paper' is a poor one in the flesh. The employer's expectations may not be satisfied by the individual when they meet.

There are some key points that will help the employer in his or her assessment of the candidates.

- Try to observe the candidate at all times. How does he or she react to situations and different circumstances?
- Make sure that any checks that need to be made have been made (such as references and certificates, etc.)
- If applicable, test the candidate. There are various ways of doing this, such as multiple-choice tests, aptitude tests, scenarios and role plays, etc.
- If there is a query or question about the background, experience or qualifications of the candidate, make sure that these are addressed.

The selection interview is a notoriously unreliable method of choosing a potential employee, but a good interviewer will be able to 'pick up on' many unspoken and unguarded features about the candidate. A good interviewer should

- ask probing questions
- always be polite
- listen well
- observe the candidate's behaviour
- check that the candidate is attentive at all times.

Notifying the successful candidate

The successful candidate should be notified at the earliest opportunity. It is also wise not to contact the unsuccessful candidates until the successful one has confirmed that he or she will be taking up the post. In some cases, the successful candidate may have changed his or her mind about accepting the position and an employer who has already told the unsuccessful candidates about the outcome of the recruitment procedure will have 'burned all his or her bridges'. The only course open then is to re-advertise and incur the expenses and the commitment once again. In some cases, it has been known for successful candidates to have accepted the offer, then after a few days (and after the employer has rejected all of the other candidates) contact the employer and say that he or she has changed his or her mind. This may be a genuine change of mind, but in some instances the existing employer (remember that the employee is probably still working out his or her notice) has offered the employee a better deal so as not to lose the individual's experience or skills.

The employer should always be aware that an individual who does not match the requirements of the job may, in the future, mean problems with that employee. It is far better not to appoint and re-advertise than to take the risk of employing someone who is merely the best of a relatively poor group of candidates.

Student activity

Following on from the previous activity and assuming that your partner has been successful in his or her application for the job, word-process an acceptance letter which confirms the appointment.

Informing the unsuccessful candidates

Everyone, at one stage or another, may receive a photocopied rejection letter following an interview. Others will simply receive a rather terse and brief phone call telling them that they have been unsuccessful. In some cases, you may not hear anything at all. Good practice in dealing with unsuccessful candidates is as important as dealing with those who have been chosen for employment.

Employers may promise to keep the details of the unsuccessful candidate on file. They may also promise to let the unsuccessful candidate know if a position arises in the future, but it is always a good idea not to make promises that the employer is unable to deliver. It is important to remember that an unsuccessful candidate may be a customer too. In this respect, careful treatment of unsuccessful candidates is as important as any other marketing technique.

Some employers are willing to give unsuccessful candidates some feedback on how they performed at the interview stage of the selection process.

In all cases, letters, telephone calls and other communication with the unsuccessful candidates should be made promptly and be courteous. The candidate invested time and effort in the application and recruitment process and should be given the respect that this deserves. Equally, if the employer promised to pay expenses for travel/subsistence, etc., to all candidates, this should be done promptly upon receipt of expenses claims forms.

Student activity

Still imagining the same situation, word-process a letter to your partner informing him or her that he or she has been unsuccessful on this occasion with your organisation.

■ Induction and training

Induction programmes

Any new employee, regardless of rank or job title, will (hopefully) feel very positive when beginning the job. This is particularly true if the organisation has planned a comprehensive induction or training programme. The employer is well advised to have organised this in advance and not simply to offer **induction** or training on an ad hoc basis.

The main aims of the induction process are

- to ensure that the new employee attains effectiveness and efficiency at the earliest opportunity
- to ensure that the new employee gains commitment to the organisation as soon as possible
- to ensure that the new employee is familiarised with the organisation, job role and procedures
- to ensure that the new employee adopts the organisation's attitudes and philosophy as quickly as possible.

Ideally, the induction package should include

- a brief description of the organisation
- number of employees
- location(s) of the organisation
- products or services offered by the organisation
- pay scales
- holiday entitlements
- pension arrangements
- hours of work
- other conditions of work
- sickness arrangements
- disciplinary and grievance procedures
- trade union membership
- staff perks (including subsidised facilities)
- travel and subsistence rules and arrangements
- medical facilities
- welfare facilities
- canteen facilities
- health and safety regulations and procedures
- education and training programmes available.

Normally, these should all be covered in a **staff handbook**. The handbook should be clear and concise and be a ready-reference volume for daily use.

Organisations have recognised that the majority of individuals who leave in, say, the first six months leave as a result of poor induction programmes. In such cases, no such induction takes place. Employers then run the risk of having individuals working for them with no real idea of the organisational structure, roles or philosophy. From the first day, they feel left out and isolated. It is no wonder that employees in such a position choose to 'vote with their feet' and seek alternative employment.

It is worth remembering that a good employer will invest as much time, money and effort on its employees as it does on its machinery.

Training and professional development

Training basically falls into four separate categories.

- **On-the-job training** is training carried out whilst at work. It may be delivered by in-house training personnel, or by 'bought in' specialists.
- **Off-the-job training** is training carried out at a location other than the workplace. It may require access to specialists or specialist equipment, not necessarily currently available in the work place.
- **Part-time training** refers to the 'mode' of training itself. This category includes day-release, evening classes and short courses. This type of training is usually paid for, at least in part, by the employer and relates directly to required job skills.
- **Full-time training** involves short- or even long-term training courses which take the employee out of the work situation for an extended period. Such training may be necessary because the employee needs to be trained in a complex area which could not be taught on a part-time basis.

Most organisations run special courses, either at the workplace or in an alternative location. The nature of the training may involve specialist management skills, health and safety or supervisory skills. It is usually key personnel who are chosen to attend these courses and they are then expected to pass on the knowledge they have acquired to the rest of the members of their work teams (this is known as **cascading**).

Personal skills development

The types of skill required for a business can range from knowledge of new software packages to more general managerial skills. The area of work which the individual is involved with will dictate the type of training he or she needs. Personal skills development has become a very popular area of training in recent years and offers guidance in areas such as time management, stress management, supervisory skills, leadership skills, management skills, communication skills, counselling skills, negotiation skills, assertiveness skills and coping with meetings.

Qualifications

Most people will start their careers with few or no qualifications. Most individuals will have at least some basic understanding of English, or mathematics, but it is only when they begin to consider what their career goal may be, that they should start to gain qualifications which will help them achieve their goal. Depending on the time and effort put in, individuals can slowly progress in their collection of qualifications. At the same time, particularly if the individual is in work, he or she will be gaining additional responsibilities as a result of the qualifications he or she has achieved.

Vocational and non-vocational training

Vocational training or qualifications are those which relate directly to the job or job area. It does not necessarily matter whether the individual is in work or not, since the programme should be designed to offer the learner the opportunity to practise the type of skills required for a particular job. This has become a very popular area, much supported by employers, who see this as the only useful and relevant way of preparing individuals for work within industry, commercial services or technology.

In some respects, you would think that the non-vocational course is the complete opposite to a vocational course. This may not necessarily be the case. Typically, a course which falls into this category will not have a direct relevance to a particular job and may be more general in nature. Alternatively, non-vocational courses may be academic and provide a wide range of knowledge which is not necessarily applied. Individuals who have followed such courses will need to undertake further training to learn how to put into practice the extensive knowledge they have gained on their academic course.

Customer needs and product training

In order to help employees understand customer needs, the organisation needs to inform employees about the following.

- Why will the customer buy?
- What does the customer want?
- What are the benefits and features of the organisation's service?

The employee must know the following about the product.

- Its appearance.
- What is it made of?
- What colours are available?
- How is it packaged?
- What is the speed and reliability of delivery?
- How does the organisation deal with faults?
- How frequent are maintenance visits (if applicable)?
- What quality levels are desired?
- How does the price compare to that of competitors?

The last consideration is how much will the customers buy? Not only is this information useful in ensuring that employees are sufficiently briefed on the customer, but it is also useful for sales and cash forecasts.

Regular training and staff development are obviously required in order to ensure that the organisation's employees are not only up to date with product availability, but intimately know the characteristics of products currently available.

■ Quality assurance

Quality assurance (QA) is an attempt to ensure that the organisation adopts a set of quality standards that have been agreed as part of a system to achieve customer satisfaction. In essence, QA tries to address the following concerns.

- The time and effort put into product design.

- The technology used in product design.
- The quality of components, materials and parts used.
- The commitment and efforts of the employees.
- The setting up of a system that monitors and records the quality issues associated with product design and production.
- The assurance that the organisation can, and will, deliver on time with the correct orders of a suitably high level of quality.
- The availability of good advice from the organisation before, during and after the sale has been made.

Quality can be rather subjective. It is only in cases where you can exactly measure the quality of the product (such as an item of clothing, for example) that any form of objective assessment can be made. One way around this is gradually to build up the image or reputation of the product to suggest quality.

Quality is dependent upon

- the appearance of the product
- the packaging
- the reliability
- the performance
- the service offered (before, during and after the sale has been made).

Many organisations institute quality audits or other mechanisms aimed at maintaining high quality standards. Obviously, the nature of this monitoring process is largely dependent upon the type of business involved. Organisations which do not necessarily produce products as such may find it difficult to make any objective quality assessment. Some ways of doing this are

- to measure the speed and reliability of response to customers' enquiries
- to maintain a strict rule on the number of 'rings' before the telephone is answered
- to ensure that administrative procedures are in place to record any customer complaints and to monitor these regularly.

■ Trade unions and staff associations

Recognition of trade unions by employers

Employers do not have to recognise a **trade union** unless they feel that it would be beneficial to the organisation. Therefore, organisations may adopt any of the following policies in relation to the recognition of unions.

- Full recognition of a variety of different unions representing different sections of the workforce within the organisation.
- Full recognition of a single union representing all or the majority of the workforce.
- Refusal to recognise any trade union.
- The establishment of a staff association as an alternative to trade unions.

As you will see, trade unions are fairly widely recognised across the country as the primary route for negotiations. In cases where there are a variety of different trade unions operating in a single organisation, there will be a joint union committee to undertake the negotiation process.

Although legislation has been passed restricting the activities of trade unions, the primary need for their existence still remains.

Functions of unions

A union exists to protect and promote the interests of its members. It acts as

- a pressure group which promotes the interest of its members
- a pressure group which protects the position of its members
- the main instrument of bargaining with the employer
- the main instrument of bargaining with the government.

All unions are formed and financed by their members. They are run by full-time officials, who are either voted or appointed by the members. Unions are independent of employers; they do not rely on them for funding. The union must also organise its own facilities and not necessarily rely on the employer to offer space within the organisation's own premises.

Trade unions carry out a range of different tasks in order to looking after their members' interests. Here are some of their major functions.

- To protect the wages of the members, particularly in times of recession.
- To negotiate the working hours required by the employer.
- To negotiate the working conditions.
- To monitor health and safety.
- To provide a range of benefits including pensions, sick pay, unemployment pay, injury benefits and strike pay.
- To represent the interests of the members in times of dispute with the employer.

In addition to these tasks, unions undertake a number of political duties relating to employment. They will actively negotiate with the government and opposition parties to further the cause of their members. With a few notable exceptions, all employees are entitled to join a trade union and take advantage of the benefits offered, both protection and facilities.

Features of staff associations

Staff associations have in many organisations either replaced trade unions or have been the only option as far as employees are concerned. Staff associations in the majority of cases tend to have the following features.

- They have been designed by the employer.
- They are run by the employer on behalf of the employees.
- They are subsidised or fully funded by the employer.
- They are generally 'no strike' organisations.
- They are the main route by which the organisation consults its workforce.
- They tend to offer a similar range of welfare facilities to trade unions.

- They are invariably separate organisations and not linked nationally.
- Membership is usually compulsory.
- They are viewed with suspicion by trade unionists since they lack the power associated with independence.

The role of unions in conflicts and disputes

The traditional view of trade unions is that their primary involvement in an organisation or industry is in the handling of conflicts and complex disputes. The term 'conflict' can, be used to describe a variety of seemingly non-contentious issues. Conflict itself occurs quite naturally whenever two parties disagree over a certain issue or the implementation of a policy. Trade union representatives within the organisation will, of course, be involved if the conflict merits their input. Equally, if the employee requires or asks for trade union involvement, then it is the union's responsibility to offer assistance.

Trade union representatives will involve themselves only in conflicts which involve their union's members. It should be remembered that employees who do not keep up their membership and the payment of membership or subscription fees may find that they are no longer represented.

Different types of union official may become involved in the handling of conflict at various levels.

- A shop steward/branch official will negotiate with management about issues within the working environment concerning his or her members.
- A regional official will be called in by the branch for additional information, guidance and authority.
- The national executive represents the union at national level and is involved in collective bargaining.

Collective bargaining

It is this final role of collective bargaining that underlines the importance of the trade union movement as far as employees are concerned. The ability to negotiate at a national level often involving hundreds of thousands of members, is a widely accepted and workable method of achieving results. Over the years many potential problems and disputes have been resolved by negotiations being carried out at national level with employers' federations, the government or other organisations.

Some organisations, for collective bargaining purposes, recognise only one trade union. This is done to simplify the negotiating process and can mean that it is no longer necessary to have discussions with a number of different employee representatives to reach an agreement.

Industrial action

In the event that a trade union believes that management decisions are detrimental to its members, it may consider taking industrial action. These actions may take several forms, such as a work to rule, and some may be more damaging to the organisation than others.

■ Discipline and grievance procedures

It is inevitable that disputes will often arise between the employer and the employees. The procedures employed by organisations and the role of trade unions or external organisations can be crucial to the settlement of such disputes.

The Advisory, Conciliation and Arbitration Services **(ACAS)** has approved the following disciplinary procedure, the key aspects of which are

- that the disciplinary procedure is written down
- that all employees have access to the disciplinary procedure
- that the employees are aware who operates the disciplinary procedure.

The flow chart in Figure 6.2 illustrates the procedures to be followed when an individual demonstrates lack of capability or poor performance.

Most organisations of any size have **grievance** procedures to deal with problems arising from their employees. The ACAS *Employment Handbook* offers the following advice.

> 'Grievance procedures should aim to settle a grievance fairly, quickly and as closely as possible to the point of origin, and help to prevent minor disagreements developing into more serious disputes. For this reason, it is usually advisable for the first stage to be between the employee and his or her immediate supervisor or line manager. This can also help to maintain the authority of the supervisor and can often lead to the issue being resolved directly between the parties without the involvement of a representative.'

It is in neither the organisation's nor the employee's interests to allow the grievance procedure to carry on for any length of time. To this end, many organisations have stipulated that

- the first stage of the procedure must be completed in 24 hours
- the second stage is completed within three days.

All organisations would obviously prefer to resolve their own internal disputes. In some cases, this is not possible and an external organisation may have to be involved or invited to help settle the issue.

Dispute procedures

Situations occasionally arise when individual employees find themselves in a position that leads to a potential dispute with their employer such as breach of an organisation's regulation or codes of practice or when an employee believes that he or she has been ill-treated. Some of the causes of disputes are initiated by the employer, whilst others are as a result of an employee's belief that a situation is unfair. The possible responses are fairly clear when the situation relates to breaches of regulations or codes of practice. However, when an employee feels that he or she has been wronged or ill-treated, the exact course that the dispute may take will differ from situation to situation.

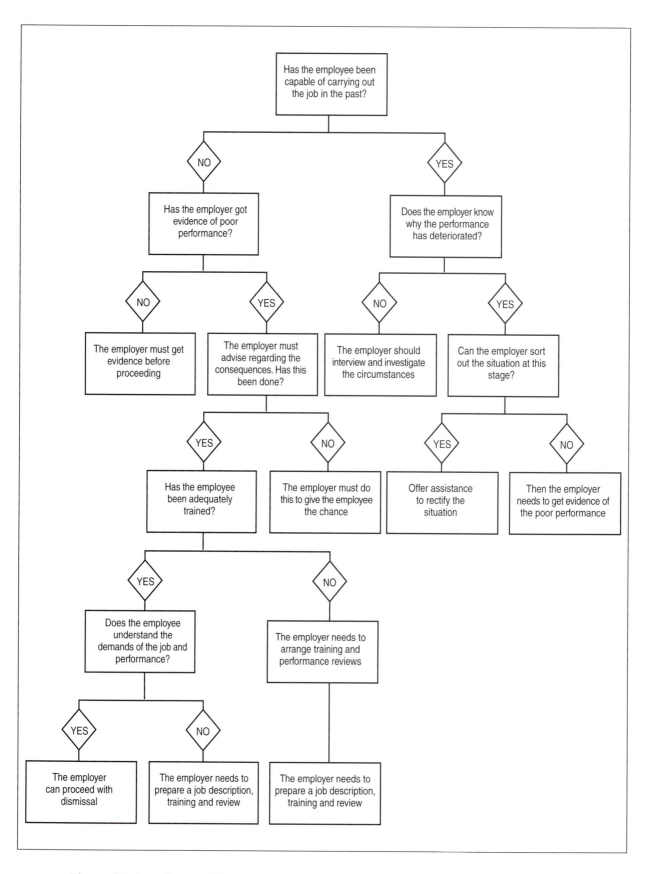

Figure 6.2 Procedures to follow when an individual demonstrates lack of capability or poor performance

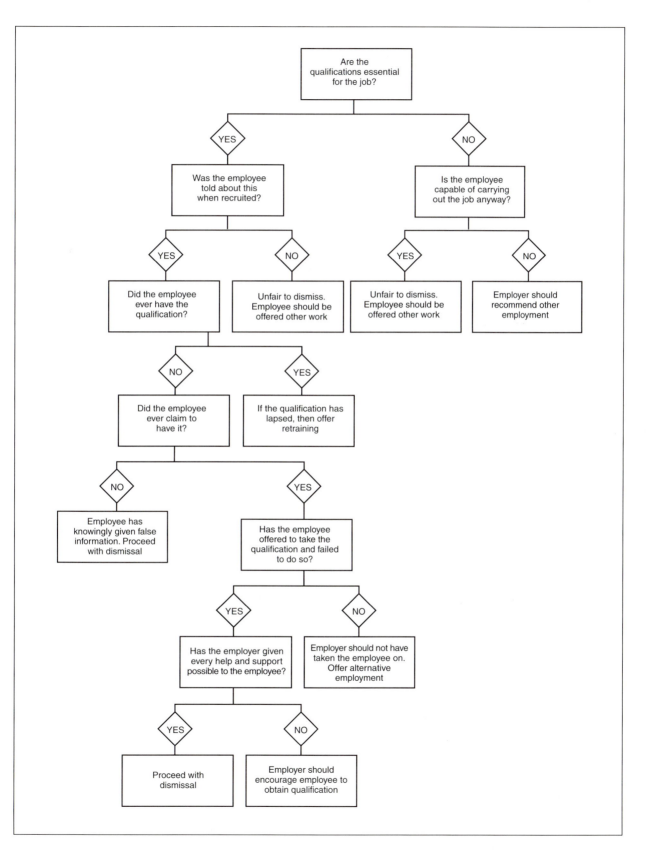

Figure 6.3 Procedure to follow when an individual lacks qualifications

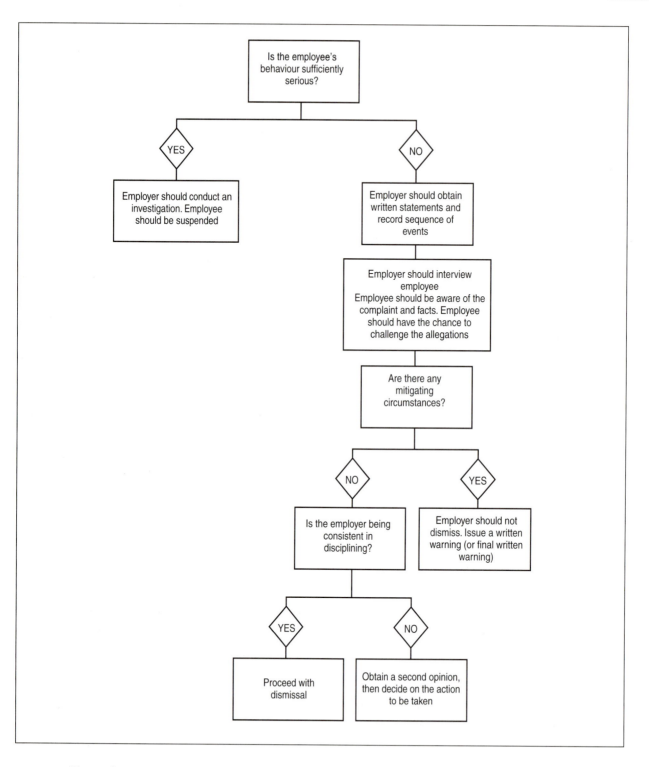

Figure 6.4   Procedure to follow if gross misconduct has been committed by an employee

The negotiations may involve internal or external bodies. The primary concern is not only to solve the dispute but also to manage the negotiation at as low a level as possible – in the first instance between the employee in question and his or her line manager. It is often not in the interests of either the employer or the employee to involve external bodies or organisations, since this heightens the tension between the two parties and may well lead to the situation getting out of hand.

Many different topics, problems or disputes may arise on a regular basis and there will usually be specified methods of conducting the negotiations on these matters. With regard to breaches of regulations, legislation and codes of practice, set procedures have been outlined by government legislation or ACAS. It is worth remembering that even at the lowest levels of negotiation, an individual employee has the automatic right of representation if he or she so wishes.

Trade unions and staff associations

In consultations and negotiations which involve pay and working conditions, the procedures begin at a significantly higher level than in situations when a simple dispute needs to be resolved. In the case of annual pay rounds or the negotiations relating to new terms and conditions of work, a trade union will almost certainly be involved at the earliest possible opportunity.

Annual pay rounds which, in effect, attempt to set the pay rises for the majority of the workforce for the next year, tend to take the form of a series of consultation meetings where differing views are exchanged. It is often important for the employees in particular to have expertise on hand in the form of a trade union official, who can relate good practice and knowledge of other pay negotiations. These consultations and negotiations are often fraught and the negotiation process is a complex one. Each side will begin the negotiations demanding more than it actually expects or hopes to achieve. Since the management of the organisation will probably have a personnel expert who will lead the negotiations on behalf of the business, the employees need to have a similarly qualified individual who can represent them.

Staff associations and, in particular, their officials play a similar role to that of a trade union representative. Their role and power is somewhat different in many cases from that of a trade union official. As you will see later, many staff organisations have negotiated away the right to take industrial action. There is a tendency, therefore, for negotiations undertaken by staff associations to be considered less important and potentially contentious by the employer. In both trade union and staff association cases the progress of the negotiation will certainly depend upon the status of the relationships between management and the workforce. Indeed, many negotiations are influenced by the course of previous negotiations and the general interpersonal relationships between the individuals involved in the negotiations.

ACAS

ACAS is an independent organisation that offers employers, trade unions and individuals the opportunity to obtain unbiased assistance when dealing with disputes. ACAS enjoys a reputation for impartiality and is recognised by employers and employees alike as being a valuable and reliable source of assistance.

As well as its primary objective to resolve disputes, it also offers a wide range of employee-related advice. In an **arbitration** situation, the two sides will turn to ACAS when they feel that they have exhausted the options open to them to resolve the problem internally. ACAS will listen to the two parties involved and consider their arguments and will then provide a solution which both parties must accept. It is a prerequisite for ACAS that both sides agree to abide by the decision made before they begin the arbitration process. On the **conciliation** side, ACAS will listen to both sides of the argument and attempt to resolve the situation by encouraging those in dispute to move closer to one another's point of view. ACAS also publishes useful statistical information regarding employee relations. It looks at disputes which have gone as far as industrial tribunals and recommends good practice in employee relations.

Industrial tribunals

Industrial tribunals are made up of individuals who have specific knowledge of employment law. The chairperson of a tribunal is either a barrister or solicitor with at least seven years' experience. The other members of the industrial tribunal include two lay people (individuals who do not have a specific allegiance to either employers or employees). These lay people are nominated either by the CBI (Confederation of British Industry) or the TUC (Trades Union Congress). The members of the tribunal all have an equal say and decisions are made by majority verdict. Industrial tribunals are somewhat more accessible than other courts. By simply filling in a form, an individual need not resort to the professional assistance of a solicitor, or, indeed, have any representation at the hearing. The tribunal does not take place in a court room and all of the usual complications that are associated with courts are avoided.

As there are no court fees, it is inexpensive to take a case to an industrial tribunal. Normally, an industrial tribunal is involved in complaints regarding unfair dismissal. The ex-employee must first ask ACAS to decide whether the case needs to be taken to an industrial tribunal.

Once a complaint has reached an industrial tribunal around one-third are upheld, ie won by the employee. Although it may seem from this that employers tend to 'win' more often than not, lessons still need to be learned by the employers who have allowed the complaint to go as far as an industrial tribunal. Individuals who have had their complaints upheld by an industrial tribunal are entitled to compensation, re-instatement or re-engagement.

Employment Appeals Tribunal

If an employer or employee makes an appeal on a point of law made by an industrial tribunal, then he or she can refer to the Employment Appeals Tribunal (EAT). The EAT consists of a High Court Judge and two lay people. It is the role of the EAT to uphold or reverse the findings of an industrial tribunal. In some cases, admittedly rare, appeals may be made to the Court of Appeal or to the House of Lords (the House of Lords being the highest court in the country).

■ Remuneration (pay)

Depending on the type of job, you will normally be paid either a wage or a salary. Wages tend to be based on the number of hours which you have worked in a particular week. Salaries, on the other hand, are one-twelfth of your annual pay. In both cases payment is nearly always made 'in arrears'. This means that you have worked for several days or even a few weeks before you get paid. As you will see, wages tend to be paid on a weekly basis (sometimes fortnightly, though) and salaries tend to be paid on a monthly basis, or every four weeks.

Student activity

In pairs, try to list as many jobs which you think are 'wage' earners and as many as you can that are 'salaried'. Discuss your findings with those of the rest of the group.

Gross pay

Whenever you are quoted a wage or salary, you must always remember that this is the amount that will be paid before income tax, national insurance or any other deductions have been made. This is known as your **gross wage or salary**. Only self-employed people will be paid the full gross amount since they have to sort out their own tax and national insurance. For the majority of people the net pay is what they will receive.

Net pay

As we have said, net pay is what is left of your wages or salary after deductions have been made. It is worth remembering that with tax, national insurance, pension schemes and other deductions, you could be left with as little as half of your gross pay. This is worth bearing in mind when looking at the wages or salaries offered by employers as you should really be thinking about what you will actually take home rather than the gross pay they are quoting.

Piece rate

Piece rate is quite common in factories and in homeworking which involves some form of assembly or hand-manufacture. For example, those working at home making lampshades, stitching clothing and addressing envelopes will all be paid on the piece-rate method. This means that every item they have completed (subject to some very close quality checks) will entitle them to a small amount of payment. For piece-rate workers to earn a good level of pay, they not only have to be fast but also they have to be accurate and their quality standards high. Piece-rate workers tend to be paid on completion of a batch of work. They will be expected to produce a basic minimum number of items over a given length of time.

Hourly rate

From an employer's point of view, paying an hourly rate is ideal for the employment of part-time or casual workers. However, a large number of full-time employees are paid on an hourly rate. If full-time employees' hours are always the same each week, then apart from the fact that they are paid weekly, their circumstances are almost exactly the same as a salaried member of staff. Part-time workers may be offered a minimum number of hours per week and then, if they are asked to do more hours, their wage will be amended accordingly. Casual workers, on the other hand, who cannot rely on a set number of hours per day or week are called in by the employer to help cope with busy periods or seasonal rushes (such as packing orders for Christmas or dealing with telephone enquiries during the holiday period).

Weekly wage

Some employers, rather than quoting an annual salary, will state how much an employee will earn per week. Again, this is based on a particular number of hours that have to be worked in order to receive that wage. It is normal practice for an employer to pay a weekly wage at the end of the week, probably at lunch time or at the end of the working day on Friday. Employees who are paid in this way may discover that by dividing the number of hours worked into the weekly wage, they will find out how much they are being paid per hour. In a similar way, by multiplying the weekly wage by 52, they will discover their annual wage.

Monthly payment

Monthly payment is the normal way to pay a salaried employee. The employer will make the payment on a particular date or day of the month, such as the 28th, or the last Friday. Some employers make this a little more complicated and actually pay their employees 13 times per year. This is because they pay every four weeks rather than each month and since there are 52 weeks in the year, 13 is the number of payments if you divide 52 by 4. This means that the pay is slightly more regular, but, of course, each payment is slightly less since you are being paid 13 times instead of 12.

Bonuses

Bonuses are usually paid to employees for two rather different reasons. These are

- if employees have personally achieved a particular target or goal set by their employer
- if the organisation as a whole has achieved a particular target or goal set to them by the management or owners of the organisation.

Sometimes, as a variation on the personal bonus, the whole department or team receives the same amount of bonus if it has achieved a particular target or goal. This serves as a way of encouraging the whole team to work together to achieve. Company bonus schemes can be quite complicated, but usually these extra payments are made either at Christmas or as soon as the organisation has worked out whether it has made a profit in a particular year. This means that the bonuses are paid at some time in April.

Some organisations, rather than offering cash, will offer prizes to their 'star performers'. For example, a sales executives who has achieved the highest sales target in a particular month may be given an expenses-paid holiday abroad. More commonly, though, the gift will be something a little more modest, such as an electric kettle or toaster.

Student activity

During the next week try to find out how many of your family or friends have earned a bonus from their organisation. What form did this bonus take? When you have collected this information, compare with the findings of the rest of the group and try to list the advantages of working for an organisation that offers this scheme.

Overtime

The term 'overtime' refers to any hours, or for that matter days, that have been worked in excess of the number of hours or days that the employee is normally supposed to work. For most employees this will mean that they are paid more for that hour or day than they would normally be paid for a standard hour or day (perhaps 'twice' the amount they are normally paid). Employers do this to encourage their employees to do the overtime rather than going to the expense of having to get in new staff to cover a handful of hours or the odd day. For some hourly paid workers, particularly those who are part time or casual, overtime just means extra hours. They may not be paid any more money for those hours than they would normally be paid for a standard hour. However, they are often grateful for the extra work and do it all the same.

As an alternative to being paid for overtime, employees may be given time off 'in lieu'. This means that they will be allowed to take the same number of hours or days off as paid leave for having done the overtime. Just as some employees are paid time and a half or double time for overtime, an extra day at Christmas, for example, may mean that they can take two or three days off in lieu for having worked that overtime. Normally, if overtime is undertaken at the weekend, particularly Sundays, or on bank holidays, the employer has to make it worth while for employees even to think about doing the overtime.

Types of remuneration

If one thing can be said about all the different forms of payment that are made to employees, then it would be that the choice of payment is nearly always the one that suits the employer rather than the employee. The employer will choose the form of payment most convenient to them without necessarily thinking about whether this is best for the employee or not. As you will see, there are three main forms of payment, although the **credit transfer** to the bank is becoming the most common.

Cash

In the past, payment by cash was perhaps the most common form of receiving a wage or salary from an employer. However, many employers do not wish to take the risk of having to arrange the delivery of several thousands of pounds on a Friday and then having to go to the trouble of splitting up that delivery into pay packets and finally giving the pay packets to the correct person. Not only is there the risk of robbery but also the expense of having to have elaborate security equipment and accounts staff on hand to sort out the pay packets. This also meant that Fridays were often disrupted by the employees having to queue for their pay packets which lost valuable time for the employer.

Cash is still a very common way of being paid as a part-time or casual worker. After all, particularly with casual workers, employees do not know when they will see the employer again, if ever, and would not wish to leave work without taking their money with them.

Cheque

Cheques are probably the most inconvenient way of being paid! After all, a cheque needs to be paid into an account or cashed at a bank. Some large employers have an arrangement with their own bank which allows their employees to go into the branch (showing suitable identification) and have the cheque cashed immediately. Whether employees then choose to take the money out in cash or have some of it or all of it transferred into their own account is up to them. One advantage a cheque does have for an employer, particularly if the cheque is being given on a Friday, is that the employee may not pay the cheque in until the Saturday morning or the following Monday, and then it has to clear (which could take as much as a week) before the cash is taken out of the employer's account.

Credit transfer to bank

This form of payment is fast becoming the most common way of receiving a wage or salary. From the employers' point of view, they only need to fill in a summary sheet which details the employees' account details and amount to be paid. For those employees who receive a regular amount at regular intervals, a standard transfer can be set up which guarantees payment on a particular day of the month. The big advantage for employees is that as soon as the money has been transferred into their account, it can be drawn out again, they do not have to wait for a cheque to clear as this is an **electronic transfer of funds** from one account to another.

Employees will, of course, receive a statement, perhaps a day or two before the payment is due to be made, which details how much is being paid into their account. The statement will also include the gross pay, deductions and net pay, along with the total amount of tax and national insurance paid so far that year.

Common fringe benefits

Rather than offering extra pay, or higher rates of pay, some employers offer **fringe benefits** to attract employees or keep the staff that they have got already. Fringe benefits are also known as 'non-financial incentives' which are aimed at providing the employees with a little extra. Types of fringe benefits include the following.

Subsidised meals and drinks

Obviously, if you work for an organisation which is involved in the catering industry, then subsidised, or even free, meals and drinks are often common-place. Many of the larger organisations which may have no association with catering offer their staff reduced rate (sometimes known as 'at cost') food and refreshment.

As an alternative to food and drink offered on the premises of the organisation, some employers give their employees luncheon vouchers. These can be exchanged for food and drink at a number of outlets, including supermarkets in most high streets or town centres. They have a cash value and some employees actually prefer to collect and keep their luncheon vouchers and spend them on an evening meal when they can fully enjoy the benefit of a free night out.

Travel

Another incentive to employees is free or subsidised travel. The nature of this type of incentive will differ from organisation to organisation. Broadly speaking, it may be one of the following.

- Free pick-up and drop-off – for employees who live in remote areas and would find it otherwise extremely difficult to get into work. In these instances the employer provides a free coach or bus service which makes pick-ups and drop-offs in a number of small villages and towns.
- Free travel passes – offered by some larger organisations, to enable their employees to travel on public transport, either in the course of work, or during their leisure time.
- Travel loan schemes – where employers pay for the employee's season ticket in order to take advantage of discounts available. The employee pays back the employer a regular amount per month interest-free.
- Company cars – key employees or those who have to travel considerable distances in the course of their work are often provided with a company car and a credit card to pay for petrol.
- Essential car user's allowance – organisations that do not offer company cars give some of their key employees a credit card or a charge account at specific petrol stations to help towards the running costs of their own cars being used for company business.
- Overseas travel – for employees who have to make regular trips abroad, the organisation provides them with the means to purchase tickets as and when they need them. This may be done either through a recommended travel agency, or by giving these employees a credit card to buy the tickets as they need them. Using a credit card, the organisation will be able to monitor the

use made of it and it will be useful to the employee for other expenses as well as travel.

■ Reimbursement – for occasional travel carried out by employees in the course of their work, organisations tend to use 'expenses claims forms' to pay back individuals for any outlay they have made in the course of their travels for the organisation

Discount on purchases

Some organisations, particularly those involved in retailing, offer their employees a discount on purchases made by them. This not only serves as a useful incentive to their employees, but also ensures that their employees use the company's products. The procedures used when employees purchase from their employer are often very carefully monitored to avoid mis-use of the incentive. Some employers restrict the amount that an employee can purchase to stop them from selling the products on to other people.

Loans

Banks and building societies, in particular, offer their employees reduced rate loans or mortgages as a very valuable incentive. Whilst the employee works for the organisation he or she can enjoy loans and mortgages at considerably lower rates of interest than the normal rate. Other organisations can give advances on salaries and wages which are, in effect, loans, and are paid off gradually by the employee. Employees need to be aware that any loans and mortgages given to them by their current employer will have to be renegotiated or paid off if they cease working for them.

Student activity

List the advantages and disadvantages of the fringe benefits outlined above. Now, without looking any further, can you think of any more?

Health insurance

Key members of staff in particular may be offered health insurance as part of their overall wage or salary package. This private health insurance often covers their families too. The employer, by ensuring that their key employees are covered by private health insurance, can be assured that the minimum amount of disruption occurs if the employee falls ill or needs medical attention.

From the employees' point of view, they can also feel secure in the fact that any serious medical problem can be dealt with as quickly as possible and they do not lose valuable time by having to wait for medical attention.

Pensions

Essentially, there are two different types of pension, since it is now a legal requirement for all employees to have a pension scheme in addition to the state pension which they will receive as a result of paying national insurance. These are

- contributory pensions – where the employee and employer both pay into the pension scheme.
- non-contributory pensions – where only the employer pays into the pension scheme on behalf of the employee.

Bearing in mind that anyone can pay up to around 17.5 per cent of their total income to a pension scheme tax free, this can prove to be quite an incentive to both the employee and the employer. The government is very keen for employees to be able to support themselves financially when they retire and has made it relatively easy to set up a pension scheme and monitor the payments. Some organisations offer one of the following.

- Company pension schemes – where a specific pension fund has been set up to pay the pension of retired employees. All employees pay into this scheme and the benefits from this joint 'saving' are passed on to the retired members of staff.
- Personal pension schemes – where the pension scheme is a more general one and is not company-based, but is related to the employee as an individual. One of the advantages here is that the personal pension scheme is movable from one employer to the next, as well as having the additional benefit of being part of a much larger overall pension fund.

In the past, planning for their future retirement was not something that many people necessarily considered. In fact, nowadays it is rare to find an employer who does not actively encourage members of staff to join a company pension scheme or set up their own private one. The key aspect of incentives to consider is whether the employer is making a contribution to the employees' pension fund or not. If the employer does not, then it is not really an incentive as such, although they may be able to take much of the complication out of organising a pension for yourself by being able to offer a company pension scheme.

Sports and social clubs

Some organisations, particularly those that value team work and team building, offer their employees a range of sports and social activities at either no cost or heavily subsidised rates. Many of the banks and other larger organisations have their own sports and social clubs, with a variety of different activities on offer. Other smaller organisations have entered into agreements with local leisure and sports clubs and have 'block membership deals' (a lump sum paid by the employer to the leisure club as payment for the membership of a large number of their employees).

Some organisations take this even further and positively encourage inter-departmental competitions in various sports and games. Others may organise day trips or visits for their employees, providing the transport, food, drink and activities at the destination.

Clothing

Despite the fact that many company uniforms are not exactly to the taste of most employees, the fact that they are provided by the employer can be seen as something of an incentive. By having to wear a company uniform, employees do not have to wear their own clothes to work and can save money by not having to buy clothes for that purpose. Most organisations provide a number of sets of uniforms to each employee, but expect individuals to make sure that they are cleaned. Other organisations merely require employees to wear a uniform whilst at work. Employees are then asked to leave the dirty uniforms so that the employer can organise the cleaning of them. Employees then simply pick up a clean uniform when they come into work the next day.

As an alternative to providing uniforms, employers may give their employees a clothing allowance. With a number of restrictions, the employer allows employees to choose their own work clothes, merely requiring them to choose particular colours or styles.

Student activity

As a group, discuss the advantages and disadvantages of the fringe benefits listed since you carried out the last activity.

Common deductions

Employees do not receive their full wage or salary. Before the money is either given to them or transferred into their account, various common deductions are made. Some are required by law, such as income tax, and others are voluntary, such as pension contributions. These deductions include the following.

Income tax

Income tax is deducted by the employer on behalf of the Inland Revenue. The employer must do this and promptly pass the money on to the government department. Although the deduction process is complicated, it follows a particular procedure.

- The Inland Revenue works out the personal allowance of the employee based on his or her marital status and other considerations.
- The employee is taxed on all money earned above the personal allowance, so the more that is earned, the more tax is paid.
- The employee is provided with a clear statement on his or her payslip, stating the amount of tax that has been deducted.
- Annually, the employee receives a slip which tells him or her the total amount of tax paid in the past year.

The tax paid by employees and business organisations funds all government spending (or at least most of it) and is used for running schools, the civil service, the emergency services, road building and many other expensive projects.

National insurance

National insurance is paid by all employees and a contribution is made by the employer too. Unlike tax there is no personal allowance and you pay national insurance on everything that you earn. National insurance funds all of the sick pay, maternity pay and state pensions paid out to people. Again, the employer is responsible for collecting the national insurance on behalf of the Department of Social Security and must promptly pass any money collected on to them. Perhaps the most important user of national insurance contributions is the National Health Service.

Union subscription

Members of trade unions will pay a weekly, monthly or annual subscription or membership fee. This will either be a standard amount, regardless of how much the employee earns, or will be on a sliding scale which increases as the employee earns more. Trade union subscriptions are, of course, voluntary, as you do not need to be a member of a trade union. However, many people realise the benefits of being in a trade union as they can offer additional insurance, legal advice, protection from unreasonable employers and representation in disciplinary matters and pay negotiations.

Pension

Although we all pay national insurance which goes towards our state pension when we retire, many people believe that the state pension will not give them a sufficiently high standard of living when they stop working. The government also encourages people to make provision for their retirement years. The different types of pensions and pension schemes are discussed on pages 170–171.

Other forms of remuneration, benefits and rewards for work

This section identifies the other main ways in which employers reward their employees for extra effort, loyalty and helping to achieve the business objectives and profit levels. These other methods include the following.

Employee share ownership

In recent years, employers have recognised that a degree of personal ownership on the part of the employee encourages much greater dedication, productivity and motivation. Organisations which use this form of participation include Marks & Spencer and the John Lewis Partnership. The availability and issue of shares is usually reliant upon the number of years' service of the employee. Normally, these shares will be made available to the employees at a particular time of the year. This share offer may occur either when usual Christmas bonuses are paid or at the end of the financial year, once the organisation's performance and profits have been calculated. Employees are not forced to take these shares instead of their bonus and they are often given the opportunity to take a cash payment instead. However, this cash payment is not as financially attractive as the shares which have been offered.

Employee shareholders and share options

The other version of this share-related participation scheme – share options – involves giving the managers of the organisation the opportunity to buy shares at a future date at a price level that is set at the time of the offer. There have been substantial criticisms of this system as it allows the managers to make huge short-term profits. They can buy the shares at a preferential price and then sell them on the market at the going rate. The upshot of this is that the managers are rewarded by this share option scheme, whereas the workforce, which, arguably, has been the cause of the increase in the value of the shares, receives no similar rewards.

■ Equal opportunities

Discrimination

In order to establish the fact that inequality exists within the working environment, it is probably a good idea to try to define what equality actually means. Perhaps an easy definition would be that all individuals or groups of individuals are not treated less favourably regardless of the situation. It is essential that equality of treatment and opportunity is encouraged to foster good working relationships within the working environment and to make the best use of all employees' abilities.

When we consider discrimination, we need to ask the following questions.

- Does any individual receive different treatment?
- Is any individual suffering a disadvantage?
- Is there any legal or other justification for such inequality?

Within employment, employees are protected to some extent by various laws and regulations. The main groups who suffer from discrimination are

- women
- ethnic minorities
- the disabled
- the young
- the old
- those with an alternative sexual orientation
- certain religious groups.

Many organisations have adopted equal opportunities policies, although they are not yet required to do this by law. The Equal Opportunities Commission has designed a standard policy which employers can use. This covers a wide variety of different situations, and includes the following:

- that to have an **equal opportunities** policy is a desirable thing
- that it should be strictly adhered to
- that all forms of direct and indirect discrimination are clearly defined
- that the organisation states its commitment to equal opportunities and further states that it is in the best interests of the organisation and employees to do so
- that all employees are made aware of the policy
- that any preconceived ideas which the employees may have regarding those

who are subject to discrimination are addressed
- that staff are trained to maintain the policy
- that recruitment and promotion are equal for all
- that training is offered on an equal basis to all
- that the employment contract does not inadvertently discriminate against anyone
- that the organisation's facilities are open to all
- that an individual is nominated to monitor the policy
- that the policy is regularly reviewed and updated according to need
- that any grievances related to discrimination are dealt with in a prompt and fair manner
- that no individuals suffer victimisation in the course of their duties within the organisation.

Case study

The Equal Opportunities Commission (EOC) was created to ensure the effective enforcement of the Sex Discrimination Act and Equal Pay Act and also to promote equal opportunities between sexes.

The EOC has the power to carry out investigations and if it is satisfied that the practices are unlawful, it can then issue non-discrimination notices which require the practice to cease. The EOC has the power to require any individual to provide information or attend hearings to give evidence. The EOC also has the power to help individuals prepare and conduct complaints in either courts or tribunals. In some cases, where issues raise important aspects of principle, the EOC will clarify the legal position.

As well as its investigations, the EOC makes recommendations to the government regarding the operation of existing law. The EOC also takes legal proceedings against individuals or organisations in their own right. It is involved in research and educational work relating to equal opportunities.

Equal Pay Act 1975

The concept of equal pay for an equal day's work is the foundation of the Equal Pay Act, which came into force in 1975. Its purpose was to eliminate discrimination between men and women in terms of rates of pay, working hours, holidays and sick leave entitlement.

The right to equal pay for work of equal value, which was given in effect by the 1983 amended Regulations, now forms a part of the Equal Pay Act. The Act may be used by workers of all ages and all forms and methods of working.

The term 'like work' can actually be defined as 'of a broadly similar nature'. In other words, if an individual can show that the work carried out is the same or broadly similar, then in legal terms, the case has been proven.

Case study

Some 20 years have passed since the Equal Pay Act came into operation. Women still earn only 79 per cent of men's full-time hourly earnings. They tend to cluster in 'women's jobs', often under-valued and under-paid. Women provide the bulk of part-time workers, with low pay and fewer opportunities for overtime or bonus earnings. The abolition of the Wages Councils has further widened the gap. Performance-related pay systems have also affected not only pay, but also training and promotion opportunities.

Britain introduced Regulations in 1984 to provide for equal pay for work of equal value. Unfortunately, due to the complexity and limitations of the legal system, they have had little impact on the 'inequality gap'. The laws and related administrative provisions have failed to provide justice for women and ensure equal pay.

Race Relations Act 1976

The Race Relations Act 1976 makes racial discrimination unlawful in the areas of

- employment
- training
- education
- the provision of goods, facilities and services
- the disposal and management of premises.

The Act gives an individual the right of direct access to the courts or industrial tribunals to gain a legal remedy for unlawful discrimination. It also established a Commission for Racial Equality. The Commission's remit includes

- enforcement of the legislation
- promotion of equality of opportunity
- the fostering of good relations between different racial groups
- advisory responsibilities to the government on the working of the Act
- acting as a principal source of information
- discretion to assist individuals who feel they have been discriminated against
- assisting organisations to implement equal opportunities.

Case study

The Race Relations Act applies to discrimination both before and after the date it came into force. The Act repealed the former Race Relations Acts of 1965 and 1968. It also abolished the Race Relations Board and Community Relations Commission.

The Act defines two specific kinds of racial discrimination – direct or indirect. Direct racial discrimination occurs when an individual treats another individual less favourably on racial grounds. The term 'racial grounds' covers colour, race, nationality, ethnicity and national origins.

Indirect racial discrimination can be best described when an individual requires specific conditions to be satisfied as a result of someone being a member of a particular racial group. It is unlawful for an employer to discriminate in relation to employment.

Positive action and equality

A solution to the possibility of discrimination is for an organisation to institute a policy of **positive action** or positive discrimination. In this instance, the organisation attempts to put right inequalities or poor treatment in the past. It positively encourages previously discriminated groups to apply for jobs and indeed, gives them preference. Within the working environment these groups are given every opportunity to 'catch up' in terms of experience and qualifications. It should be noted, however, that overt positive action, particularly in the recruitment process, may, inadvertently, discriminate against others.

Achieving equality within the working environment is essential to the organisation both morally and legally. Taking the latter example, the employer may be required to pay compensation for any unlawful discrimination. In order to maintain equality the organisation should ensure that

- procedures are in place which take account of objectivity and equality
- training and guidance are given to all employees
- regular checks are made regarding procedures, practice and policy
- immediate action is taken when necessary
- records are kept to show that reasonable steps have been taken to achieve equality.

Commitment to equality is also essential, not only relating to those to whom legislation is applicable but also to all employees and groups of employees. Employees should be made aware of the employer's policies regarding correct behaviour in terms of discrimination. The employer, as we have mentioned earlier, is responsible for ensuring that the non-discriminatory legislation is adhered to within the workplace.

Whilst it is an organisation's right to choose an individual for a particular post, there are a number of pieces of legislation which limit this freedom of choice.

Under the Disabled Persons (Employment) Act 1958, an employer with more than a certain number of employees is required to employ registered disabled persons as a minimum of 3 per cent of the workforce. The only exception to this is if the organisation has an exemption certificate.

Similarly, the Rehabilitation of Offenders Act 1974 protects ex-offenders from discrimination on the grounds of their past life. The Act states that an individual who has a past conviction need not mention 'spent' convictions on his or her job application forms or at interview. He or she must, however, mention any convictions that are not 'spent'. (The length of time that must pass before a conviction is 'spent' depends on the gravity of the offence.)

Under the Employment Protection (Consolidation) Act 1978 an individual cannot be discriminated against on the basis of union membership.

Keywords

The keywords that you should know for this chapter are listed below. Check to make sure you understand the meaning of each word. Discuss those you are unsure of with your tutor.

ACAS	industrial tribunal
arbitration	mission statement
cascading	on-the-job training
conciliation	positive action
contract of employment	quality assurance
credit transfer	rate card
electronic transfer of	referee
funds	remuneration
employee share ownership	short-listing
equal opportunities	staff association
fringe benefit	staff handbook
grievance	trade union
gross wage or salary	

Examination practice

Short-answer questions

1 Give four examples of points that would be included in a contract of employment.

2 What is remuneration? Give three different common types.

3 State two laws that aim to ensure equal opportunities.

4 Explain what is meant by vocational and non-vocational training.

5 How soon does a contract of employment need to be issued to a new employee?

6 What is gross misconduct and how would it be handled by the employer?

7 Briefly state what you would expect to be told during an induction programme.

8 Outline the main differences between trade unions and staff associations.

9 Briefly list the main stages in a disciplinary procedure.

10 What steps could employees take in the event of a grievance with their employers?

Essay questions

Your role in the personnel department of a growing manufacturing organisation has meant that you have become involved in a number of new areas relating to recruitment, selection, induction and training of new employees. You are also the first point of contact in the personnel department for disciplinary matters and for employees who have a grievance.

1   Your personnel manager has asked you to draw up a simple job advertisement to be included in the local newspaper for the following positions: accounts clerk, word-processor operator and administration assistant to the production manager. You will need to carry out the following tasks:

   a   draft a suitable advertisement which includes the three available posts.

   b   briefly outline a person specification which details the ideal characteristics or skills required for each of the above posts.

   c   suggest ways in which your manager could short-list suitable candidates.

2   In your role as an assistant to the personnel manager, you have been asked to prepare a memorandum which outlines the key disciplinary and grievance procedure as recommended by ACAS. Your manager has decided that these guidelines will be the ones which will be followed. You will need to state clearly the following:

   a   under what kind of circumstances would disciplinary procedures be commenced?

   b   what are the stages of the disciplinary procedure and how do they relate to one another?

   c   what advice could you give an employee who has a grievance against the organisation or another individual?

3   With the continued growth of the organisation, the personnel manager has decided that it would be a good idea to set up a staff association. Since the organisation does not have very many trade union members, the main purpose of the staff association will be to provide welfare and recreational facilities for the employees. You will need to set your ideas down as a proposal which the personnel manager can take to the board of directors.

   a   You must include a clear definition of what a staff association is and what its purposes are.

b You must also include a list of the probable facilities or activities that should be offered by the staff association.

4 In the past, the majority of employees were on permanent full-time contracts with the organisation. However, with additional work from the new contracts acquired by the organisation, there has been a need to employ individuals on an alternative basis. In this respect, some employees do not receive standard wages or salaries. The personnel manager wants to review the way in which some employees are paid and has asked you to prepare some notes regarding alternative remuneration methods. This should include:

a the different sorts of remuneration

b the circumstances in which these different types of remuneration could be appropriate to particular employees.

7 The working environment

■ Introduction

It is in the employer's and the employees' interests to have the most efficient and effective office environment. The nature of the working environment and the way in which individuals operate within that environment is the subject of this chapter. In order to understand fully the needs and pressures of the modern office environment it is important that you consider the following. However, it is worth remembering that each and every office has its own peculiarities and demands and no one office is likely to be exactly the same as another.

- How work is planned and by whom.
- How work is organised, scheduled and workloads established.
- How each individual's work area is organised according to the type of work that he or she is expected to undertake.
- How most offices are organised in terms of the layout and design of the work areas and the divisions of different parts of the organisation's operations.
- How equipment is taken care of, by whom and why.
- How certain aspects regarding all of the above features of the modern office environment are often controlled and set out by government and European Union legislation.
- How Health and Safety legislation ensures that employees work in a safe and healthy working environment.

■ Work planning, organising schedules and workload

Organisational skills are very important to anybody who is working in the administration section of a business. In fact, organisational skills should also be very important to anybody who is undertaking a programme of study. Sometimes you may feel a lot more organised than you do at other times. In business, there is so much paperwork and information involved in day-to-day duties, that someone who is very disorganised could do the business a great deal of damage. Some organisational skills include the following.

- Being neat and tidy in your desk area.
- Keeping a diary of dates and times when meetings should be attended. A record should also be kept of any expected visitors (who may be customers or prospective customers) to the organisation.
- Having an efficient method of storage and retrieval of documents, whether this is paper based or computer based.
- Having a follow-up procedure in place so that documents are always available at the correct date and time.
- Managing time efficiently. Time management does not apply just to those people who are in authority and have many responsibilities at work. It is

important for all of us to be aware of the need to monitor the way in which we either waste or make the best use of our time at work.

■ Having a 'to do' list. This list can be weekly and/or daily and should list the duties that have to be carried out. Prioritising duties (putting them in their order of importance) is necessary if you are to be well organised. It is also very satisfying to end the day with a list which has successfully been completed.

Student activity

In order to ensure you are well organised, design a 'to do' list which you could use for your course work. Allow for the title of the job, any deadline that needs to be met and a section which allows you to indicate when the job has been completed. Also include a section which enables you to monitor in case there is a problem.

Diaries and other methods of planning work

The use and updating of a diary is essential in the organisation of work and the planning of activities. Secretaries are often responsible for keeping a diary for their boss. In most cases, the secretary will have a diary as a back-up to the main diary. In other cases, the boss may have a pocket diary and the secretary may be in charge of the main desk diary. The first problem is making sure that the two diaries are consistent with one another. The diaries need to be updated and cross-referenced. Failure to do this may result in information being missed and appointments ignored.

Here are some useful suggestions for the efficient keeping of a diary, whether this is for yourself or for your bosses.

■ Make sure that you write clearly, print the names and write down individuals' telephone numbers where possible.

■ If you make a tentative arrangement, put it into the diary in pencil. Once it has been confirmed, overwrite with pen.

■ Make sure that you put into the diary all of the information that you think that you need. There is nothing worse than looking at a diary entry that just has a name and a time. The chances are that you will not remember what the appointment is about.

■ When you book in an appointment, take a look at the rest of the day's commitments. Otherwise you may find that you have put in an appointment at the office when you need to be somewhere else either immediately before or after. Also try to make sure that you leave a reasonable amount of time for a lunch break, or a gap between appointments so that you can 'draw breath' at some point during the day.

■ Remember that appointments may be just part of your overall work during the day. You should try to avoid them getting in the way of your other commitments and routine duties.

- If you need to make a appointment outside of the office, make sure that you allow enough time for travelling – remember that you may encounter delays or bad weather.

- For appointments outside the office make sure that you have precise details of the location. Ask the individual you are meeting to fax you a map if you are unsure about where to go.

- Try to make allowances for the unexpected. If you book appointments directly after a meeting that normally overruns, try to give yourself enough time to compensate for this.

- You will need to see your boss at certain times during the day. If you overbook your boss, you will not have time to take any instructions, guidance, dictation or have a planning session.

- Make sure that you put aside a few minutes each day to coordinate and update the diaries which you are using. You may also need to change tentative arrangements and make them confirmations in your diary or your boss's diary.

Electronic diaries

As an alternative to the usual form of diary, some organisations may use the **electronic-diary** method of logging appointments and meetings. This information can be stored

- on the main computer system
- on a lap-top computer
- on an electronic personal organiser or database.

The electronic diary enables the user to scroll forwards or backwards by day, month or year. It can store around 5 years' worth of days and dates. Provisional or confirmed appointments can be stored, holiday periods blocked out and various reminders can be set for particular days or weeks or months in the future. The electronic diary can also be used to detail appointments out of office hours and can also cross-reference various appointments or tasks which have to be completed before appointments. In all, the electronic diary is an invaluable tool which can enable the manager or secretary to have instant access to all current and future commitments.

As with diaries, these systems need to be accessible, but not necessarily open to all members of staff. The diaries may contain confidential information, either directly related to the organisation itself, or of a more personal nature. The most important considerations if these systems are used are

- that access is limited
- that access can be made if authorised
- that any portable or stand-alone system is compared with or updated by another system housed in the office
- that there should be some procedure which reminds the users to not only back up the system but also to check regularly to see that appointments and meetings have not been overlooked.

Wall planners, wall charts and planner boards

These are other typical systems which enable work planning to be carried out more efficiently.

Office wall planners can either be calendar-based or simply a series of boxes which can allow important dates and other information to be in full view of all office staff. Versions of these include single-use, paper wall planners or long-term use, wipe-off boards or even magnetic formats.

Blank wall charts and boards are useful for noting down a number of different messages which may be relevant to some or all members of staff. Typically, these would be used to detail the movements of employees or inform office staff of an impending meeting or deadline.

Slotted planner boards consist of a number of slots cut into a sheet of metal which is then mounted on the wall. Specific projects and work can then be illustrated by using a number of card inserts which are placed into the slots. Typically, these planner boards will have weeks and months running across the top and at a glance individuals can see who is involved in a particular project, over what period of time and what other commitments they may have during this period. This serves as a useful way of allocating available human resources to particular short-term projects and activities.

Student activity

Representatives from six of your major customers are intending to visit your organisation to look at your facilities and meet some of the key personnel. You will have to organise their entire visit based on the following information.

Date of visit: Monday 25 June 19–
Length of time available: 3 hours
Start time: 1030 hours.
Finish time: 1330 hours.
Refreshments required: coffee and biscuits on arrival, light buffet lunch.

You may wish to consider some of the following.

- Which individuals will they need to meet?
- Where will the meeting point be?
- How will they spend their time?
- What travel information do they need?

You should log this information on a diary page and prepare an itinerary for the day.

Time management

Given the various demands upon individuals in the workplace, it is important that various **time management** techniques are used in order to make the most of the working day. The following list details some of the techniques which could be used in order to improve time management.

- Try to review your current commitments and priorities at the beginning of the day.
- Spend a little time at the end of each day reviewing how far you have got with the priority work.
- Make sure that you have blocks of time allocated to finishing off a particular job. During these times you should not make yourself available to anyone
- Set up regular review meetings so that you can ensure that you are updated on current priorities by your manager.
- If you can, convince your employer to allow you to develop your skills either through in-house training or by external courses. The short-term loss of your presence will be more than compensated by your improved abilities.
- If you are not sure of how you spend your average working week, consider maintaining a time log which shows how long you spend at meetings, on word processing, on taking telephone calls and dealing with the public.
- Make sure that you fill in the necessary routine documents that may be required by other departments. These will need to be in on a particular day and should probably take priority.
- If you need to, consider re-prioritising your tasks so that you do not waste time on jobs which have a low priority.
- Try not to read every single word of the various documents and other paper-work which passes across your desk. You will need to develop the ability to skim-read or scan.

■ Organising individual work areas

Even though new employees are allocated a particular area in which to carry out their duties when they join an organisation, it will be their responsibility to maintain this work area and to ensure that it is used in the most efficient and effective manner possible. An individual's work area should always be kept neat and tidy, both from an efficiency point of view and that of health and safety. Obviously, the organisation would have to ensure that the individual has sufficient work space in order to comply with the Health and Safety at Work Act, as well as ensuring that there are no hazards in the area.

Individuals, however, will have to make sure that they make the best use of the space they have been allocated. This can be done by trying to establish a system which addresses the following points.

- Is all the information regularly required, such as telephone numbers and addresses, readily to hand, eg in a card index on the desk?
- Is there a supply of regularly used stationery, such as company headed paper and envelopes or compliments slips?

- Are the filing cabinet drawers up to date and any borrowed files accounted for?
- Are the extension telephone numbers of key personnel readily to hand?
- Is all confidential material locked away?
- Is the office furniture suitable for the user, eg is the chair giving suitable support to the back?
- When using a computer system, is 'good housekeeping' being practised with regard to the files stored on the hard drive? Good housekeeping is a term used for the regular and sensible naming and saving of material. If floppy disks are used for the storage of material, the user should ensure that back-up copies are made.

Student activity

As a group, can you think of any other considerations relating to your individual work area? Do you expect to have a specific work area allocated to you? How would your needs change if you had to share desk space with another member of staff?

■ Office layout

It has certainly been the case that the majority of organisations have tried all forms of office layout and design over the years. Some have decided to make the best use of the space that they have available and reduce the number of individual offices. Others have retained the more traditional approach and kept the individual office. Many organisations and their employees consider that an individual office is both a status symbol and a reward for a position in the hierarchy. Whatever the reason behind the allocation of space within the office environment, it is certainly true that the majority of organisations will seek to make the optimum use of the floor space by adopting an attitude of gradual development and change, in consultation with the employees and their managers. Equally, as the nature of the work carried out within the office changes, there will be a need to rationalise the work space to incorporate access to information (traditionally stored in filing cabinets, for instance), or to enable more employees to gain access to key pieces of equipment that are used on a daily basis, such as the photocopier, fax machine or computer-linked laser printers.

The cellular office

Given the fact that the majority of offices are rectangular, of a medium size and have a number of windows and doors, we can see that office layout and design may be hampered by the constraints of the physical environment. This more traditional 'space' is often referred to as the **'cellular office'**.

Advantages

- Each of the individual offices are lockable, thus providing the organisation with the ability to restrict access to certain rooms during the working day, and particularly at night. In addition to this, confidential information can be kept within a controlled environment and valuable equipment can be made safe when the office is not regularly occupied.
- Each of the individual offices is private, enabling the employees to carry out their work with the minimum of disruption and confusion that may be caused by other activities in the office, such as alterations and building work. Each office is self-contained, enabling meetings to take place and customers and clients to have private meetings with customer-liaison staff and managers if required.
- Each office contains a discrete work team involved in activities that may entail the participation of all those in that team. They will have the ability to interact with one another without the possibility of being interrupted or interrupting other employees.
- Each office has a specific purpose, and some may require additional ventilation, heating or lighting. These extra environmental considerations can be accommodated according to need, such as 'dust-free' environments for computer hardware, extra lighting for designers or draughtspersons, or additional heating for those in offices that have more window space or are closer to exits and other more open-plan areas such as the warehouse or machine areas.
- Each office can be purpose designed to accommodate a certain number of employees or different types of office machinery. Equally, the more noisy office machinery, such as printers, photocopiers and telex machines can be

housed in relatively sound-proofed areas that will not interfere with other work or contravene legislation covering the office environment.

Disadvantages

■ Each individual office means a number of walls, doors and windows will have to be incorporated into the building. Not only are there costs attached to this, but also these all take up space. In the majority of cases, space is the principal concern and, to this end, the organisation needs to make the best use of all of the space that it can afford. The siting of doors mean that desks and office equipment will need to be placed in such a way that they do not obstruct access or serve as a hazard if the building needs to be evacuated. Each partition that is put up in the office space will mean that more floor space is used up. This may mean also the resiting of cables and electrical points, all adding to the cost of the office for the organisation.

■ Each office brings with it the costs of redecoration, heating and lighting, all meaning that the individual costs of each room will be considerably more than would be the case if the office was open plan. In addition to this, the needs of each of the rooms will be different, and so the organisation may not be able to have a uniform look throughout the whole of the suite of offices.

■ Each set of employees within individual offices will have to be supervised by a manager or a supervisor. Whilst the number of managers and supervisors can be cut down for the open-plan office, the management will need to keep a close eye on the activities of the employees in all of the separate offices.

The open-plan office

The more integrated and **open-plan offices** have found considerable favour in the past few years. Despite this, there is still a need to have partial partitions

and some individual offices. The use of screens to show the limits of one department or section of the organisation is fairly commonplace, but some offices do not have any visible means of splitting up the office space. In these types of offices, it is common to find all grades and levels of employees from clerical workers and typists to managers and directors.

Advantages

- Allows for easier supervision of employees. All of the members of staff are in constant view of one or more supervisors or managers.
- Allows greater flexibility and communication between departments.
- Should mean greater efficiency in terms of work flow, as work will move freely from one desk to another without having to be transferred to another separate office area.
- Often adopted as part of the organisation's move towards centralisation of activities, staff and resources (see below).
- Should give managers and supervisors a better understanding of the nature and the demands of the work carried out by the rest of the employees. They will actually see the work being done and will be able to make an assessment as to the needs of the employees and their workloads.
- Cheaper to maintain and considerably more economical than smaller office rooms. As there is less space lost because of a lack of walls and other physical blocks, lighting, heating and cleaning are often simpler and cheaper.
- Offers considerable flexibility in terms of layout and space allocation. It is easy to change the look of the office and the amount of space given to each of the separate departments or sections.

Disadvantages

The disadvantages apply to most, although not all, open-plan offices.

- Quite noisy because of the lack of partitions and walls.
- Suffer from a considerable amount of 'through-traffic' with employees moving around the office in the course of their work. This may cause interruptions and disruption to those who are trying to concentrate.
- Subject to the problems of reduced security and the possibility of theft. The advantages of having most of the equipment and information readily to hand means that unauthorised individuals may gain access to materials and machinery that they should not be allowed to use or see.
- Lack of private areas for confidential meetings and secure areas to store sensitive information. The office may have to incorporate separate office areas for these purposes. Banks, for example, with their open-plan approach to the majority of the work space, will still have rooms available for confidential meetings to take place as and when required. Some of the offices will not be in constant use, but can be used by any authorised individual upon request. Normal procedure would involve some kind of booking system.
- A source of infection and illness. Common colds and other ailments can be passed on as a result of the intermingling of employees and the lack of physical barriers.

- Still needs areas that are partitioned off to house equipment and machinery that are too noisy to be used in the general office area.
- Private offices still required for the senior management of the organisation. They will expect to have a discrete area given to them as a sign of their status in the organisation.
- Standardised lighting and ventilation may not suit everyone's tastes and needs.
- Few walls to hang pictures, charts and tables. As a result, the impression may be very impersonal or bland.

Student activity

Individually, consider either the college/centre or your place of work in terms of comments which we have made regarding office layout. Firstly, identify the type of office environment in which you work or study and then try to identify specific advantages and disadvantages of the layout used. Make some suitable suggestions regarding improvements to the office layout. Feedback your thoughts and conclusions to the rest of the group.

■ Legislation affecting the working environment

Most organisations recognise the fact that if they provide pleasant and clean working environments, their employees will be more inclined to work more efficiently and effectively. This is not to say that good work cannot be carried out under difficult and poor conditions, but an adequately organised office that offers a degree of privacy and quiet is more likely to provide the right results.

Recognising the fact that some offices operate in the worst possible conditions, the government has gradually framed a number of laws which aim to control and eliminate the worst excesses of poor conditions and management of the office environment. The main points that need to be considered are found in the **Offices, Shops and Railway Premises Act 1963** and the **Health and Safety at Work Act 1974**. As we have already seen in the previous chapter, they cover the following:

- At least 40 square feet of floor space should be allocated per employee.
- The temperature of the office must not be less than 16°C after the first hour of work.
- There should be an ample supply of drinking water, which is accessible to all employees. This must be maintained and come directly from the mains water supply.
- There should be adequate first-aid facilities available to the employees. There must also be at least one first-aid box available for the first 150 employees and another for each 150 employees (or part thereof).

- The employer is required to have a fire certificate from the local fire authority if there are more than 20 employees. This means that the premises must have been inspected and that all of the necessary standards relating to fire precautions have been met. This will include the installation of fire alarms and fire doors if appropriate.
- There must be a simple and clearly understood system by which accidents are reported. This will usually take the form of an accident book.

Other important statutory requirements include the following.

Management of Health and Safety at Work Regulations 1992

This major piece of legislation, an updated and modified version of the Health and Safety at Work Act 1974, aims to provide a systematic and well-organised set of guidelines covering health and safety. They include the following.

- Employers are required to assess any potential risks that employees may have to face and take preventive measures to cope with them.
- This risk assessment must be continually monitored by a group of employers working closely with at least five employees.
- Employers are required to employ specialists whose sole responsibility it is to implement the preventive measures, as well as to provide information for all other employees within the organisation.
- Employers are further required to carry out regular screenings of their employees to make sure that they have not suffered any ill-effects as a result of carrying out their duties. If appropriate, any health hazards which have been identified should be addressed immediately.
- Employees who have been given the duties of safety representatives should be regularly consulted, provided with time and space to carry out their investigations and given the authority to act on them.

Health and Safety (Display Screen Equipment) Regulations 1992

This act is designed to protect employees who spend considerable amounts of their working hours in front of a computer screen. The main points of the legislation are as follows.

- Employees must receive sufficient breaks from the screen.
- Work should not be repetitive and the employee should be given a variety of tasks.
- Basic safety requirements must be satisfied covering the screen itself, the design of the keyboard, as well as the shape and height of the desk and chair being used.
- Regular eye tests must be provided by the employer and if the employee needs special spectacles in order to carry out his or her tasks, they should be provided by the employer.
- Efficient lighting and proper ventilation should be provided in the room where the employee is using the computer.

Provision and Use of Work Equipment Regulations 1992

This act covers all equipment from major production-line machinery to hand-held tools. The legislation requires employers to

- Take into consideration how and where equipment will be used, and choose the least hazardous methods of production.
- Purchase only equipment that conforms with any applicable EC safety directive.
- Ensure that employees are given sufficient information to enable them to use any equipment safely – where appropriate, training and retraining should be offered.
- Ensure that all equipment is serviced regularly.
- Ensure that potentially dangerous machinery has appropriate guards to prevent injury.
- Provide protection for those using hazardous materials.
- Ensure that work is carried out in an environment which has sufficient light.
- Display any relevant warnings regarding potential dangers.

Manual Handling Operations Regulations 1992

These Regulations were implemented to try to prevent unnecessary injury at work. They cover lifting, pushing, pulling, carrying and moving objects at work, and offer advice as to the correct manner in which these should be carried out.

Personal Protective Equipment at Work Regulations 1992

The term 'personal protective equipment' includes life-jackets, harnesses, head, hand and foot protection, glasses and goggles, and clothing designed to be visible at all times and in all conditions. The Regulations state that the protective equipment must be fit for the purpose for which it is intended, as well as actually fitting the employee. The equipment must conform with EC regulations and it must be suitably stored, cleaned regularly and replaced if defective. In addition, employees must be trained in the correct use of the equipment.

The Factories Act 1961

This act covers a wide range of different organisations, focusing on the use of machinery. The key features of this piece of legislation are as follows.

- The employer must provide toilet and washing facilities.
- Premises should be adequately heated and ventilated.
- The employer must make sure that floors, stairs and passageways are not obstructed in any way.
- All floors should have a non-slippery surface.
- Potentially dangerous machinery should be fenced off to protect employees.
- The employer must ensure there are adequate fire escapes, which are well sign-posted and maintained regularly.
- Fire doors themselves should never be locked or obstructed.

■ Health and safety at work

The employer's responsibilities

All employers must comply with the following health and safety requirements.

- To provide a safe working environment.
- To provide adequate welfare facilities.
- To ensure entrances and exits are safe.
- To ensure equipment and systems used are safe and regularly serviced.
- To make sure that items needed for use in handling or storage are safe.
- To make sure that dangerous or toxic (poisonous) materials are housed in safe containers.
- To provide instruction, training or supervision regarding working practices and materials used.
- To ensure that all accidents are rigorously investigated and the causes are dealt with promptly.

If the employer is negligent, he or she may be prosecuted.

An employer must provide a reasonable standard of health and safety, which covers

- employees
- visiting workers (such as individuals servicing machinery or production-line equipment)
- customers
- visitors and representatives from other organisations
- the general public.

It is also worth remembering that this responsibility extends beyond the premises themselves, to any health and safety problems which may arise from the work undertaken within those premises.

Bearing in mind that the local authority has the right to enter the employer's premises at any time, the management of health and safety regulations should be an on-going process. An inspector from the Health and Safety Executive may insist on examining equipment and legally enforcing the requirements of the various health and safety legislations.

Ideally, a new employer should

- notify the local authority responsible for health and safety of the new business and state the company name and address
- contact either the Environmental Health Department (in the case of offices, shops, restaurants and warehouses) or the Health and Safety Executive area office (for other businesses)
- obtain employer's liability insurance
- display the insurance certificate in the workplace
- prepare a written statement of health and safety policy (this applies if the employer has more than five employees)
- display the Health and Safety at Work Act poster, or distribute a leaflet which contains this information
- make an assessment of the potential risks within the workplace
- maintain a written record of this risk assessment (if the employer has more than five employees).

The employee's responsibility

Employees have a legal responsibility to cooperate with their employer on health and safety matters.

If an employee is negligent and causes injury to himself or herself or another person, the employer may be faced with a problem. The employee may claim that it was not really his or her fault. As long as the employer provides safe working conditions, then apart from the accidents caused by negligence, there should be no real concerns here.

Another possible area of concern is when an employee deliberately puts someone else's life in danger. Depending on the circumstances, he or she could not only be dismissed but also be the subject of criminal and civil proceedings.

Protection of individuals and the workplace

There are a number of incidents that might happen in the workplace that could put people in danger. Above all, before you consider the workplace itself, the employees or other individuals must come first. Remember that premises, equipment and other items are replaceable, people are not. It is therefore very important that you make sure that the people are safe before trying to sort out the damage or danger to the premises. Never put your self at risk for the sake of possessions or property. Tackle a problem only if there is little or no risk to yourself or other people.

There are a number of ways of protecting the workplace without putting yourself or others in danger. Fire extinguishers, alarms and other equipment are designed for you to protect or save the premises from danger. As you will see, you should always make sure that you know how to use the equipment that is available and never try to use something that you have not been trained for. There are other 'in-built' systems that can help to protect the workplace. These include sprinklers, fire alarms and smoke detectors. If all of these are working correctly, the systems should be able to deal with the majority of problems.

It is said that all accidents occur as a result of 'failures of control'. This means firstly that the organisation has not made sure that there are physical safeguards in place, and secondly, it has not organised effective safety control systems.

Organisations are keen to improve their safety record and many

- set practical goals for health and safety that everyone can understand
- encourage employees to work together in a safe manner
- encourage employees to meet the safety goals within the limits available to them
- make sure that employees use the available resources to the best effect
- make sure that employees accept responsibility for health and safety
- make sure that ways are developed so that health and safety can be measured against a particular standard.

Student activity

Try to find out how to turn off some of the machinery at your college. The computers should have a wall-mounted junction box that cuts off the electricity to all of them. Where is it?

Medical emergencies

The **medical emergencies** that could occur in the workplace may be as a result of fire, electrical equipment, hazardous substances.

You should never attempt to tackle a fire unless you have called the emergency services and made sure that you are not putting yourself at risk.

All employees should treat electrical equipment with care. Always remember the following key safety points.

- Make sure that you understand the instructions before attempting to use an electrical appliance.
- Switch off the machinery or electrical appliance before plugging it in.
- Make sure that you report any damage or fault that you find. This includes the cables.

There are various regulations that are aimed at protecting individuals from the dangers of hazardous substances that might contaminate them at work.

- Make sure that you follow the organisation's safety procedures when dealing with hazardous substances.
- Read the hazard warning signs and labels on containers. They should tell you whether the substance is dangerous and whether it may cause injury if it touches your skin or if you inhale it.
- Make sure you know the actions that you should take if any of the substance spills on to your skin or your clothing.
- Make sure you never take clothing or protective equipment home with you that is stained or soaked by hazardous substances.
- Make sure that you never transfer hazardous substances into smaller containers that do not have the right labels on them. Unlabelled containers are a potential hazard to all who might come in contact with them.
- Make sure that you work in a dust-free environment. Continued exposure to dusty air can damage your lungs and, in time, other parts of your body.

Coping in an emergency

Rapid and clear thinking is the key to ensuring that panic and additional dangers are avoided in the event of the need to evacuate the building or in the vicinity of an accident. In the case of fire, remember that it can spread quickly. You must warn anyone who could be at risk; then alert the emergency services immediately. Always try to be calm – people tend to panic in these situations.

Some incidents may mean simply that a room or an area of the workplace should be evacuated. This may be as a result of a machine or piece of equipment becoming dangerous or faulty. It is better to be safe than sorry and no one should be put at risk if there is a problem.

Student activity

What would you do in the following situations?

1 A computer screen has exploded and pieces of glass are scattered about the room.
2 A hot-water tap has ruptured and there is scalding hot water spraying into the room.

If materials become dangerous, usually as a result of fire or some other problem, you should do your best to make sure that as much of the material is moved away from the source of danger as possible.

Assuming that you respond quickly enough, there should not be any reason to worry about injuries at this point. If the worst has happened and someone is hurt, then you should do your utmost to make sure that the casualty is removed from immediate exposure to the danger before raising the alarm. The injured should be your priority, provided that you are not putting yourself in danger as a result. Without putting yourself at risk, you should always try to follow the steps given below.

- Do your best to make sure that everyone is out of the building or at least out of immediate danger.
- Shut all doors behind you. This is a double check that a room has been cleared and, in the event of a fire, it will help to stop it spreading.
- Look out for notices that give you the location of the fire points and assembly points. Fire exits will also be marked. Head for these and do not deviate from the routes that are shown unless the route is blocked.
- Familiarise yourself with the guidelines in operation at your workplace. Always follow these instructions in the case of an evacuation.

Student activity

What would you do in the following situations?

1 A colleague's eye has been hurt. He says that it is only sore and does not want you to make a fuss.
2 A colleague has just slipped on the floor. She is not hurt, but tells you that this is the third time that this has happened.

Student activity

Two people are painting the walls of a building. Suddenly, the scaffolding on which they are standing gives way and they both fall about 6 metres to the ground. They both appear to be seriously injured. You saw what happened and are a qualified first-aider.

What will you do? Discuss this in pairs, then feedback your suggestion to the rest of the group.

What would you do in the event of an accident?

We hope that the suggested way of dealing with the situation was something like this.

1 Give first aid to the two people.
2 Make sure that someone has called an ambulance.
3 Clear the area – the rest of the scaffolding might fall on someone.

Student activity

Your colleague is using an electric drill, the wiring is faulty and he receives a severe electric shock. The drill falls on to a metal table and your colleague collapses. You are a qualified first-aider.

What will you do? Discuss this in pairs, then feedback your suggestions to the rest of the group.

So, what were the right actions to take? It was a little more tricky this time.

1 Switch off the power – otherwise you would get a shock, too.
2 Give first aid.
3 If the casualty needs it, and he probably will, resuscitation may be needed, ie you will have to help him to start breathing again.
4 Get medical help.

Student activity

Here is the last situation to try out. Some poisonous and inflammable liquid has spilt out on to two of your colleagues. It is all over their clothing. You see what has happened and must act fast. You are a qualified first-aider.

What will you do? Discuss this in pairs, then feedback your suggestions to the rest of the group.

There are a number of points to think about here.

1 Assuming that the liquid is not giving off toxic (poisonous) fumes, your colleagues should be able to get out of the area themselves, but they would need to take off the clothing and be checked for injuries by a medical expert.
2 If they cannot get out of the area themselves, then it would be a priority to get them out. You would need help here.
3 Once they are clear of the area, you should give first aid and call for medical help.

Reporting an accident

There are some very important reasons for reporting accidents at work.

■ To help ensure that further accidents are avoided, and that safety measures can be brought into effect in the future.

ACCIDENT REPORT FORM

Employee's name ....

> This is your own full name, or the name by which you are known at work.

Employee's address ....

....

....

> This is your home address – you should include your full address and postcode.

Particulars of accident

Date ....**Time** ....**Department** ....

> You should put the date and the time of the accident. You should also put in the name of the department in which it happened (if not appropriate, then put down your own department).

Treatment needed

....

....

> You should detail the treatment given to the accident victim at the scene of the accident, whether this was given by you or another person.

Hospital treatment

....

....

> If known, you should write down the nature of the treatment given to the accident victim in hospital.

Nature of injury

....

....

> State exactly what physical injuries the victim sustained.

Treated by ....

> Again, both at the workplace and the hospital, who treated the accident victim?

Witnessed by ....

> Were there any independent witnesses who saw how the accident happened? If so, who were they?

Description of accident

....

....

> Describe exactly what happened, ie how did the accident occur?

Activity undertaken at time of accident

....

....

....

| What was the accident victim doing immediately prior to the accident? You should describe this in detail. |

Was the person authorised to do this activity?   **YES/NO**

| This is an important question and has a bearing on who was to blame for the accident. If the injured person was not authorised to do the activity that caused the accident, then the employer may not be liable for the injuries. |

Was the accident caused by machinery?   **YES/NO**

| Another important question: did a machine actually cause the accident? The employer and the safety inspectors may want to know whether the machine was safe to be used. |

Was the machine in operation?   **YES/NO**

| If the machine was being used at the time, and was found to be the cause of the accident, it is important to find out whether the operations of the machine whilst it was working had caused the accident itself. |

Were the protective guards being used?   **YES/NO**

| Legally, they should have been, but many operators do not bother with the guards that are meant to protect them. This would be a breach of the Health and Safety Regulations and the injured person could be held responsible for the injuries. |

Signed .... **Date** ....

| Make sure that you sign the report so that your signature can be read, and date it. |

Figure 7.1   How to fill in an accident report form

- To make sure that any insurance claims can be made. If a person is hurt at work, he or she will have to prove that it happened there and not somewhere else.
- To make sure that additional precautions are taken in the future as the accident may have revealed a risk that had not been considered before.

If you witness an accident at work and it is not serious enough to have to call the emergency services, then it should be reported at least verbally to your superior. Your manager will have the responsibility of making sure that action is taken to avoid this situation occurring again.

You may be expected to fill in an **accident report form**. This will detail the nature of the accident and a full explanation of the situation as and when it happened. Figure 7.1 looks at a sample accident report form and considers each of the various questions.

Safe working practices

The main responsibility for making sure that **safe working practices** are adopted lies with the employer. Whether you work in an office, shop, factory or any other form of workplace, it is essential that you try to prevent accidents. Here are some common accidents that could occur at any time and in any place.

- People tripping over things left on the floor.
- People slipping on wet or over-polished floors.
- People bumping into things because the work area is too cluttered.
- People injuring themselves on sharp edges or corners of furniture.
- Boxes, for example, being stacked too high and falling on people when they attempt to move one.
- Sharp tools or equipment that cause injury when they are picked up.
- People hurting themselves by having to work their way around blocked passageways.

Many things that we do can cause temporary or long-term injuries. One of the most common is Repetitive Strain Injury or RSI. The main causes of this injury are.

- incorrect posture
- having to work too hard for too many hours
- having to make repeated movements, particularly awkward ones
- having to sit awkwardly with arms or head in an uncomfortable position
- not resting enough between periods of work.

Student activity

Do you know anyone suffering from RSI? How has he or she suffered and what could have been done to prevent this happening? Make a list of your findings.

Safety checks

In order to make sure that the workplace is a safe place to operate in, it is a good idea to make sure that a number of regular checks are made. We can identify these as falling into the following areas.

- Fire prevention.
- General office safety.
- Hygiene.
- Machine safety.
- Dangerous substances.
- Transport and handling goods.
- General maintenance.

Figures 7.2, 7.3 and 7.4 provide some checklists that you could use for inspection of the various areas mentioned above:

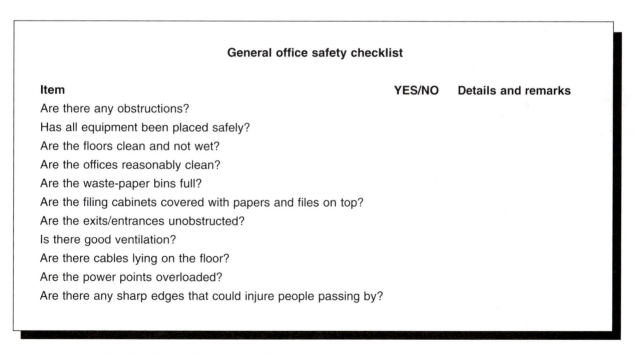

Fire prevention checklist

Item	YES/NO	Details and remarks
Are the fire extinguishers clearly accessible?		
Have the fire extinguishers been inspected recently?		
Are the fire alarms working?		
Are all of the fire doors clear?		
Have the sprinklers been checked recently?		
Have the fuse boxes been checked recently?		
Has the fire alarm been checked recently?		
Are all the inflammable materials and liquids labelled?		
Are all the inflammable materials and liquids stored correctly?		
Do all of the employees know what to do in the event of a fire?		

Figure 7.2 Checklist to identify fire hazards in the workplace

General office safety checklist

Item	YES/NO	Details and remarks
Are there any obstructions?		
Has all equipment been placed safely?		
Are the floors clean and not wet?		
Are the offices reasonably clean?		
Are the waste-paper bins full?		
Are the filing cabinets covered with papers and files on top?		
Are the exits/entrances unobstructed?		
Is there good ventilation?		
Are there cables lying on the floor?		
Are the power points overloaded?		
Are there any sharp edges that could injure people passing by?		

Figure 7.3 Checklist to identify general office hazards in the workplace

Hygiene checklist

Item	YES/NO	Details and remarks
Is the area regularly cleaned?		
Are the toilet facilities clean?		
Is the protective clothing regularly cleaned?		
Is hot water and soap available?		
Are there clean towels or disposable towels available?		
Is there any sign of mice, rats or insects?		

Figure 7.4 Checklist to identify hygiene hazards in the workplace

Student activity

In groups, choose one of the following and draw up a checklist similar to the ones shown above.

- machine safety
- dangerous substances
- transport and handling goods
- general maintenance.

Keywords

The keywords you should know for this chapter are listed below. Check to make sure you understand the meaning of each word. Discuss those you are unsure of with your tutor.

accident reports

cellular office

electronic diaries

Health and Safety at Work

medical emergencies

open plan office

RSI

safe working practices

time management

work schedules

Examination practice

Short-answer questions

1 What is an open-plan office?

2 The cellular office may have a number of disadvantages, but state at least three advantages.

3 Give three basic ways that employees could organise their individual workload.

4 What is RSI?

5 Outline three time management techniques.

6 What is an electronic diary?

7 Give three tips on how to organise your own work area.

8 Briefly describe the purposes of the Health and Safety at Work Act.

9 State three possible causes of fatigue in the workplace.

10 State three things that should be included in an organisation's safety policy.

Essay questions

You work as an administrative assistant in a busy, open-plan office in the centre of a small town. Although the office is quite spacious, there are a large number of individuals working there all with their own computers, printers and filing cabinets. As new employees have joined the organisation, people have been moved around in a haphazard way and additional desks and terminals have just been squeezed into any available space. The office manager has recognised that this has begun to affect the efficiency of the office and has set up a working party to look at the overall office environment and general layout.

1 You have all been asked to prepare a list of the features you would like to see in an ideal office environment. Specifically, you will need to suggest the following:

a how a large office could be set up in such a way as to minimise the amount of disruption and noise from other workers.

b how an ideal individual work area should be laid out.

2 There is still a tremendous amount of paper-based filing and other traditional forms of note-taking and messaging. Since the organisation is keen to improve the efficiency of inter-departmental communication, you have been asked to suggest a number of ways in which new technology could improve work planning, scheduling and workloads. You will need to consider the following:

a what specific new technologies could be employed to improve the services provided by the various secretaries?

b how could the organisation generally improve communications within the organisation?

3 Many of the staff are unaware of the various pieces of legislation which relate to office work. You have been asked to prepare a short summary of all the relevant legislation, including the Health and Safety at Work Act, which could be circulated to all existing employees, as well as being included in the induction pack for new starters.

4 As an experienced member of staff you have been asked to design a short training programme for new employees. It is intended that this training is part of the organisation's attempts to improve efficiency and overall communications. You will need only to outline briefly all the major considerations which should be included in the training programme. Your attention is drawn to following areas:

a how to plan work, schedule and organise workloads

b how to organise you own individual work area

c how to ensure that your own computer works efficiently and that no vital information is lost.

Administration functions and procedures

8

■ Introduction

In this section of the book we intend to look at the procedures an organisation may have in place in order to ensure the following.

- the role and duties of the receptionist with particular reference to dealing with customers and clients
- the methods used to ensure adequate stock control
- the opening and distribution of incoming mail
- the preparation of mail leaving the organisation.

Obviously, all of these activities are very important in ensuring that the business maintains suitable records and that the company image is upheld.

■ Roles and duties of the receptionist

The work of receptionists may be extremely varied. This will depend upon the nature of the business in which they are working and the size of the operation. Typically, the role will include some of the following

- typing
- operating a switchboard
- using a computer
- filing
- giving out brochures and sales literature to customers and other visitors
- opening and arranging incoming mail (including registered mail, parcels and other deliveries)
- making tea or coffee for visitors
- ensuring that the reception desk is never left unattended
- the ability to give basic first aid, should the need arise.

It may be that the person calling at the business is a first-time caller. He or she may be making an enquiry regarding the services, products or activities available at the business with a view to placing an order or negotiating a long-term contract. Because this is the first time he or she has had contact with the business, it is very important that the impression this person receives is a good one. The receptionist should deal with an initial enquiry in the following way.

- Greet the caller promptly in a polite and courteous manner.
- Identify the best person to deal with the caller.
- Contact the person concerned to find out if they are free.
- If the person concerned is available and willing to see the caller, the receptionist should direct the caller to the office or ask the caller to wait for a member of staff to accompany him or her to the relevant department.

If the person concerned is not free, the receptionist should

- ask the caller if he or she is prepared to wait, and if so, make the individual comfortable by offering refreshment and magazines

- ask the caller if he or she would like to make an appointment for another day/time
- ask the caller if he or she would prefer to see someone else, and, if so, contact that person.

The receptionist should log the caller in the **visitors book** and make a mental note of the name of the person so that he or she can be greeted by name in the future. It may be that during the course of the day receptionists will have to deal with a series of requests from both members of staff and from visitors. In order to deal with these requests efficiently, receptionists will have to ensure the following.

- A good knowledge of the personnel within the business.
- A good knowledge of the layout of the business in terms of the location of particular individuals and departments.
- Up-to-date information regarding client and customer telephone numbers, fax numbers or addresses, plus the names of those people who are regular contacts at other organisations.
- The ability to remember people's names and to be able to recognise voices on the telephone.
- A good knowledge of the work being carried out within the business and any new products and services which are planned.
- An understanding that no confidential information should be given to anyone without the appropriate authority.

Receptionists may have to deal regularly with suppliers who are calling at the organisation. These suppliers may or may not be expected. Often sales representatives will make appointments to call at regular intervals to take orders for goods they sell. On the other hand, it may be that they will call simply because they are in the area. Receptionists will get to know the suppliers by name and know who they wish to see when they arrive. They will also know whether the supplier is a welcome visitor to the organisation. They should use tact and diplomacy if dealing with an unwelcome visitor.

Most suppliers will use a **business card** which states their name and organisation plus their telephone and fax number. The receptionist should take the business card from the supplier and contact the person he or she has called to see. If the supplier has an appointment he or she should be directed or taken to the office concerned. If not, then the receptionist should contact the member of staff the supplier wishes to see and make alternative arrangements.

Routine callers are usually those who are expected. The receptionist would be aware of their visit as they would have been logged in the **appointments diary**.

Student activity

Compile two lists, one of good experience, one of bad, when visiting an organisation for the first time. Compare your list with those of the remainder of the group.

It should always be remembered that individual organisations will have their own systems in place to which their members of staff should comply. This would be true whatever the type or size of an organisation. During your time at the institution in which you are studying at present, you will be instructed to carry out tasks to a particular standard or layout. When you commence your working life, it may be that the organisation which employs you has different standards and procedures. Once employed, it will be your duty to follow such policies and procedures as are set down by your employers. These procedures may be concerned with the layout of a business letter, or the logging procedures carried out whilst on reception duty. The procedures will be made clear to you when you commence work and you should ask for assistance if they are not clear.

First impressions and physical appearance

As we have said, the impression given to clients and customers is vitally important to the image of the organisation. With the reception and its staff being the first contact with the organisation that a client may have, the way the receptionists present themselves is of prime importance.

That does mean to say that receptionists need to spend large amounts of money on clothes and personal grooming. In fact, very often large organisations supply their reception staff with a uniform which is worn during working hours. You need only to look at the counter staff in building societies and travel agents to see that these are not really uniforms, but interchangeable outfits which carry the corporate image of the organisation.

Student activity

As you are currently studying this course, it is assumed that you are expecting to find employment in the near future. Think about the clothes you have in your wardrobe or cupboard at the moment. Are they suitable for work? What changes would you have to make once you are working for five days a week? Write a list of the items you may need to buy and their expected cost.

Logging procedures

Diaries

An appointments diary would be kept within the department (probably by the secretary) to show when each member of staff would be either engaged or entertaining a visitor.

Staff in and out book

It could be that the employees of the organisation have to leave the premises during the course of the working day to carry out some of their duties. For this reason a **staff in and out book** would be kept on reception for them to complete as they leave and then when they return. The receptionist would need to ensure that this is done each time so that a record is kept of the whereabouts of each member of staff.

Personal telephone calls

It may be that it is organisational policy that employees using the telephone for personal use are billed at the end of a certain period for the calls made. The calls would be logged on a form.

Petty cash

It may be that the organisation keeps a small amount of cash for use on a casual basis. It may be used to pay the taxi or bus fares of employees who need to leave the office during working hours to collect goods, or to purchase small items of office stationery or equipment which may be required urgently. Obviously, this will not be a large amount of money, but it will still be important that a check is made on how and where the money is being spent. The person requesting the money will have to complete a **petty cash voucher.** The details of each petty cash voucher will then be transferred to the petty cash book by the petty cashier (the holder of the money).

Expenses claim forms

If it is organisational policy to reimburse its employees for any expenses incurred whilst travelling on behalf of the company, then the logging of these expenses is a requirement. An expenses claim form would be completed as a one-off exercise if it were an unusual trip, or as a matter of routine if the employee travels regularly for the organisation.

Stamp purchase record

If stamps are used for the dispatch of outgoing mail from the organisation, a record will be kept of the stamps used.

Staff holiday rota forms

It may be part of the duties of the receptionist to keep a rota of the dates and duration of staff holidays within the organisation. This could be completed using a wall chart. These are available complete with stick-on coloured symbols, so that each member of staff could be allocated a different colour or symbol. This allows for the complete staff requirements to be shown on one chart.

Stationery requisition form

It could be that one of the duties of the receptionist is to issue and monitor stock to other members of staff. In order to log all these stationery requirements, a stock requisition form could be completed by the member of staff and handed to the receptionist each time an item of stationery is required. If it is the case that the receptionist is responsible for issuing stationery, then he or she will also be responsible for ordering new stocks to replenish those which have been issued. Every so often it will be necessary to order more routine items of stationery. In order to keep a check on these items arriving in the reception and being issued out of the reception, the person in charge of this process will complete a **stock control card**. The receptionist will deal with all the logging procedures mentioned above, perhaps on a daily or weekly basis. She or he will, however, find it necessary to be familiar with other documentation which will arrive at the organisation, or, similarly, will leave the organisation on a regular basis.

■ The reception area

An added feature of the reception area is that the organisation can take advantage of this space to advertise itself. For example, in the reception area of your college, there are probably some displays which advertise other courses and programmes of study available now or in the future.

Organisations may use the reception area to advertise new and existing products. They may also display photographs of key personnel within the organisation, as well as those of any parent or subsidiary companies. In addition, should the organisation have received any certificates or awards, for example, the Queen's Award to Industry, these will be displayed in the reception area to help promote the reputation and image of the organisation. Alternatively, photographs of recent presentations, perhaps for long-service awards or retirements, may be on show there.

All of the above ways of displaying information help organisations to be seen as innovative, forward-thinking and caring, each of which help with the image they are seeking to promote. It would be one of the duties of the receptionist to ensure that the display boards are neat and tidy and that the information contained on them is up to date.

With so many people visiting the premises via the reception area each day, health and safety is an important aspect. To ensure a safe working environment, as well as the health and safety of other employees and visitors, receptionists need to consider the following.

- Are the floors torn, worn, slippery or soiled?
- Is there sufficient light for working?
- Are there any trailing cables, or do any have loose connections?
- Are any of the corridors leading from reception cluttered, making them difficult to walk through?
- Is any item of furniture in an unsafe position, eg with drawers in front of doors of passageways, or in an unsafe condition, eg with loose legs?
- Are fire exits labelled and easily accessible? If the area is a no-smoking zone, are there adequate signs?
- Are the facilities for making refreshments for visitors safe? Is the kettle easy to reach or are wires trailing?
- Are the filing cabinets situated in a safe place? Does the receptionist ensure that drawers are closed?

Naturally, with so many visitors passing through the reception area, the organisation would need to take steps to ensure that its equipment, materials and information are kept securely. A great deal of confidential material could be available within the premises. If the reception area is not secure, open access to other offices would be available should anyone require it. For this reason, the following steps should be taken.

- Reception should be staffed at all times. Cover should be a priority for lunch and coffee breaks and for holiday and sickness periods. Some larger organisations employ gate-keepers who vet visitors before they even reach reception.
- Receptionists should ensure that all the documentation regarding visitors, ie the appointments and visitors books are completed accurately. This will help ensure that nobody is on the premises without their knowledge.
- Telephone conversations of a confidential nature should not take place when a visitor is in the reception area. The receptionist should offer to call back if the information cannot be discussed at the time.
- Paperwork should be kept out of sight of any visitors. Receptionists should ensure that their work is placed face-down on the desk until they can deal with it.
- Similarly, current work on the VDU of a word processor should not be displayed when visitors are waiting in the reception area. The receptionist should tilt the screen in a direction suitable for ensuring this.
- The receptionist should not enter into any conversations with a visitor which could be of a confidential nature.
- Filing cabinet drawers should be locked.

■ Stock control systems

These are the procedures which are required in order to ensure that stock is ordered, delivered and otherwise handled with efficiency. It is also essential that stock control encompasses dealing with customer demand in the most cost-effective manner. As we will see, good stock rotation incorporating re-ordering systems are an integral part of stock control.

The principal focus of stock control is on the re-order quantities or re-order levels which determine the level of stock when a new order is placed. An essential part of this is **economic order quantity (EOQ)**. This attempts to calculate the level of stocks which will minimise the costs. Essentially, economic order quantity considers

- the costs of holding stock
- the fact that the more stock which is held the higher the costs
- the average cost of ordering stock
- the fact that larger orders mean that unit costs and delivery costs are reduced.

Buffer stocks

This is the desired minimum level of stock which will be held by a business. It will always hold this minimum level in order to account for problems in production or, perhaps, being let down by its suppliers. Other reasons for holding **buffer stock** are that some suppliers may deliver substandard materials or that demand may unexpectedly rise.

Theoretically, the more efficient the organisation, the lower the buffer stock. If an organisation wishes to be a true **'just-in-time'** producer, buffer stocks can be eliminated. Obviously, there are enormous advantages in not having any buffer stock, the principal one being that **capital** is not tied up in stock holding when it could be used more profitably elsewhere.

Re-order levels

Again, this is a way of establishing a minimum level of stock before an order is placed. In order to arrive at an appropriate **re-order level**, the business needs to consider

- how long it will take the supplier to deliver once the order has been placed (this is known as the lead time)
- the level of demand for the particular product
- the level of buffer stock currently held.

There are three basic ways of establishing a form of re-order level.

- **Fixed re-order levels** – using the EOQ, the business can make repeat orders at varying intervals.
- **Fixed re-order intervals** – although this system ignores EOQ, it does make sure that stock levels are regularly replenished. As a direct consequence of using this system, the business may have wildly fluctuating stock levels.
- **Two-bin systems** – this is a simple system but quite effective. The stock is split into two parts or bins. Once one of the bins is empty, a new order is placed with the supplier. It is important to make sure that stock is removed

from bin one if this is the bin in use; if stock is removed from the second bin, this would upset the system. When the supplier has delivered the replacement stock, the first bin is filled and the second bin is now the one in use.

Maximum and minimum stock levels

There are obviously some advantages and disadvantages related to holding too much or too little stock. We will begin by looking at having too much stock. The key points are

- storage costs will be high
- the stock needs to be insured
- the stock will occupy a greater space
- the space could be used for more productive means
- the funds tied up in stock cannot be used for other more profitable purposes
- inevitably, there may be unsold or unused stock, particularly if the organisation is concerned with products which have a definite life span or are superseded by more up-to-date products
- there may be an increase in the amount of shrinkage as a result of theft.

The points to consider if too little stock is held include the following.

- The business will not be able to cope with unexpected increases in demand.
- The business may be faced with the problem of having to tell customers that it cannot supply them.
- There may be severe implications the production process if suppliers are unable to deliver urgently needed materials or components immediately.
- Order costs may be high since the business will have to pay a delivery cost per order and if these orders are low, then the unit costs will be much higher.
- Unless the business has agreed an annual turnover figure with its suppliers, it will not be able to take advantage of bulk discounts for large orders.

Stock rotation

This is an administrative and physical process that aims to ensure that older stock is used before newer stock. This process is absolutely essential as it aims to prevent unnecessary wastage. Some products could become obsolete, pass their sell-by date or become otherwise unsaleable (through deterioration, etc.).

The most common form of stock rotation is known as **Fifo** (first-in-first-out). This form of stock control and rotation identifies the stock by date and ensures that the oldest stock is the first to be used or sold. Fifo is very common within UK businesses.

Lifo, or last-in-first-out, aims to eliminate inflation from the business's profits. It makes the assumption that the stock being used or sold at the moment is the last stock that was purchased. This means that the stock that is left is assumed to be the oldest stock. In other words, the old stock was purchased at the old, pre-inflation price.

Both of these stock rotation systems have their advantages and disadvantages. Broadly speaking, they relate to their effects on the profit and loss statement and the balance sheet. Lifo, by pricing the stock at the earliest price, cushions the effects of rising prices on the organisation's costs. It does not allow the organisation's profit position to be increased artificially. When there is inflation, Lifo does give the organisation a rather more accurate profit figure. However, the advantages here are counterbalanced by the fact that the stock is undervalued on the balance sheet.

Stock wastage

Typically, wastage involves the inefficient use of resources. A good stock control system aims to minimise any stock wastage. Stock wastage tends to occur when the business has not adequately rotated its stock. If the business fails to use old stock before it uses its newly acquired stock, there may be a danger of discovering that the old stock is no longer useful to it. There may be a number of reasons for this.

- The specification for a particular stock item has changed.
- The stock item has a definite use-by date. This is particularly true of consumable products such as food.
- The stock has suffered damage or deterioration as a result of being stored for too long.

The business needs to consider ways in which it can reduce stock wastage and this may have to include a radical restructuring of the stock control systems. One of the principal reasons for stock wastage is over-ordering.

Information technology and stock control

Databases are used extensively by businesses which have computerised stock control systems. Individuals involved in stock control are responsible for adding and subtracting stocks from the records in order to give the business a clear picture of the current stock levels. In order to make sure that the computerised system is being used correctly, businesses institute a series of regular stock checks in order to identify discrepancies or inconsistencies in the recording systems. Many of these computerised stock control systems trigger an automatic re-order once the re-order level has been reached. As we will see, this system is even more sophisticated when we look at retailers who use bar coding systems which automatically record when an item of stock has been sold and will then place this on an order which can then be consolidated to the supplier.

Bar coding and scanning

Bar coding is a system of recording data in such a way that it can be read instantly by a laser beam. Most supermarkets and many other retailers have phased in this system over the past few years. The vast majority of manufacturers produce their products in packaging which incorporates a bar code. Simply by passing the product's bar code across the laser beam, the transaction can be recorded. This allows the business to maintain accurate stock records. Scanning bar codes in a warehouse or storeroom is becoming commonplace. Typically, the products and components may not necessarily have a bar code attached to each individual item, but there will be a bar code on the shelf or attached to the bin in which the item is stored. Employees can therefore remove stock from the storage areas and record the fact that they have been used by employing a portable bar code scanner. The information stored on these portable machines can then be downloaded on to the main stock control computer. Again the business will have accurate stock information and can act upon this for re-ordering purposes.

Communications and stock control – EDI and networks

Electronic Data Interchange **(EDI)** is an on-line communication system that links computers with mainframes. It can be used to download stock levels/ requirements from geographically distant parts of a business to the main office. In this way the central purchasing and storage facilities can be warned about impending requirements for particular products and other items of stock. Effectively, the branches can then request replacements from the distribution centre and the distribution centre can use EDI to request orders from its suppliers.

Networks similarly employ computers in order to facilitate easy communication between separate parts of an organisation. They can be used to request orders or re-supplies from the distribution centre. Another useful application of networks is to enable various authorised individuals to gain access to the stock systems and investigate the current stock levels in anticipation of their need for components and materials at a later date. In this way they can be alerted to deficiencies in stock levels and request action to be taken in order to rectify the situation.

■ Stock control duties and procedures

Inevitably, the basic stock control of consumable items will be the responsibility of one or more individual. Normally, the duties of a stock control clerk responsible for stationery supplies include

- the receiving of orders for stationery from the different departments within the organisation
- the booking out of stationery stock against the orders that have been received
- the adjusting of the relevant stock record cards to take account of the stock that has been issued
- the ordering of new or additional stock either directly from the supplier or by raising a stationery requisition form to instruct the purchasing department or buyer to order stock from the supplier
- making sure that the stock does not fall below the recommended minimum stock level
- ensuring that the area in which the stock is kept is maintained, tidied, logically organised and safe from damage or accidental harm

- carrying out periodic stock checks to ensure that the amount of stock 'on paper' tallies with the actual level of stock that is believed to be in the stock area.

When dealing with deliveries of stationery stock, the individual responsible should follow the procedures below to ensure that the amount of stationery that has been delivered tallies with the actual order.

- Unpack the delivery and ensure that the amount that has been delivered is the same as both the amount on the delivery note and the original order.
- Count all of the delivery carefully and check that none of the items are damaged or otherwise faulty.
- If some items have been omitted from the delivery, this may be as a result of the supplier being out of stock. Normally, this would mean that the stock item has been marked on the delivery note as 'out of stock'. There will also be a note which will say 'to follow'. The individual checking the order should make a note of this and tell the accounts department when the items are delivered. This will also remind the checker to follow up the supplier should items not have been delivered after a reasonable period.
- Some items may be marked as 'discontinued'. This means that the supplier is permanently unable to supply these items to his or her customers. In some cases, the supplier may have delivered a replacement or substitute item to replace the items that have been discontinued. In most instances, this item will be very similar to the one that was originally ordered. If it is not a suitable replacement, the item should be returned to the supplier.
- Occasionally, the supplier may have forgotten to include certain items in the delivery despite the fact that they are on the delivery note. In these cases, the supplier should be contacted immediately and informed of the short order.
- In all cases when the items that have been delivered do not match the delivery note or the original order, the accounts department should be informed so that it does not pay the invoice (when it arrives) in the belief that the delivery was correct.
- Sometimes the supplier may have incorrectly added items to the delivery – these may or may not be on the delivery note. In any case, the supplier may realise that he or she has made a mistake, so it is advisable to tell the supplier about the additional items before he or she contacts you. If they have been included on the delivery note (and were not ordered), the accounts department needs to know so that it does not pay for them when the invoice arrives.
- On other occasions, the supplier may have got the delivery totally wrong and will have delivered items that bear no resemblance to the original order. The supplier needs to be told about this and the accounts department should also be informed.
- Deliveries may include items that have been damaged in transit. The packaging may have been inadequate or the boxes may have been broken during transportation. There is also the possibility of items that do not work

(particularly equipment and delicate items such as computer disks, etc.). The supplier should be willing to replace these immediately, but should be informed at the earliest possible opportunity.

- The supplier, following the instructions from your order, may have delivered items that you ordered by mistake. Most suppliers will take these back, but you should be honest and contact the supplier about the problem immediately.

When stock needs to be issued to a particular individual or department this should occur only when an authorised stock requisition order has been placed. As many organisations operate on the basis of charging the appropriate individual or department, the cost of the stock will be set against the appropriate budget. Some organisations will allow stock to be ordered only at a particular time of the week. This is to ensure that a member of staff is not constantly involved in getting orders together for individuals and departments. It also acts as a useful way of ensuring that the users of the stock in the organisation take some care in planning their stationery needs.

From time to time, there is a need to ensure that the amount of stock matches the amounts that are on the stock records – a **stock reconciliation**. There is no other way of doing this apart from counting all of the stock that is being held and checking this against the amounts that are supposed to be there. If the stock control clerk has ensured that the items are stored correctly and that only one box of items is opened at a time, this job may not be as difficult and boring as it could be. If there are differences (these are called 'discrepancies'), the stock control clerk should inform the manager or supervisor. Assuming that the stock control clerk has made sure that all items that have been issued have been entered on to the stock record cards, then when the time comes around for a stock reconciliation, the task will be relatively easy. There are other occasions when the stock record cards need to be adjusted.

- If stock has been damaged.
- If stock has become obsolete (this is may be as a result of a change in the stationery or when the use of a particular item has been phased out).

Before any stock is thrown away, you should be aware of the following.

- All damaged stock should be checked to ensure that it is no longer worth keeping.
- Obsolete paper and forms could be used as scrap paper.
- Obsolete stock and old stock may have a resale value.

It is of vital importance that any removal of stock, for the above reasons, is entered on to the stock record cards so that when the stock is audited, the actions will be remembered.

Periodically, the organisation will need to carry out a **stock audit**. This will involve undertaking

- a full stock inventory (the physical counting of all of the items in stock)
- a calculation of the total value of all of the items in stock

- a calculation of the cost of all of the stock that has been issued to the various individuals and departments in the course of the period since the last stock audit
- a careful noting of all of the adjustments that have been made to the stock
- a costing based upon the issued stock and the adjusted stock.

Student activity

Consider the following cases and suggest a solution to each of them.

1   You receive a delivery of staples, which, unfortunately, are the wrong size for the staplers that you use in the organisation. When you check the order, you discover that the supplier has sent the ones that you ordered. However, you misread the appropriate line in the price list and put down the wrong item number.

2   A large order of photocopy paper arrives. You check the number of boxes and know that there are five reams in each box. The number of boxes ties up with the number ordered. Five days later, after having used some of the boxes, you discover that one of them contains five reams of yellow photocopy paper instead of white.

3   Having fallen out with your original photocopy paper supplier after the last problem, you order a new supply from a company that you have never dealt with before. The paper is cheaper, it is delivered the same day and you feel happy. Unfortunately, this does not last. By late afternoon several people have complained that the paper jams in the copiers and that the quality of the paper is poor. You compare the paper to the stock delivered by the previous supplier and discover that there is a major difference in the quality.

In each of the above cases, if relevant, find out what consumer legislation covers the problem. Compare your findings with those of the rest of the group.

■ Mail handling procedures

Many larger organisations have mail room staff who deal with both internal and external (incoming and outgoing) mail. Other organisations, particularly smaller ones, give the responsibility of dealing with the post to one or two individuals as part of their regular duties.

The individuals distributing the incoming mail may also collect some items for the outgoing mail during the course of their deliveries. However, the busiest time is usually in the afternoons when the day's post is ready for sending out. It could be that the mail room stipulates a deadline or final collection time, after which no mail will be accepted. This may be necessary to ensure that its staff process the mail in time for final posting times at the post office.

It has become common in recent years for the mail room to deal with all aspects of the outgoing mail. Departmental staff sending a written communication simply prepare the envelope and leave it sealed in the outgoing mail tray. A member of the mail room staff collects this and the envelope goes into the batch of mail for either first or second class or special delivery posting.

Sorting mail

Whoever is responsible for dealing with the organisation's post each day will have to be aware of several guidelines regarding both incoming and outgoing mail.

An organised routine is important if the mail is to be opened, sorted and distributed quickly. The following is a guide to the procedures and steps needed to ensure this routine is adopted.

1. *Sort the envelopes,* take out any envelopes marked 'private' or 'personal' as these will not be opened but delivered to the individual still sealed.
2. *Open the mail* using a letter knife along the edge of the envelopes. This will ensure that the contents are not damaged in any way. Sometimes electrically operated letter openers are used – this removes a tiny strip of paper from the edge of the envelope.
3. *Date stamp the documents.* Sometimes the time will also appear on the stamp. Care should be taken not to mask any typed or written information. Personal or private mail should be date stamped on the envelope.
4. *Check the mail for enclosures.* An enclosure is an item which has been sent with the letter. These could be cheques, leaflets, photographs or catalogues. Any paper-clips should be removed and the enclosures stapled to the accompanying documents. This will ensure that the items are not parted during the distribution of the mail.

   Some organisations record the receipt of cheque payments at this stage in a remittances book. This lists the date the remittance (amount of money) was received, from whom, the amount received and includes the signature of the person opening the mail. In addition, it is also the policy of some smaller organisations to keep a register of incoming mail.

5. *Sort the mail by addresses.* The exact destination of the mail may not be immediately obvious so look for a 'For the attention of' line, or the subject heading on the letter, or a reference given at the top of the letter.

   If none of these items appear, you would need to read quickly through the letter to determine who should receive it within the organisation. It may be that several people need to see the one letter. In this case it should be photocopied and copies sent to the various individuals, or a circulation slip or routing slip should be attached to the original. The most common use for one of these slips would be for books or magazines which would be expensive to copy for several people. The slip would list the names of the people to see the document, their department and a column for them to initial once they have read the literature. It would also state the name and department of the person to whom the document should be returned.

6 *Distribute the mail.* In a small organisation the person responsible for this job may have to walk only from one room to another with the post. It is, however, much more involved the larger the organisation becomes. Distributing mail in a very large organisation can be a full-time job for several employees. They would be involved in taking vast amounts of mail to several floors of a large establishment. They may use trolleys, sectioned into the names of individuals, much like filing cabinets, to do this.

Often, the person delivering the incoming mail to each department or section within the organisation would also collect their outgoing mail at the same time. This would be taken back to the mail room for sorting.

Student activity

A magazine has arrived in the mail which needs to be seen by the following members of staff.

Mr Thompson, Sales Manager
Mr Sharman, Marketing Director
Ms Blundel, Promotions Manager
Mrs Chapman, Product Manager

Create and complete a circulation slip. The magazine should be returned to you by 25 June 199–.

Some smaller organisations keep a record of outgoing mail in the same way that they would the incoming mail. This record allows them to keep a check on the amount of money spent on postage stamps and confirms when mail was actually dispatched out of the office. This method of recording postage would normally be the responsibility of one individual and allows costs to be monitored.

Dispatching parcels

Another duty of the mail room assistant is to weigh any parcels which have been prepared ready for dispatch from the organisation. This would be done within the department and the parcels would be taken to the post office with the rest of the mail at the end of each day.

Wrap the parcel sensibly, taking care to ensure that it is secure and not likely to be damaged during transit. The Post Office deals with hundreds of parcels each day, and although it takes every possible care, it is inevitable that some parcels will meet with knocks and bumps on their way. Any damage to parcels can cause delay or loss and expense to your organisation.

Tie-on tags can be used for parcels, and care should be taken to make sure these are attached securely. The name and address of the sender should also be displayed clearly on the parcel so that it can be returned should there be a problem with delivery. A further precaution is to include the name and address of both the sender and the recipient inside the parcel.

Weigh the parcel using manual or electronic scales. Electronic scales automatically calculate the postage due. When using manual scales, the operator would need to refer to the *Postal Rates Guide* issued by the Post Office. *Frank a label* with the correct amount of postage and stick it to the parcel. Add any necessary sticker such as 'fragile', 'urgent' or 'handle with care'. The parcel is now ready to be taken to the post office for handing over to the counter clerk.

All parcels and packages that are being sent overseas need a declaration label which describes the contents. This includes airmail and surface mail. The reason for this is to inform customs officers in the country to which the parcel is being sent of its contents. Some articles require a tax to be paid on them by the recipient. This is called a **duty**. Duty is put on some goods to discourage people from sending them. Gifts may be allowed in duty free in certain countries if described on the label as 'gifts'.

Student activity

You are going on holiday for two weeks and you need to leave a detailed list of instructions for the temporary member of staff who will be dealing with the outgoing mail in your absence. Ensure that you include in your guidelines details regarding the preparation of parcels.

Franking machines

Unless the organisation is very small, it is usual for a **franking machine** to be used instead of stamps. A franking machine prints in red the value of the stamp. In addition, it allows space for an advertisement by the organisation, as well as the time and date of posting.

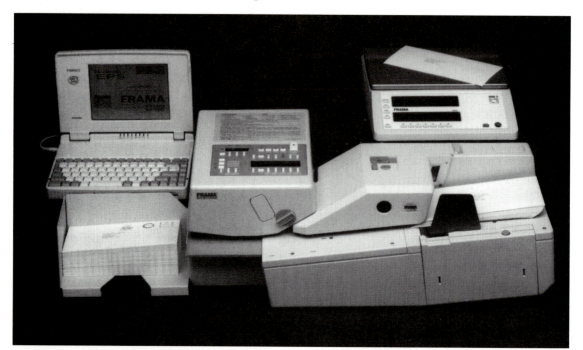

A franking machine can be hired or purchased from the manufacturers, although a licence has to be obtained from the Post Office before the machine can be used. Although there is no charge for this licence, the Post Office will set the meter on the machine to keep a record of units bought, used and still in credit to the organisation on its franking machine. The value of the postage being franked can be changed very easily, in much the same way as a date stamp is changed.

Once the credit left in the franking machine reaches a certain predetermined level, the machine will have to be recredited by contacting the post office. On the latest machines this can be done via the telephone. They are fitted with a mini-modem which is linked to the franking machine via the telephone. With these newer machines it is no longer necessary for someone in the organisation to take the machine into a post office. However, those machines which are not linked to the telephone line will do the same job, although it is more time consuming to have to take them to a post office to be credited. It is also necessary for these machines to be accompanied by a book which the post office clerk will complete each time the machine is credited with units.

Regular envelopes can be franked directly; more bulky items need to be franked using an adhesive label, which is then stuck on to the mail. Once the mail has been franked it can be handed over the counter of a post office. It is either tied in bundles or placed in a special Post Office bag designed for this use.

Student activity

As in the previous activity, you are to prepare a list of guidelines for the temporary member of staff who will be carrying out your duties whilst you are away. Write a list of procedures for franking the mail for him or her to follow.

■ Royal Mail and other delivery services

The Post Office uses the postcodes to help speed the sorting of mail. If the correct postcode is used on envelopes, parcels and packets, this speeds up delivery. The Post Office provides a vast range of other services to its customers which can speed up delivery and can provide cover for compensation.

- **Inland mail** – Inland mail is usually regarded as first and second class letter services which are used more than any other service. The letters do not receive any special security handling.
- **Recorded delivery** – The recorded delivery service provides proof that the mail has actually been posted and that it has reached its destination.
- **Registered mail** – Registered delivery is a secure way of sending valuables or money of up to £500 in value. It also guarantees delivery by 12.30 pm the next working day. Registered Plus provides compensation for loss or damage up to a maximum of £2,200 and guarantees delivery by 17.30 the next day.

- **Datapost** – This service guarantees overnight delivery within the UK as well as a quicker than normal delivery overseas.
- **Special delivery** – Special delivery guarantees that urgent mail reaches its destination by 12.30 pm the next working day. This type of mail gets priority over all other mail.
- **Parcel post inland** – Parcelforce guarantee delivery of parcel post with inclusive cover either by the next working day (Parcelforce 24 and Datapost) or within two working days (Parcelforce 48).
- **Business reply service** – This service is used by organisations who wish to obtain a reply from their customers. By using this service the replies will be paid for by the organisation rather than the customer. The envelope is posted in the normal way, but no stamp is required. It can be used with both first and second class mail.
- **Freepost** – Freepost also allows the organisation rather than the customer to pay the postage. The word 'FREEPOST' is included in the address of the organisation. Letters are sent only by second class mail.
- **International reply coupons** – These are exchanged in practically all countries of the world for a stamp or stamps. The person for whom the coupon is intended takes it to the nearest post office and exchanges it for a stamp used by their own country. An international reply coupon is a convenient way of 'prepaying' the cost of a reply from abroad.
- **Swiftair** – This is an express airmail service available for an extra fee for all letters to Europe and most other countries.
- **International datapost** – This offers an express guaranteed delivery service to over 170 countries and territories worldwide.
- **Accelerated surface post (ASP)** – This overseas service is cheaper than airmail and quicker than ordinary surface mail. Items that are to be posted by ASP should be put into separate bags, labelled ASP and then the Post Office will collect them.
- **Bulk airmail** – This airmail service for printed papers sent overseas bases its costs on the weight 'pence per kilo'. It also has to be kept in separate bags and labelled ready for collection by the Post Office.
- **Parcel post international** – Datapost and International standard offer an express guaranteed delivery of parcels overseas. International economy offers a basic international delivery service of parcels overseas.

The Post Office also offers: certificates of posting which are a way of making sure that your letter is posted; a registered letter can be insured against damage or loss by taking out consequential loss insurance; cash on delivery enables the postman to collect the payment from the recipient and pass on payment to the sender by special order.

Keywords

The keywords you should know for this chapter are listed below. Check to make sure you understand the meaning of each word. Discuss those you are unsure of with your tutor.

appointments diary	just-in-time
bar coding	Lifo
buffer stock	petty cash voucher
business card	re-order level
capital	special delivery
datapost	staff in and out book
duty	stock audit
economic order quantity	stock control card
EDI	stock reconciliation
Fifo	visitors book
franking machine	

Examination practice

Short-answer questions

1 How could an electronic diary assist a receptionist?

2 List 5 qualities and 5 duties of a good receptionist.

3 'Maintaining the reception area' is a very broad term. Write an explanation of what this task involves.

4 What items would appear on a Stock Control Card and when would this be completed?

5 Write a paragraph which explains the terms 'minimum order level' and 'maximum order level' when considering stock control systems.

6 What is the purpose of a circulation slip and what is it otherwise known as?

7 Give two examples of a mailing or delivery service that would ensure next day delivery.

8 Where does the mail that has been passed through a franking machine go after leaving the organisation?

9 State which Royal Mail service you would use if you wanted to send money through the post.

10 State which Royal Mail service you would use if you wanted to ensure a letter is waiting for someone at a hotel when they arrive.

Essay questions

1 You are the main receptionist in a very busy organisation. Several times you have encountered the problem where it is impossible for you to take a lunch break because the reception area is too busy and nobody comes down to relieve you. This makes you very frustrated and over-tired and leaves you feeling very short-tempered and irritable. In addition, you are constantly having to ring around the different departments in order to

contact individuals who have visitors waiting in reception. This is very time-consuming and gives a bad impression to the visitor(s). You have complained to the Head of Administration and s/he has said you should put your complaints in writing. You should consider the following:

a what steps are needed to ensure continual cover on the reception desk?

b when is the reception the most busy and how could you improve the service offered at these times?

c how could the problem of locating individual members of staff be overcome?

d how would such improvements help the image of the organisation?

2 One of your duties is to ensure an adequate supply of stationery and office sundries in the department in which you work. This is quite a thankless and sometimes a time-consuming job, as people tend to take items from the stationery cupboard without telling you and only manage to complain when they go to the cupboard and find that the last item has been taken. The main items which seem to 'walk' are sellotape, computer disks and liquid correcting fluid. You have suspected for some time that you had a petty thief in the department, but have never been able to place the blame on anyone in particular and you have no evidence that someone is helping themselves to the items. You have reported the on-going problem to your line manager, who has asked you to write down some suggestions which could improve the situation. Itemise your suggestions and state why they would improve the current problem.

You work as an administrative assistant in a busy engineering company. One of your main duties is to deal with both the incoming and outgoing mail. You are likely to be away on holiday for three weeks in the middle of August and you have been informed that one of the office juniors is to take over this role for you. Your line manager is concerned that this office junior may find the job tedious and so will cut corners. You have been asked to provide her with a detailed list of instructions. You should carry out the following:

3 Prepare a list of the regular duties you carry out regarding the dealing of the mail (both in the morning and early afternoon) which arrives at the office. Make sure you cover:

a how to make sure the mail gets to the intended destination as soon as possible.

b how to make sure no mail gets opened which should not be.

4 The office junior will also be responsible in your absence for the outgoing mail. As you have to deal regularly with large parcels and items which have to have a guaranteed 'next day delivery', it is very important that she has all the information necessary to enable her to use the correct services and couriers. You should:

a prepare a booklet which lists the services you regularly use and identify the types of mail to be sent by each.

b prepare an instruction sheet which she can have readily to hand when dealing with the outgoing mail.

Processing information

9

■ Introduction

In this section of the book we intend to look at the procedures organisations may have in place in order to ensure the following:

- adequate sources of information for use by their staff
- sufficient storage and retrieval systems and procedures to ensure that documents are stored safely and are easy to find when needed
- efficient and effective communication systems, both from an internal point of view and externally
- facilities for the printing of all types of documents and resources available for the reproduction of original documents (reprography)

■ Sources of information

It would be very difficult to identify all of the potential sources of information that could be considered relevant and are used regularly by business organisations. Apart from the more obvious sources of information, which include the following list, we have attempted to include the more general information sources which are available at a variety of different levels and detail.

Broadly speaking, there are three main sources of information that the business researcher may be interested in.

- Information within the company which already exists but which may not be in a particularly usable form.
- Information external to the company which again already exists and is much more expensive to track down.
- Information which may or may not be within the company, and is usually external to the company, but which does not exist in a usable form. Commonly, this information is customer opinion, attitude or buying traits.

The two ways of researching information are known as **secondary research** and **primary research**. Primary research involves finding out new information by way of research opinion polls, interviews or questionnaires. Secondary research involves accessing information through sources which already exist. The information required may be internal or external to an organisation.

Secondary information

Before an organisation goes to the expense of paying for primary research, it is worth looking at what information is already available. Secondary data is often in the form of published materials which have been collected by someone else.

Published data in book form available in most reference libraries include titles like *Regional Trends* or the *General Household Survey*. Some of the more simplified sources of information include reference books such as the *Yellow Pages Directory* and *Local Thomson Directories*.

In addition to these 'manual' types of reference it is also possible to gain a vast array of information from computerised versions, for example CD-ROMs, the Internet as well as Ceefax and Oracle services which are accessed via TV. Other sources are local chambers of commerce, which have good libraries and links and leads to other sources of information.

- CD-ROMs are small optical disks which can contain in computerised format a huge amount of information such as reference books and national newspapers.
- the Internet contains a large variety of information stored on a computer. It can be located by the use of a modem link to a service provider. The World Wide Web provides access to a vast array of 'sites' which contain information on news, travel, statistics and commercial information from business organisations.
- A wide range of information is available through teletext which is accessed via TV. Teletext is available as Ceefax and Oracle and provides a wide range of current informatio, including weather forecasts, sport, travel and news headlines.
- Prestel is a viewdata system available through a computer and modem. This service is provided by BT and offers access for a fee to general information and specialist information. Some information is restricted to specific organisations.

Government statistics

Perhaps one of the more useful and often-used aspects of government statistics is the standard industrial classification. It essentially breaks down the different markets and organisations which make up the economy into ten distinct divisions. These are

division 0 – agriculture, forestry and fishing
division 1 – energy and water supply industries
division 2 – extraction of minerals and ores, manufacture of metals, mineral products and chemicals
division 3 – metal goods, engineering and vehicle industries
division 4 – other manufacturing industries
division 5 – construction
division 6 – distribution, hotels and catering, repairs

division 7 – transport and communication
division 8 – banking, finance, insurance, business services and leasing
division 9 – other services.

It is not just the UK government that produces useful statistical information but other government-related organisations and bodies also produce a wide variety of data. These include

- the European Union which publishes the *General Statistical Bulletin*
- the United Nations which produces a *Demographic Yearbook*
- the Organisation for Economic Cooperation and Development (OECD) which publishes *Main Economic Indicators*
- the International Monetary Fund (IMF) which releases a *Balance of Payments Yearbook*.

Other published statistics

There are a number of different agencies or commercial research organisations which produce a variety of statistical information relating to very many different topics. These agencies and research organisations collect or buy information which they then compile in report form and sell on to other organisations. Typical examples of agencies or commercial research organisations include

- **Mintel**, which produces short reports on a single specific consumer market and includes details
  - market size
  - projected growth
  - market share of main competitors
  - advertising spending
  - market trends
- Euromonitor, which produces keynote reports (at around 75 pages each, these give a broad outline of the nature and specifics of a particular market)
- Retail Audits, which collects data from supermarkets and other large retail chains on sales figures of particular products. This audit service is very useful for suppliers in assessing how effective their marketing has been and its impact upon other organisations' sales and market share.

As an alternative to these commercial organisations, the many trade associations produce some very useful data. Examples include the Market Research Society, the Advertising Association and the Chartered Institute of Marketing.

Marketing research – primary information

Research makes a positive contribution to a business by helping in the decision-making process. There are many different types of marketing research. The main ones are as follows.

Market and sales research

- Estimating market size of new markets.
- Estimating potential growth of an existing market.
- Identifying market characteristics and segments.
- Identifying market trends.
- Sales forecasting.
- Collecting data on existing customers.
- Collecting data on potential customers.
- Collecting data on competitors.

Product research

- Customers' attitude to new products.
- Comparing competition with own products.
- Finding alternative uses for existing products.
- Market testing proposed products.
- Investigating customer complaints.
- Packaging research.
- Generating new ideas for new products.

Research on promotion and advertising

- Choosing the right advertising medium.
- Analysing effectiveness of advertising.
- Establishing sales areas.
- Evaluating present sales techniques.
- Analysing salesforce effectiveness.
- Establishing sales quotas.

Distribution research

- Location of distribution centres.
- Handling products (efficiency).
- Transport costs and comparisons.
- Storage efficiency and needs.
- Retail outlet locations.

Pricing policy

- Demand.
- Perceived price.
- Costs.
- Margins.

Student activity

Using the above marketing research lists as a clue, identify the particular departments within a typical business organisation that would be interested in the kinds of information that could be collected on those information areas. Compare your ideas with those of the rest of the group.

The scope of marketing and market research is very broad. In fact almost every aspect of the production, promotion, sales and after-sales life of a product is scrutinised at some point for one particular purpose or another.

Student activity

Visit your local public library or college library and look in the reference section to see what is available in the way of resources. Try to identify the following

a Where you would find details on the more successful and well-known organisations in the UK. This should include their turnover and profitability.

b The name of your local councillor.

c Details of the local unemployment figures.

Sources of information, advice and assistance

In this section, we have identified some of the useful information sources that would be able to provide general assistance, or more specific advice, to the majority of business organisations.

Federation of Self Employed

The Federation of Self Employed provides a network of regional and local groups to assist and support those engaged in self-employment. The organisation itself and, indeed, via the members, provides a wealth of information and advice which is the accumulation of many years' experience.

Federation of Small Businesses

The Federation of Small Businesses (FSB) aims to assist the 400,000 new enterprises which are established each year. Under the financial support of Mercury Communications, the FSB is a leading campaign and pressure group.

With nearly 60,000 members, it is concerned with bringing about favourable changes in legislation, particularly in relation to the protection and promotion of small businesses. One of the key services which it offers is a 24-hour legal advice scheme. In its booklet 'Getting Started in Business' the FSB offers valuable advice on a number of issues, including finance, tax, premises, marketing, customer care and problem-solving.

Chambers of Commerce

The network of chambers of commerce and industry offers substantial support, services and facilities to businesses. These include

- export advice
- adult and youth training
- advice on British Standards, company legislation, import and export documentation
- access to directories and mailing lists
- representation to local and central government
- subscription to magazines and newsletters
- office support services
- European information
- formal and informal social events.

Service providers

The service providers such as banks, solicitors, accountants, estate agents, design consultants can all provide information relevant to their area. For example, a bank can provide financial facilities such as loans, overdrafts and specialist services such as free banking in the first year for new businesses.

Training and Enterprise Councils and Local Enterprise Companies

There are 82 Training and Enterprise Councils **(TECs)** throughout England and Wales. Scotland has 22 Local Enterprise Companies (LECs). Both of these organisations offer training and support for small businesses in the interests of addressing the needs of the local community. Each TEC and LEC has its own particular programme. Generally speaking, the training opportunities include

- enterprise awareness events, which aim to alert potential new businesses of the demands and problems associated with setting up a new business
- specific business training aimed at assisting the setting up or development of businesses
- open-learning skills programmes – business skill seminars on such topics as management and marketing
- information and advice on Investors in People programme
- training programmes for employees
- coordination and planning for small firms' training loans.

TECs and LECs are also involved in the following business services.

- Training access points (TAPS) – these provide information about local and national training opportunities. TAPs can usually be found in libraries and high-street locations, as well as in TECs and LECs.

- Counselling and advice – TECs, LECs and Local Enterprise Agencies also offer advice to both new businesses and existing businesses through the services of a personal business adviser.
- Consultancy – the Enterprise Initiative Consultancy Scheme enables small businesses to employ consultants in specific areas.
- Investors in People – based on the assumption that training and development of employees is crucial in the successful development of a business, this initiative helps businesses address this consideration. Operating with national standards, the TECs and LECs offer guidance in this matter.

There are a number of other services and initiatives which are handled by the TECs or LECs, which include the following.

- Business Development Centres – these provide informal advice, information and guidance, as well as other business services. These may be contacted via a Freephone number.
- Enterprise 2000 – this scheme is designed to give specific help and support to individuals starting their own business. It offers impartial advice from experienced business counsellors as well as seminars on marketing, finance, business administration and preparing a business plan.
- Business Development Fund – this service provides information on everything individuals need to know in terms of financial support for their business. It has been primarily set up to help small to medium-sized business (ie those with up to 100 employees).

Department of Trade and Industry

The Department of Trade and Industry **(DTI)** itself offers a lot of advice and networking facilities to new businesses. Business Link is a business support network for new businesses which calls on the considerable resources of the DTI. It aims to provide a flexible business advice service on a single site where the new business can obtain information relating to all the DTI services from that location. Part of the Business Link is a personal business adviser (PBA) who is there to help small firms with problem-solving, production of action plans and access to business support services.

There are a number of regional assistance programmes related to the four main government departments involved in business-related matters. These government departments are

- Employment
- Trade and Industry
- Environment
- Transport.

Recently, the four departments have been integrated into offices known as Government Offices (GOs) for the regions.

Councils

County councils, in particular, and, indeed, all borough councils offer access to information and advice for small businesses and those considering self-employment. They produce a number of useful booklets which can be used as a checklist for accessing the names and addresses of relevant organisations. Nearly all councils have their own business advisers or, at the very least, they have a business library usually located in a central library location.

Companies House

Companies House holds the public records of more than a million companies. Companies House itself has four major statutory functions. These are

- to incorporate and dissolve companies
- to examine and hold documents presented under the Company's Act and other legislation
- to make this information available to the public
- to exercise certain powers in relation to companies on behalf of the Secretary of State for Trade and Industry.

Local Enterprise Agencies (LEAs)

There are over 400 Local Enterprise Agencies (LEAs) throughout the UK which offer business advice and counselling to new or expanding businesses. They also offer extensive assistance in the formation of business plans. The LEAs have very good links with various businesses and organisations in the local area. They are able to offer either direct assistance or referral to an organisation which can provide that help.

The Prince's Youth Business Trust/Prince's Scottish Youth Business Trust

These organisations offer grants or low-interest loans to individuals between the ages of 18 and 29. Specifically, they will provide assistance to those who are encountering difficulties in raising finance from other sources. They also provide advice, training and marketing opportunities to businesses.

■ The Data Protection Act

Use of information

The **Data Protection Act** attempts to ensure that stored information is put only to specific lawful purposes. Whilst is difficult to maintain this degree of certainty about the user of the information, most organisations tend to use stored information for its specifically stated purpose only. Problems will inevitably arise when there is an interchange of this information between different organisations. The organisation which initially collected the data may have had a specific purpose in mind. However, the organisation which has acquired the information may have different motives altogether. The transmission of sensitive information from one organisation to another can pose considerable problems both to the individual and to the Data Protection Registrar. In particular,

information stored regarding an individual's creditworthiness may include a number of inaccuracies which have not been identified. If the individual subsequently discovers these inaccuracies, then it is a difficult task to trace the transmission and use of the original inaccurate information in order to ensure that all information stored at whatever location is, indeed, accurate.

Student activity

How would you go about discovering whether the information stored about you as an individual is correct? Discuss this as a group.

As with any data storage facility, the organisation will take steps to ensure that unauthorised access is avoided. The Data Protection Act, however, makes this a legal requirement and, therefore, unauthorised access can mean fines for the organisation which has suffered the breach of security. The sensitivity of some of the material stored is such that it could be used for criminal or other unlawful purposes by an unauthorised entrant. The sensitivity of the information is further heightened by the fact that the individual whose information is stored in the system may be unaware that it is actually there. If unauthorised entry is gained and this information is used by others, the individual may suffer as a result.

Student activity

Information regarding customers is regularly traded between organisations. How would an organisation ensure that the information being passed on does not adversely affect the individual or the organisation itself? Discuss this in pairs.

Most organisations keep detailed records which may include

- customers' names and addresses
- customer transactions
- customer credit information
- specific information regarding customers, such as their political affiliations (in recent years certain high-street banks have admitted that they keep details of customers' political allegiances)
- staff records
- personal information regarding employees' domestic situations
- disciplinary action taken against employees.

Organisations obviously store a great deal more information than this, but the Data Protection Act relates specifically to the way in which this information is used. The Act attempts to prevent this information being used to harm an individual. The Act requires all organisations or individuals who hold personal details regarding other individuals on computer to register with the Data Protection Registrar. If an organisation or individual fails to do this, they may be fined up to £2000.

The Registrar must ensure that the data conform with the Act. Specifically, this means that the Registrar must ensure that the information complies with the following codes.

- The information must be collected in an open and fair manner.
- The information should be held only for lawful purposes.
- The uses to which the information is put must be disclosed to the Registrar.
- The information held must be relevant to the purpose for which it is held.
- The information must be accurate.
- The information must be up to date.
- Any irrelevant or inaccurate information must be destroyed.
- Individuals can be told about the existence of the information.
- Individuals can challenge inaccurate information.
- The information must be kept confidential.
- The organisation must take steps to ensure that unauthorised access is avoided.

Student activity

Consider, from a personal point of view, the Data Protection Act and try to assess the range and amount of information which may be stored by organisations concerning you. Write a list of any considerations you can think of and then compare your list to those of the remainder of your group. How much do they vary?

Accuracy of information

The Data Protection Act states that 'personal data shall be accurate and, where necessary, kept up to date'. The Act gives further guidance on interpreting this. 'Accurate' means correct and not misleading as to any matter of fact.

The Act contains special provisions which apply to information obtained from the data subject or from third parties. These are dealt with fully within the Act. Stated briefly, a data user who wishes to rely on these provisions must ensure that both the fact that the information has come from such a source and any challenge by the data subject to the accuracy of the information are recorded. If these requirements are complied with, the fact that the personal data are inaccurate does not result in a breach of this principle.

The Registrar will seek to establish that there is a factual inaccuracy and will also wish to see whether the data user has taken all responsible steps to prevent the inaccuracy. The matters which the Registrar may wish to consider will include

- the significance of the inaccuracy
- the source from which the inaccurate information was obtained
- any steps taken to verify the information
- the procedures for data entry and for ensuring that the system itself does not introduce inaccuracies into the data
- the procedures followed by the data user when the inaccuracy came to light.

If an individual suffers damage because of inaccurate personal data held about him or her by a user, he or she is entitled to claim compensation from the data user. An application for compensation must be made by the individual to the court. The Registrar cannot award compensation.

Responsibilities of the organisation

An organisation's activities may be subject to the Data Protection Act if it uses either word processors, microcomputers, minicomputers and/or mainframe computers. An organisation should be aware that it makes no difference whether the equipment is owned or leased. It is not the equipment itself that is important, but the use of that equipment for the storage and processing of data. The control of the data is in the hands of the organisation. If any of the above are used by the organisation, the following questions need to be addressed.

- Is the equipment used for the processing of accounts payable and accounts received?
- Is the equipment used for the checking of credit ratings?
- Is the equipment used for the payroll and storage of personnel data?
- Is the equipment used for marketing and sales information?
- Is the equipment used for the storage of general management information?
- Is the equipment used for the production and manipulation of letters and text?
- Is the equipment used for the transmission of electronic mail (e-mail)?

If the organisation uses its equipment for any of the above, then these activities are not restricted by the Act.

On the other hand, if the organisation can identify that it stores and uses personal data and has to ensure that they are properly secured, then this does require special attention. The data protection laws frequently refer to specific types of personal data which are either prohibited or which must have special safeguards. These data relate to

- racial origin
- political opinions
- religious beliefs
- health.

Student activity

There are several exemptions and restrictions set down in the guidelines relating to the Data Protection Act. Obtain a copy of these leaflets and research the following.

a What data are exempt from the regulations?

b What disclosures are prohibited by law?

c How likely is it that data relating to one individual could be accessed and purchased by another individual or organisation?

Present your findings in the form of a word-processed report.

Costs of implementation of the Act

Obviously, one of the negative effects of the implementation of the Data Protection Act for an organisation could be the costs involved. If the organisation is large and the amount of information stored is of a nature to require registration with the Registrar, then some expense will be involved in the overseeing of the input of such data. It may be necessary for the organisation to employ an individual to control and monitor this process. Such a data protection officer would have the responsibility of monitoring the additions, deletions and use of information. This could involve a great deal of staff time and expense in terms of salary for the organisation.

Student activity

Again, as in the previous activity, obtain copies of the guidelines regarding the implementation of the Data Protection Act. You will find that your college/centre or local library will have copies. Try to estimate the cost to an organisation of complying with the legislation. Does it cost more for an organisation than it does for an individual? Discuss your findings with the rest of your group.

■ Storage and retrieval of information

The words 'storage and retrieval' can often be confusing when one has not worked in an office. In fact, they mean 'filing' or 'indexing'. This involves a logical and effective way of recording documents and storing them in an efficient system which will allow the easy retrieval of that information when required. Nowadays, however, storage and retrieval also includes the computerised systems of storing and retrieving information. The safe and secure storage of information and the easy access or retrieval of that information is essential if an organisation is to function successfully and efficiently.

Filing is the basis of record-keeping and entails the processing, arranging and storing of the documents so that they can be found when they are required. The documents are placed in consecutive order and preserved in that system until they are required for reference. This can be carried out in any number of locations – a telephone directory is an index of alphabetical names and addresses. Your own address book is also a method of indexing in alphabetical order.

Different people and different organisations can often interpret the word 'system' in conflicting ways. The word can be used when referring to filing in any of the ways we have listed below.

- It can mean the method used for filing the documents, ie in alphabetical or geographical order.
- It can mean the equipment used for filing the documents, ie a lateral or vertical filing cabinet.
- It can mean the location used for filing the documents, ie in one department or office, or in a centralised filing department.
- It can mean the physical way the staff file the documents.

So what are the basic techniques required to ensure that the storage and retrieval of information and documents is efficient? Let's look at these in some detail.

- Ensure that the papers which have been passed for filing have been marked in some way to indicate that they are ready for storing.
- Sort the papers into order so that they are grouped in the required way.
- Remove any paper-clips and staple documents together – this will ensure that they do not get separated during the filing process.
- Each individual file should be in date order, with the most recent documents at the top or front.
- Be careful with the documents – curled edges can easily become torn.
- File daily if possible – this makes it less of a chore and also ensures that the files are up to date.
- Follow organisational procedure regarding borrowed files 'out' or 'absent' files (see page 244).
- Follow up all overdue files regularly, ie when they have been borrowed by another member of staff or department, by using a bring-forward system.
- Use a cross-reference system (see below) whenever a file is known by more than one name.
- 'Thin out' files when necessary. There will be an organisational policy regarding the length of time documents are held in the system. When they

become obsolete or out of date, they may be transferred to the 'archives' – an additional storage area where files are stored in boxes in case they are required for reference.

- Be aware of health and safety regulations regarding filing cabinets. Always close drawers after you have used them and lock drawers and cabinets before leaving the office at night.
- Always ask for help if you are unsure where something should be filed, and do not be afraid to offer ideas if you think the system could be made more efficient with some improvements.

Methods of filing

When documents are filed, it could be that they are done so using any of the following systems. Different methods will prove suitable for different circumstances.

Alphabetical

This method refers to the filing of documents according to the first letter of the surname. This is normally the first letter of the surname of the correspondent, although in a personnel department the files could be arranged in alphabetical order, determined by the first letter of the surname of the member of staff.

Advantages
- It is a convenient and easy-to-understand system.
- It requires no indexing.
- It is useful for incorporating miscellaneous documents.

Disadvantages
- It can become very large and cumbersome.
- Confusion can occur when names are the same or similar.
- Cross-referencing is necessary as there is a possibility that files may be requested under different titles.

Student activity

Place the following list of names in alphabetical order.

Hewitt, David	Canwell, Alun
Cowley, Maurice	Hurle, Peter
Hunt, Peter	Aliffe, Burt
Woodhouse, John	Sergio, Maria
Jones, Nick	Sergio, Despina
Sutherland, Joshua	Watson, Susan
Hewitt, Ross	Gowen, Susan
Canwell, Stuart	Darby, Owen

A quick way of putting a list into alphabetical order is to put it into numerical order first, by writing the position (number) where each one will appear next to the name, and then writing the list out again in numerical order.

Numerical

This method is linked by means of index cards to the alphabetical method. Each document or folder is given a number and these are filed in numerical order. The information contained within the files is sorted into alphabetical order.

Advantages

- The numbered files are more easily found.
- The numbered files are less likely to be returned to the wrong place.
- The number reference can be added to any correspondence.
- The numbered files can be easily increased, thereby expanding the system.

Student activity

Place the following list of numbers in numerical order.

134	310	180	333
176	245	76	17
95	88	21	
109	213	54	

Geographical

The files are arranged in alphabetical order according to the location of the correspondent. This is a common system used in sales departments where the documents are filed under the area or region. Local authorities would also use the geographical method of filing documents as the area itself would be more frequently referred to than the inhabitants of that area.

Advantages

- For some organisations geographical location is the prime consideration.

- It is possible to file the documents directly.
- Statistics can be gathered easily from the filing system without the need to retrieve too many individual files.

Disadvantages

- The filing clerk would need to know the system well and be good at geography!
- Confusion can occur if regional or county boundaries change.

Student activity

Place the following list of towns and cities in geographical order, ie alphabetical order.

Ipswich	Portsmouth	Oxford
Norwich	Aberdeen	Saffron Walden
Southwold	Colchester	Great Yarmouth
Bury St Edmunds	Gants Hill	Walpole
Cambridge	Braintree	Liverpool
Newmarket	Bristol	Edinburgh
Plymouth	Bath	Chelmsford

Subject

Again, this system also uses the alphabetical method of filing, but the subject determines the order. Your own filing cabinet or folder may be arranged by subject. You probably have divider cards which are arranged into the subjects that you study during the course of the week.

Advantages

- It is easy to understand.
- It is straightforward; no indexing is required.
- Expansion is not a problem, as additional files can be added.
- Confidentiality is not a problem, as no names or addresses are used.

Student activity

Place the following list of subjects which may be studied at your college/centre in subject order.

Accounts	Media studies	Human biology
Typewriting	German	Geology
History	Greek	English language
Biology	Italian	French
Geography	Word processing	Spanish
English literature	Psychology	Russian

Disadvantage

Confusion could occur where more than one person is responsible for filing, as the two may not both consider the document is related to one particular subject.

Chronological

Chronological filing means that documents are stored according to the date, with the most recent date being at the front or top of the file. Travel agents are likely to use this method; as they receive travel documents for clients they would be filed in date order, either of departure, or of payment dates.

Student activity

Place the following list of dates in chronological order, putting the most recent at the top.

25 January 19–	24 August 19–	17 November 19–
1 August 19–	24 April 19–	18 June 19 –
27 June 19–	17 September 19–	21 December 19–
6 May 19–	15 June 19–	6 April 19–
15 November 19–	11 November 19–	
21 September 19–	20 July 19–	

Types of storage equipment

Vertical filing cabinet

These are used for storing papers vertically in files with their strips or labels on the top edge of each file.

Lateral filing cabinet

These are used for storing papers where the files are suspended laterally with their strips or labels vertically on the front. A bring-forward system is important to ensure that documents are where they should be when they should be. It may be necessary to use only a diary to enter bring-forward dates for a small number of documents. However, for a large number, a special cabinet system would prove useful, with the additional use of system sheets.

A follow-up system would contain sections for each month as well as a current monthly section (with 31 insert folders, one for each day of the month) and would operate in this way.

- When a file needs to be followed up at a later date, the person needing to do this would complete the form designed for this purpose.
- The form would be filed in the follow-up cabinet under the date requested.
- It would be the responsibility of the clerk each day to take any forms from the current daily folder and find the papers to which they refer. He or she would then pass the forms and papers to the person whose signature appears on the form.

- Once the form and papers had been dealt with, they would be returned to the clerk. If necessary, another date would be entered on the form for the follow-up process to continue.

An efficient organisation would need to keep track of the whereabouts of all files housed within its filing system. In order to do this a file 'out' or 'absent' card would be inserted each time a file was borrowed. In this way the clerk would always know the exact location of a particular file, when it was borrowed and by whom. Individual pieces of paper or documents should never be removed from a file. To ensure that nothing is lost or misplaced, the whole file should be taken from the drawer.

It is possible that one file could be known by more than one name. It is often necessary to update files, for example when an organisation changes its name, or when a personnel file changes name because the member of staff marries. This could cause confusion as some people might still refer to the file, or look for it, under the old name. For this reason a system has to be in place which enables the clerk or anyone else seeking the file to find it without too much difficulty. A cross-reference slip would be placed either in the old or in the new file, directing the person seeking the file to the correct place.

Databases

Databases are based on the idea that a common 'pool' of information can be organised in such a way that all those using the system can be satisfied. Therefore, instead of each department within an organisation keeping and maintaining its own set of files, they are grouped together to form a database.

Such databases have advantages over traditional filing systems.

- There is no unnecessary duplication of information, which is more economical, and is also more effective in keeping information up to date.
- There is less chance of inconsistency of information.
- Comprehensive information is more readily available.
- Any enquiries can be dealt with 'on demand' rather than going through the normally tedious process of obtaining files.

Electronic databases are normally defined under two main systems.

Centralised systems
In a centralised system, all processing of information is carried out by one computer. This central computer is responsible for the processing, even though it may be linked to terminals. This means that each of the offices or departments may have its own terminal, but the information is stored and retrieved by the central computer.

Distributing systems
This system allows for some processing of information to be carried out by the terminals. These terminals have their own storage and retrieval programs, so information can be input and manipulated on them, rather than just on the central computer.

Computer-based filing systems

Microfilm is a method of using film to condense the space occupied by documents. This, to some degree, helps to replace the paper which so often builds up within an organisation. Additionally, microfilming is used to preserve old or valuable documents, thus ensuring they are not handled too much. Nowadays, libraries tend to use this method of storing information and it helps alleviate the mountains of documentation which could be found in the normal library. The process for using microfilm is as follows.

- The original documents are photographed and processed on to the computer.
- The computer is used to access the information required, by 'scrolling' through the film. The specific page of a document can then be viewed on the screen of the computer, and if necessary, printed.

Obviously, all information stored on computer must also be protected. Organisations which use this method of storage and retrieval must ensure the following.

- Back-up copies of disks must be made and safely stored.
- Passwords must be used by the staff using the computer, and these should be changed regularly.
- As an addition to passwords, user codes can also be used. These codes are known only to those who are authorised to access the information and relate to specific files or documents stored.

■ Common communications systems and use of office technology

You must be able to communicate well and effectively to both the people you work with and also the customers or suppliers of the organisation. Communication may be

- non-verbal
- spoken or verbal
- hand-written
- text produced using a keyboard and involving the use of telecommunications.

A much more comprehensive look at the nature of communication can be found in the companion book *Business Communication for Secretarial Certificates,* but for our purposes, we need to have a look at the communication systems that are more common in the majority of business organisations.

Telecommunications

Telecommunications have had a drastic impact on the communications systems of organisations. At a stroke, many of them have replaced traditional forms of communication.

Telephone systems

In recent years, telephone systems have been developed to provide many new features, including

- visual display of number dialled
- a re-dial button
- a secrecy button
- a timer so that the call cost may be estimated
- a memory facility for all regularly dialled numbers
- the day, date and time
- conferencing.

Switchboards, too, are much more sophisticated and allow the telephone operator to assess the status of each individual line on the system. They can also identify which extension should be dialled in response to a particular call. Switchboards also have the facility to log calls and record them. This assists in the monitoring of unauthorised personal calls made by employees. The logging itself enables the cost of the call to be attributed to a particular department and its budget.

Cellular phones enable individuals to be contacted in remote locations and important information to be transmitted wherever that individual may be. With regard to car phones in particular, a hand-free system has been developed in order to avoid the perils of telephone use and driving.

Radio-pagers

An alternative to cellular phones, and in many respects cheaper, is the **radio-pager**. This enables the individual carrying the radio-pager to be contacted and given a short message or telephone number. Additional facilities available on a radio-pager are

- using the PABX system (private automatic branch exchange), an individual may be 'bleeped' to inform him or her that there is a message

- a visual display consisting of either the telephone number to be contacted or brief details of the message

Multiple radio-pagers may be 'bleeped' simultaneously.

Answering machines

Answering machines have become a vital part of business communications, despite the fact that people are not keen on talking into machines. When the individual called is not available, or when there is no one to take the message on an extension, the answering machine can receive the message.

Fax machines

Another way an organisation may choose to communicate with its customers or clients or other companies within the group located on different sites is by the use of the facsimile machine, colloquially known as the 'fax'. The word 'facsimile' means an exact and faithful reproduction of, and applies to text, photographs and graphic images. A fax machine is capable of relaying documents and graphics via the telephone network to another location in just a few seconds. This means that an added benefit of a fax is that an organisation is not limited in what it can send. It is also useful for organisations which may need to contact companies overseas. A fax machine is left on for 24 hours a day, and it does not have to be continually monitored through the night. This means that the time differences between countries are not a problem.

Student activity

Design your own covering sheet for a fax message. Remember to include any necessary details. The headed paper used by an organisation for other correspondence could also be used.

Telex

Although using much the same principle as the fax machine, the telex is more limited in its use. For this reason, the fax has really replaced the telex in most organisations. It is not possible to transmit charts and diagrams via the telex. However, the same advantages apply regarding the transmission of messages to countries overseas. Telex messages can also be prepared and saved on electronic file and transmitted at a later time when they are dispatched automatically.

Electronic mail and computer networks

Increasingly, information is transmitted electronically. The days of waiting for letters or documents have, for most organisations, long gone. Nowadays, the tendency to use electronic processes to transmit information is more the 'norm', particularly in larger organisations.

Electronic mail **(e-mail)** offers all of the facilities provided by fax and telex, but is paperless. It offers the advantage of being able to store messages when the destination terminal is busy. E-mail systems offer a variety of common features, including

- terminals to prepare and store messages
- a communication link with other work stations within the network
- a central controlling computer
- a directory of addresses
- a central mail box
- a system which dates the message
- a function that notes that the message has been received by the addressee
- a facility to multiple-address so that all members of a particular working group are sent the message simultaneously
- a prioritising system so that messages can be identified as important or routine
- a storage facility in order to keep in the memory those messages that have not yet been received
- compatibility with existing equipment and computer systems.

E-mail offers a number of advantages over other forms of communication, including

- savings on stationery and paper costs
- savings on telephone costs
- rapid transmission
- integration with other systems
- recording of all transmissions so that accurate costings may be obtained
- allowing employees to telework
- allowing addressees to peruse their e-mail when they wish.

Another version of the e-mail system may be found in the electronic data interchange which enables individuals to exchange business documents using the same communication system.

Rather than rely on the traditional methods of sending information on hard copy through the post, electronic mail offers the opportunity to transmit information instantaneously to remote but linked computers. A further advantage of this system is the alarm device which informs the recipient that the message is awaiting them. Networking, or linking computer systems together, helps to improve the processing of information as well as communication within an organisation. Networks can be classified according to their location.

LAN (Local Area Network)

Most commonly, this is a network confined to one building with work areas containing microcomputers. These can be extended over an area of two or three miles.

WAN (Wide Area Network)

This is a computer network which is distributed nationally (or internationally) and makes use of telephone or satellite links.

By making use of the LAN or **WAN** networks an organisation has control over its own information processing, but also has access to the main database which may be held at head office. It also allows branches to communicate easily and quickly with each other and with head office.

What has made a lot of the computer facilities available is the change from analogue signals, which were required to transmit at different frequencies, to a more flexible system called digital. Digital signals are pulses which can be understood by computers. These signals are sent from one computer to another via a modem or similar device and may be accessed instantly.

Conferencing

Since the increasing input in recent years of new technological developments, it has become common for conferences to take place on a national or international basis by the use of telecommunications. Such systems are available to allow the users to 'link' to each other using any of the following.

- an audio telephone system – where all those involved can hear each other and are able to communicate with all the members involved in the conference

- audio-visual conferencing – where members involved in the conference, whether it be national or international, can both hear and see one another and communicate as if they were all in the same room
- computer conferencing – where the different terminals communicate with one another, allowing the independent users to send messages via the central computer
- interactive software conferencing – where computers which are linked and share the same software can communicate by sending images and messages to one another.

Student activity

In groups of four, investigate the available computer technology within the college/centre/place of work at which you are presently studying or working.

Discuss the different uses to which the computers are put and whether there is a need to widen their availability.

■ Reprographics and printing

Reprography is a term used in the office world and simply means 'making a copy of'. This can range from a simple photocopy to producing thousands of copies of one original document. We intend to look at all the different methods used to copy documents, and to compare them with regard to cost, speed, quality and effectiveness.

However, it is useful to mention at this stage, the **Copyright, Designs and Patents Act 1988.** This piece of legislation is intended to protect the publisher or copyright holder of documents. Any document showing the copyright symbol is protected by this Act and copies may not normally be made without permission from the originator.

The 'fair dealing' provision of the Act allows for one copy to be taken for research, private study, criticism, or review. However, the copying of a substantial part of the work is not allowed without written permission from the copyright holder.

Photocopiers

The range of photocopiers available makes it impossible to describe exactly what the machine will look like, or even to list the facilities it will offer. However, they range from small desktop copiers, which individuals would use for their own material, to large industrial heavy-capacity copiers, which would be used for large operations.

'Intelligent' copiers are capable of volume copying and can accept information directly from a computer. The original is converted into an image, which in turn is converted into an electrical signal. This signal triggers a laser which reproduces the image and processes it, and then transmits it to other locations. Such machines are capable of producing up to 150 copies per minute.

Colour photocopiers are also available, and these machines produce impressive material using a combination of colour toners, lasers and heat.

Photocopiers available in more recent years also have the added facility of sorting, collating (collecting together in the right order), stapling and binding documents together, thus making the process much quicker than in the past. A good stock control system for the maintenance of supplies of paper toner cartridges and fastening and collating materials for the photocopier should be in place.

Obviously, one of the main considerations when dealing with reprographic material is the fact that the information may be of a confidential nature. The person responsible for this task should always ensure that all confidential material is placed face-down on a desk and is sent through the internal mail using a 'confidential' internal envelope.

Student activity

Try to gain access to the photocopying machines used in the college/centre in which you are studying/working. Find out to what purpose they are mainly put – are they used to bulk copy, or for smaller copying purposes? Are the members of staff who use the machine happy with the service it provides? Would a colour photocopier be cost effective?

Desktop publishers

Desktop publishing computer software programs allow the production of artwork combined with text and graphics. Documents such as letterheads, forms, advertising material, newsletters, journals, manuals and brochures can be produced. In addition, slides and overhead projector transparencies can also be designed.

Duplicating machines

Although very rarely used in the modern office, some smaller organisations do make use of ink duplicating machines. Briefly, a master is made, either by hand, or by using a typewriter or word processor. The master is attached to the drum of the duplicating machine and automatically inked. The number of copies produced can be hundreds and this is a very cheap method of producing substantial amounts from one original.

Offset lithography

Again, **offset lithography** has been replaced by the photocopier in business organisations, although for large runs of documents, they are still commonplace in commercial printing organisations.

The copies are reproduced in ink from a plate containing a 'greasy' litho image. A litho image is the reverse image which is put on to a plate using an offset-litho machine. It is then transposed when duplicated.

Company efficiency and cost-effectiveness

Naturally, any organisation which makes use of a reprographic department, or which finds itself producing an increasing number of copies of documents, will need to make some comparisons between those systems currently in operation and those available to them. How organisations compare efficiency and cost-effectiveness is discussed below.

The cost-effectiveness of the systems used is of prime importance and may be the largest comparison an organisation has to make. It could be that a very sophisticated desktop publishing system is currently being used, but not to its full potential. The purchase of another program may mean that it can produce more effective material, but at a higher cost.

The organisation would have to make quite detailed investigations into the cost-effectiveness of the current system and those available on the market. It may be considered sensible to provide a series of desktop copiers, rather than one or two multi-function large machines.

The organisation would need to consider whether leasing or hiring a machine would be more cost-effective than purchasing one outright. In addition, the overheads incurred as a result of a new machine or adaptation of existing equipment would need to be considered.

The speed with which the machine can carry out the reprographic function is of prime importance. The image being produced may be of particularly good quality, or extremely inexpensive, but very slow. The organisation would need to consider its financial situation and the amount of time being lost whilst waiting for work to come back from the reprographic department. It may be that it would benefit the organisation to purchase or hire another machine which would produce equally good copies, but in a much shorter time. Additionally, a more sophisticated machine may cut down on the amount of time being spent by the administrative staff in collating, binding and stapling documents.

The quality of reprographic material is important for several reasons.

- The document may be illegible if not copied to a sufficiently good standard.
- The document may be going outside the organisation, perhaps for advertising purposes.
- Colour might be needed as an integral part of a document.
- It may be necessary to reduce or enlarge some sections of the document.

- The long-term developments envisaged in this area of work would also need to be carefully considered.

Student activity

Look at the following list of quantities of documents to be produced. Select the most appropriate method of duplicating, taking into account the quantity required, the cost of duplication and the quality of copy required.

a   10 copies of a page from a magazine
b   20 copies of the minutes of a meeting
c   2000 copies of a new form to be used within the organisation
d   500 copies of a notice to be circulated to all personnel

Keywords

The keywords you should know for this chapter are listed below. Check to make sure you understand the meaning of each word. Discuss those you are unsure of with your tutor.

Chamber of Commerce
Copyright, Designs and
    Patents Act 1988
Data Protection Act
DTI
e-mail
intelligent copies
lateral filing cabinet
Mintel
numerical filing

offset lithography
primary research
radio pager
reprography
secondary research
standard industrial
    classifications
TEC
WAN

Examination practice

Short-answer questions

1 Briefly state the procedures for sending a fax.

2 What is E-Mail?

3 Bureaufax is one example of electronic mail, give one other example.

4 Give two advantages and two disadvantages of alphabetical filing.

5 Give three advantages of numerical filing.

6 What is chronological filing.

7 How can computer databases aid filing?

8 When should filed documents be destroyed or 'weeded out'?

9 What is the purpose of a pager?

10 Give three main ways in which the Data Protection Act can protect individuals from unscrupulous organisations.

Essay questions

1 Your immediate line manager has to write a very complicated and detailed report. He asks you to assist him in the research of some of the information. You need to state where you would find the following information and provide him with a list of the most suitable sources:

  a details about main industries in the different European countries

  b the population figures of certain European countries

  c the main educational qualifications obtained in certain European countries

d the major considerations when seeking employment in certain European countries.

2 You work in a busy accounts department as an administration clerk. Your main duties include the maintenance, care and filing of all of the records. Although you 'inherited' the system from the previous clerk, the system works reasonably well. Your manager, however, wishes to make significant changes to the way in which the records are filed and housed. At present, they are alphabetically filed, but your manager wants you to suggest another way of filing them and propose some systems to combat the following problems:

a files are automatically opened on potential customers or suppliers before any goods have been purchased or sold to them. This seems to be a waste of filing space, as in your experience, less than half of them actually become 'live' files.

b when customers and suppliers change their trade names, the files are still kept under the old name. This is because many of the accounts staff still know these organisations by their old names. The new names are simply written on to the front of the file as a reminder.

c Many files are taken out of the system and either not put back or are misfiled.

Set out your ideas in the form of a short informal report to your manager.

3 Your organisation has had increasing problems recently regarding the inefficiency of its current communication systems. At present you have no computerised systems in place and it is proving more and more difficult to ensure that all the appropriate staff are kept up-to-date and suitably notified about developments and forthcoming events. Your departmental manager has allocated you the task of researching the possibility of installing some new office technology which would solve this problem, and which would improve the communication process both internally and externally. Your line manager has asked you to come up with 5 ideas of the types of technology you think would help to improve the situation. You should produce your considerations in the form of a memorandum addressed to the Head of Department.

4 You work in a relatively small organisation and you are one of five secretaries who all work for different groups of individuals. You share one very old and out-dated photocopier. Recently you have all been experiencing serious problems, such as indicator lights

appearing which claim that paper is jammed when it isn't, toner being out when it isn't and very poor copies. You all seem to be complaining a lot, but nobody is doing anything about it. You have offered to present the problem to the Managing Director and to request that a new photocopier be acquired. You know that the old one is owned by the organisation, but that money is scarce. One of the other secretaries suggests that hiring one may be more cost-effective. Prepare your notes for discussion with the Managing Director, ensuring that you cover all the benefits of a new machine, with the facts for him to consider regarding either the purchase or hire of another photocopier.

Index